A Round-Heeled Woman

A Round-Heeled Woman

My Late-Life Adventures
in Sex and Romance

JANE JUSKA

VILLARD 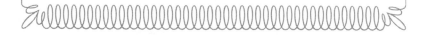 NEW YORK

Copyright © 2003 by Jane Juska

Library of Congress Cataloging-in-Publication Data
Juska, Jane.
   A round-heeled woman : my late-life adventures in sex and romance/ Jane Juska.
      p. cm.
   ISBN 1-4000-6011-7
   1. Juska, Jane. 2. Aged women—United States—Biography.
3. Aged women—United States—Sexual behavior. I. Title.
HQ30 .J87 2003
305.26'092—dc21
[B]   2002033155

Villard Books website: www.villard.com

Printed in the United States of America on acid-free paper

4 6 8 9 7 5 3

Designed by Cassandra J. Pappas

To Gene

Acknowledgments

To Jim Gray and the Bay Area Writing Project for turning me into a teacher who writes.

To Mary Ann Smith, Jack Sayers, Bob Presnall, and Susan Reed, whose patience and encouragement made this book possible.

To Bill, who told me I had a story to tell so tell it.

To my son, Andy, and his beautiful wife, Karen, who put up with my antics and loved me all the same.

To Elyse Green, at the William Morris Agency, who rescued me from the slush pile and sent me on.

To my agent, Ginger Barber, who gave me a new life.

To my editor, Susanna Porter, who made me a better writer.

To J., who dragged me out of the slough of despond more than once and set me to work.

Contents

A Round-Heeled Woman

ONE

At the Movies

Love is a great comedy, and so is life,
when you are not playing one of the roles.

—LOUISE COLET, in a letter to Flaubert

D o you think you're a nymphomaniac?" Bill wants to know.
We sit on my couch close enough for him to grab me
should I offer the right answer. Bill obviously thinks there is a
strong possibility, and inches closer. He is an attractive man of
sixty-one, six years younger than I. He is rich, his jacket cashmere, his trousers a finely worsted wool. He drives a BMW and
an Alfa Romeo, though not at the same time. He has brought me
a bottle of expensive Chianti, a book he enjoyed, and a cactus
fully in bloom. Shortly, we will walk out onto College Avenue
and choose a restaurant where we will have dinner. Bill will order
everything on the menu that looks interesting, and we will dip
into four or five hors d'oeuvres and entrées. We will share a bottle of wine, French. We will return to my cottage, where Bill will
continue to quiz me on my sex life.

A few months ago, I turned sixty-seven. My hair is mostly
white, with glints of what once was: blond, brown, gray; my face

is lined—with wisdom, ahem; my eyes—blue as ever they were—are bifocaled. My teeth, not as sparkling as they used to be, remain American: sturdy, straight, and made to last. Signs of age notwithstanding, dressed—with all of my clothes on—I look pretty good. Undressed is a different matter: my body is not twenty-five or forty-five; it's not even fifty-five; and, because it has never been interfered with by plastic surgery, what once was firm is loose, what once went up goes down. Intimations of mortality are all about me. Now, though, sitting fully clothed next to Bill, I have possibilities; I can see he thinks so, too. Still, I am an unlikely candidate for the title of Ms. Nymphomania. How is it I am even in the running?

I may turn out to be the hero of my own life or the villain, who knows, but this I know for sure right now: I am easily aroused. And I offer this as a partial answer to Bill's question. I am aroused by the sight of meadows, the sound of rushing creeks, by print. Not even erotic print. Sometimes, as I lie on my futon reading, say, the *Times* or *The American Scholar,* I will feel the familiar tickle between my legs. But mostly, I am aroused by men, parts of men. I love men's asses, even the ones that aren't perfect. I am aroused by the sight of John's neck, of Bill's forearm, of Sidney's voice, Robert's hands, Graham's legs. Men have fabulous legs, no fat, long muscles. Walking down the street in the summertime, all those men in shorts, is a thrill for me. And I adore penises. They are different one from one another, straight and crooked, long and short, thick and thin, endlessly fascinating at rest or attention. They do wonderful things for me and I do wonderful things for them. Freud wrote that men desire women but women desire men's desire of them. I suppose so, but, to my mind, women are missing a lot if they're satisfied only with flared nostrils and heavy breathing.

———

My heels are very round. I'm an easy lay. An easy sixty-seven-year-old lay. 'Twas not always so. As these pages will show.

Psychologists say that a significant change in one's life is preceded by a particular, specific event or experience. So it was with mine.

In the fall of 1999, when I was only sixty-six, I sat in the darkened movie theater, malted-milk balls pulsing in their paper bag, and stared at the screen where Eric Rohmer's soignée heroine smiled coolly across the table at a gentleman clearly her inferior. I popped a ball and once again gave up the notion that I could make them last as long as the movie. With malted-milk balls, my urge was immediate, my discipline in short supply. Aided by the wisdom of advancing age, I no longer crunch the balls as I did when I was thirteen; now, to make them last, I suck on them until they begin to dissolve in my mouth. At exactly the right moment I will bite down (I would never do this to a man; they are so vulnerable there) on the small but rewarding hard center and smile inwardly at the little crunch. Malted-milk balls, like a lot of things, were better when I was young; today's balls have a chalky taste, and I swear they are smaller. I know they are bad for me, another reason I like them so much. I have become a historian of balls.

Lately—have you noticed?—old people, people living on fixed incomes, people like me, have started to bring their own food to the movies. This is tacky. And it is noisy. The paper bags they bring from home filled with cold popcorn they have popped in their microwaves make noise when the old people rustle around in them. Professional movie sacks, like the one that holds my malted-milk balls, are made of softer material; professional sacks are very quiet. Occasionally, I turn and stare nastily at the miscreant. Mostly, the offender just glares back and continues to rustle. Sometimes, it seems to me, they rustle even louder. And in the dark of the theater, when I shush them, they look at me and their eyes turn red, like wolves' eyes on nature programs, or like my grandmother's when I forgot to say thank you. These people are my age; they are my peers. Why do they persist in embarrassing me?

Then there is the talking, which they do whenever they damn well feel like it. At what age—I want to know—does one get to ignore everybody but oneself? How old do you have to be to be rude? With this talking, sometimes, it is a wife explaining the movie to her hard-of-hearing husband, who has refused to wear his hearing aids: "What did he say?" the man will shout, and the wife will answer, in tones loud enough for the people back home to hear, "He said he's going to kill her." Then there are the ones who come in late: "I can't see a thing," one of them will call, though to whom is unclear since no one answers. And there are the folks who don't seem to realize the movie has begun and who continue the conversation they started in the parking lot: "I told her she should call her daughter, she lives right down the street. . . ." Once, by mistake, I went to a movie at noontime, unaware that this particular showing was for deaf people. It was the best audience I have ever been privileged to be a part of—totally quiet. I seek them out now.

This movie, this *Autumn Tale*, engaged my attention at once, so that the claws of the elderly scuttling along the bottoms of their popcorn sacks went unnoticed. I like French films. Everything about them—the scenery, the people, even the plots—is interesting to me. Where the French live, what a middle-class apartment looks like, a café, a hotel room, what the French wear, is fascinating to me. I trust French filmmakers to show me

French life. I do not trust American filmmakers to render a true picture of American life. What I see on the screen—a small town, a farm, a prison—is what Hollywood thinks those places ought to look like. So we get the perfect small town in *State and Main,* not a real one. I don't learn anything except about Hollywood. *The Matrix? The Sixth Sense? Traffic?* It seems to me that French movies show the extraordinary in everyday people; American movies show extraordinary people who are, inside, just folks. So in France, in the film *Belle de Jour,* we have an ordinary, beautiful (she is, after all, French) woman living an ordinary life, who, by virtue of her own ingenuity, lives a secret and very sexy other life. In America, we have Julia Roberts, who, as Erin Brockovich, foul of mouth and pushed-up of bra, wants what we all want: security with a little justice on the side. I'd rather have a sexy secret life. And I will. Watch me.

The French are grown up. The French are cool. They are understated, like in this film, *Autumn Tale:* a wedding, and the guests, all except for a bold young thing in red, are dressed in the colors of autumn. They are subtle. They are elegant. All the women are tall and thin; that's French, too. The men? Not one of them can hold a candle to the women even though they are married to them. That is definitely cool, making the men look ordinary, making the women smart to have seen beneath the surface to the steadiness below. Not one of those men is handsome, I thought, as I gazed at the screen. And all the women are. I love it.

The plot, the events of this movie that will change my life, is not unfamiliar: two best friends, women in their late forties, one married, one not. The married friend secretly places an ad in the personals column of the newspaper for her friend and complications ensue. In the vineyards of the Rhône Valley (a very cool place I have never been to), the movie ends happily, though maybe not. The French always leave room for the maybes; ambiguity is another sign of grown-upedness that the French do very well.

Though more than twenty years older than the women in the film, I identify with the unmarried one, the one for whom the ad was secretly placed. The woman is independent and stubborn; she is proud and she is lonely. Divorced and cynical, devoted to her work, she swears she wants nothing to do with men. And yet we see the downturn of her mouth, the nervous rubbing of her fingers, the torn cuticles, the careless tumble of her hair. My own cuticles will take a beating in the months to come. And I hear something of my own voice in the abrupt defensiveness of her speech, her insistence that her work is quite enough. All of us in the audience—young and old, noisy and not—know that the absence of men in her life, while bearable, is not desirable. We can see that she is just plain scared to do anything about it. I know the feeling.

I was divorced thirty years ago. Except for a few skirmishes with men that ended sadly, I lived a full and, in many ways, satisfying life. Teaching was my passion. I was lucky to have found it. It was work that demanded my energy and attention. A single parent, I had a son who demanded the same. And, just in case I found myself tempted, I got fat. No man would look at me. I was safe. Then came 1993. I retired from teaching. My son was grown up and gone. And I was no longer fat. However, men did not come flocking; no man came at all. My stage was bare; in fact, without a classroom I had no stage at all. At age sixty, I had put myself out to pasture after thirty-three years of thriving on a live audience: 150 kids during the day and one feisty son at night. So I was okay. Except there was no one for me to touch and no one to touch me.

Garrison Keillor once wrote that, of all the sensory deprivations, the deprivation of touch is the most severe. I was severely deprived. It was not that I had gone around touching my high school students; I was fully aware of the impropriety of touching kids, even at my advanced age and with my sound reputation. But with all those kids coming and going into and out of my classroom each day, there was bumping, there was rubbing, there was so much life that some of it rubbed off on me. I felt touched even if I wasn't.

But I didn't know that then. I knew I couldn't live on my pension, but I didn't know that my newly empty stage was another reason I took a part-time teaching job at a nearby college only months after retiring from high school teaching. I didn't know it was my own deprivation that made me eager to become a volunteer teacher at San Quentin State Prison across the bay. I didn't know this deprivation was present and serious until, at age sixty, I began a five-year journey through my unconscious aided by a skillful analyst. Although an M.D., my analyst would not prescribe drugs no matter that I wept and wailed, cursed him loudly, and begged to be hospitalized. It was surgery without anesthesia. It was, as a scholar has written, "no consolation but a sober and complex estimation of reality." It was the hardest and most important thing I have ever done in my life. But don't listen to me; listen to Emily Dickinson:

> One need not be a chamber to be haunted,
> One need not be a house;
> The brain has corridors surpassing
> Material place.
> . . . .
> Far safer through an Abbey gallop,
> The stones achase,
> Than, moonless, one's own self encounter
> In lonesome place.

Psychoanalysis has lately gotten a lot of criticism, often by people who would benefit from it. Talk therapy, under the guidance of a good analyst—and there are lots of them—is invaluable. It costs money, but so does lying flattened on your own bed, able to live a life only dimly lit. Analysis saved my life and made me rich. I had to learn to read the sober and complex book that was me. With the help of the best teacher I will ever know, I learned to appreciate me, to be analytical and sometimes critical of me, to not be scared of me. Learning all that made the world a different place, a place with plenty of room for me to live a full life.

At sixty-six, one year postanalysis, I felt good. Psychoanalysis had cleaned out a lot of gunk; it had insisted on teaching me to think, it had forced me to stop wallowing in the self-pity of narcissism, it had offered me its couch, and at the end of five years I was strong enough to rise and go forth. And try as I might to revert to a lifetime of repression, I could no longer pretend that my life was complete. One of the truths I had had to accept during my years on the couch was that pleasure was not bad, that it was natural for people to desire pleasure, that denying oneself pleasure was not healthy. This was contrary to the teachings of my mother; it was contrary to the mores of the small Ohio town in which I grew up, where the anhedonic life of the Mennonites formed my community. So it was no easy task to realize and accept the fact that I liked men. They are different from me. They are stronger, usually, their voices are deeper, they are taller, most of them. And lots of them are sexy. So I began to look around, and, oh god, failure and rejection waited just around the corner.

It was a dark and stormy night, New Year's Eve 1998. My friend Nathalie at the wheel, we were on our way into San Francisco to a singles party. This was all her fault. "Look," she said, "we can always leave." She had convinced me that anything would be better than one more New Year's Eve home alone. So here we were on our way to the Golden Eagle Bar and Grill. The wind howled, the rain pounded against the windshield. Nature was telling us to go home.

At the Golden Eagle Bar and Grill, some seven hundred people had braved the elements. The place was jammed. Where were the people my age? The range looked to be between thirty and fifty, and where the hell was I supposed to sit? To stand? To fall down? "Come on," said Nathalie, slim and youthful in her Paris black. Nathalie bought her clothes in France; I bought mine in Berkeley. Nathalie was forty-three; I was sixty-two. This would be a long night.

At the bar, I asked for white wine. It came in a huge glass, practically a bowl. It was full of wine. I had two and the world looked better. I did what I had done before in large gatherings, fueled by alcohol. I began to shop for Nathalie. "Sit there," I told her. "I'll be back shortly." And off I went to introduce myself to young men presentable enough to squire Nathalie through the heterosexual world. I met lots of men that way. And then I saw a man my age. His hair was as gray as mine, his face as lined. Of course, as a man, he looked better; he looked great. And he looked scared. He stood, his back against the wall, as a pack of women—there they were, women my age—moved in closer and closer to their prey. He looked terrified. Who would save him? Not me. I turned away, embarrassed by my sex and ashamed deep within myself of the hunger that I knew was as strong as those women's. "Let's go," I begged Nathalie. We went.

It would be a long time before I could bring myself to try again, to go on hikes with the Sierra Club, to attend alumni association events, to agree to a blind date. The women at these functions outnumbered the men at least three to one. I grew tired of talking to interesting women, of watching women more aggressive than I tree the few men present. Finally, I gave up. Celibacy was better than humiliation.

So I returned to my longtime sexual partner, myself, and found comfort in the knowledge that at least I had tried. It wasn't my fault I was alone. I wasn't even especially lonely. Except for this: every once in a while, as I walked down the street or folded towels or filled my gas tank, this thought, completely unbidden, would leap into my brain lickety-split before I could repress it: What if I never have sex with a man again? It made my stomach churn, it made me dizzy, and it kept me awake sometimes like lightning flashes in a summer night.

In the darkness of the Elmwood Theatre, I decided on a happy ending for the lonely woman in *Autumn Tale*. On my walk home, the cool evening invigorated me. Suddenly, the thought came to me: I could do that, just like in the movie. I could write an ad. I knew at once where I would send it. By the time I got to the corner of my street, I knew what I would write. It went like this:

Before I turn 67—next March—I would like to have a lot of sex with a man I like. If you want to talk first, Trollope works for me.

It was the absolute truth.

TWO

The Library

Read, read everything.

—WILLIAM FAULKNER

The day after composing my ad, I walked to my library, which is 225 steps up the block from my cottage in Berkeley, California. Like Ann Arbor, Gainesville, Madison, like all university towns, Berkeley is a wonderful place to live. Rich people and poor people live here, all different colors of people live here, young and old, homeless and not. I live a mile and a half from the university and feel much smarter than I did when I lived in a suburb in the house where I reared my son. My house in Orinda was redwood and glass, as a California house should be. It sat in the middle of two acres of wildflowers, live oaks, and bay laurels. Alongside the deck, which I entered from my bedroom, ran a creek. In the middle of the creek was a tall rock. Every winter, when the rains came often and strong, the water rushed over the rocks and made a waterfall, my own private waterfall. I could barely afford the house when I bought it in the seventies. By the nineties I was running out of money and the house needed work. So I sold it. Sometimes I miss it, though mostly I don't.

I am a renter now. My cottage is one fifth the size of my house, four hundred square feet down from two thousand. Here there is no dishwasher, no washing machine or dryer, no creek, no decks. Instead, it has French doors that open onto a wonderful garden cared for by my landlady and her gardener. It has a flagstone patio, where I sit in the sun to do the crossword puzzle. Renting my cottage gives me a life uncomplicated by the burdens of homeowning: a rotting roof, a plugged-up sink, peeling paint, loose tiles, etc., etc., etc., ad absurdum, ad nauseam. It also gives me an insecurity about what would happen to me if my landlady sold or moved or . . . or . . . or . . . And, once I placed the ad, I began to worry about where I live: What if a man actually answered the ad? What if he came to collect? What if I liked him? Where would we do it? Where I sleep is not actually a bed. It's more like a slab of foam on top of built-in storage units. It is longer than a regular bed and narrower, kind of French now that I think of it. For me, it is comfortable; for two, well, maybe if we were stacked on top of each other. And what would my landlady say or think? She and her family live in the main house on the other side of the garden. What would she do if she saw men coming and going? Even one man coming and going? Would she throw me out? Besides, did I really want to welcome a stranger into my home? Oh my, oh my. Already I was doing a "yes, but": the kind of thinking that had kept me walled off from risk, change, excitement. Hell, I would figure this all out. "Do not borrow trouble," my grandmother, who did it all the time, used to say. Probably no one would answer the ad anyway.

Outside the gate, I walk everywhere: to concerts, to football games, to the movies, to restaurants. I walk to my library every day to read *The New York Times,* a ritual necessary to fuel my lifelong fantasy of a week in New York, where I would see every play on and off Broadway, hear every concert in Carnegie Hall, and eat knishes from the corner stands. What was a knish, anyway?

The library is my candy store. I can have whatever tastes good at the time: my daily *Times* fix, poetry, fiction old and new. At the end of my thirty-three years of teaching high school English, I ran, not walked, to the library and booted onto the screen the love of my life: Trollope, Anthony. There he was—eighty-four entries! I was set for life. Except not long after, maybe two years later, I was out of Trollope; I had read all his novels and loved all of them, the good and the not so good. What an amazing writer, a man who admired and respected the women of his time and who sympathized with their vulnerability in the Victorian world of men. In case you're thinking about befriending Trollope, know that he is not clever the way Dickens is clever, though he sometimes tries to be (and fails). But Trollope is ever so much more confident and talented in the rendering of women as genuine people. And with titles like *Can You Forgive Her?* and *He Knew He Was Right,* how can you resist? Forgive me, but the answer to the first is yes, only a fool would not forgive her; to the second, Trollope says, No, he wasn't right, just look at all the trouble he made.

So now you see why Trollope appeared in my ad. He had been a significant man in my life. Wouldn't it be nice if a live man shared my affection for him?

A favorite section in my library is the biography section. Here are all these famous people, some more famous than others, some surprises. Like Hadley Richardson, Ernest Hemingway's first wife. There she sat, on the shelf, waiting for me just the way she sat on a real-life shelf from which Ernest Hemingway plucked her. "I wish," he wrote, "I had died before I could love anyone else." Now, if Scott Fitzgerald had married Hadley instead of Zelda, he would have lasted longer as a writer and as a man. But Ernest dumped Hadley for the designing Pauline.

Fitzgerald would probably have dumped Hadley, too—she was so nice. Zelda, now, was not so easy to get rid of. My library is full of wonderful people. Margaret Fuller is there. She is a hero of mine, too.

For now, in late October, in this library, I sat at a table, the recent issue of *The New York Review of Books* spread out before me. Outside, the rain slapped the sidewalks. Inside, the homeless were gathering, bringing the smell of the streets with them, adding their own pungency. Not much like Rohmer's Rhône Valley.

The New York Review of Books is a periodical for serious readers. It claims to review books written on serious subjects, and it does. More than that, though, very smart people write very thoughtful, very long essays on everything from Freud to Jon-Benet Ramsey. It's also expensive, which is why I read it in the library. I save the best part for last: the personals, the most distinguished personal-ad column in the country, how about that? I was about to join it.

Most of these ads did not sound as if they had been written by very smart people; to wit: *"Blue-eyed female college grad, 49, 5'6", seeks nonsmoker, Jewish, male college grad to share, from concerts to museum openings."* Often, while I was reading the ads, my attention would wander to vacation rentals and I would fantasize about *"Greenwich Village. 1 BR plus study. Lg. music room, library, balcony. $4500/month."* Oh, well. Now, however, I was serious about becoming an advertiser of myself. Now, for I was sure smart people answered these ads, I wanted somebody to answer me. I wanted touching and talking and I wanted it sooner, not later—now, not tomorrow. For I was about to turn sixty-seven.

$4.55 a word, the *Review* charged. This called for Aristotelian discipline. It would have to be short. It would have to have purpose and an understanding of audience. Honed to its essence, I had to do it. The ad in my head—"Before I turn 67—next

March—I would like to have a lot of sex with a man I like"—
would that be enough? Could I leave out Trollope? Without
Trollope, the ad would cost $91 if they didn't count dashes,
$100 if they did. With Trollope, $136.50! Shouldn't I specify Bay
Area? That would cost two words more. Did they take Visa?

Behind me, the schizophrenic in his red beret roamed the
young people's reading section, spinning the carousels and swearing at the books as they spun. "Lousy fuckers, no hitting the
sky." The beret, torn and damp from the rain, fell to one side of
his head as he continued his tirade. I knew better than to shush
him. Once, outside the library, when I was on my way home
carrying a bag of groceries, he came at me from down the
street, his red beret bright as a signal light, cursing and yelling,
"Spare change?" He saw the baguette sticking out of my grocery bag, stuck his face into mine, his eyes, blazing with fury,
and bellowed, "How about a little bread? Can you spare a little
bread?" I walked quickly on by, trying to decide whether to use
the special number the police had given the residents of my
neighborhood. "If any of these street people give you trouble,
call us. We'll be there immediately," they promised at a neighborhood meeting. I had never used that number, nor had any
neighbor I knew. The people in my neighborhood feel guilty
enough keeping their porch lights on all night every night, to
discourage the homeless from sleeping there. We all feel guilty
and helpless and angry at the disgrace heaped upon our heads
by a government—local, state, national—that chooses to ignore
the poor and the sick. Is it Thoreau who said the measure of a
society is the care it takes of those unable to care for themselves? Our measure is very low.

In the library, I put my hands over my ears and kept reading.
*"DWF seeks intelligent, sexy, witty, emotionally available, erotically confi-
dent, professional man . . ."* She doesn't want much. I wondered
what she'd settle for; how old is she—*"early sixties."* She'll settle.

"SWF seeks that special idyll with a literate, caring . . . " Nonsense. I
counted the words: 34, at $4.55 a word—that ad cost $154.70! It
seemed to me that all the ads but mine played around with the
truth: *"long walks along the beach . . . love of nature . . . opera . . ."*
Somewhere I read that personal ads projected what the writers
of them would like to be, not what they were: men's ads included the out-of-doors; women's, fireside coziness. It seemed
to me that men wanted a way out, women a way in. It also
seemed to me that women placed ads, men answered them. In
the issue before me, twenty-four of the thirty-two ads were
placed by women. What does that mean? Probably not much.
Just that women have to work harder to get the attention of
men than men do to attract women. It also reflects the fact that
there are just more of us than there are men. We continue to
compete with one another long after we are past childbearing,
long after we seek protection from the male. I kind of think
Plato was right when he said (actually, Aristophanes says it in
The Symposium) that *"In the beginning, we were whole; we combined in us
both the male and the female."* And then, we got uppity and angered
the gods. Zeus struck us in two: half of us became male, the
other half female. Zeus told Apollo to compose our forms. *"He
molded the breast and took out most of the wrinkles, much as a shoemaker
might smooth leather upon a last; he left a few, however, in the region of
the belly and the navel, as a memorial of the primeval state."* Since then,
we have wandered the earth in search of wholeness. Alas, our
search is never successful; we are doomed to a severed state and
the erotic urge is a sort of compensation. If he is right, the
erotic urge is hugely important. That's what I think is underneath all these ads, that very urge to find completion. Where it
happens—the beach, the opera—is irrelevant; that it does happen is necessary to life. To refuse it is to court death.

  I liked my ad. The urge was there. I was open to all comers.

And Trollope went in. What the hell, I didn't plan to spend this kind of money again.

The woman who occupied the same chair every day once the rains began, whose pretty face was lined and windburned from living out-of-doors, was staring at me. *People* magazine dangled from her fingers, then dropped onto the plastic bag she always carried, crammed with scraps of material, hats, scarves. I looked back and smiled and the woman dropped her eyes. Her shoes, showing beneath the long black skirt, were wet; from the look of her ratty black jacket she was soaked through. Her dark hair, curly in the dampness, shone in the light of the library. What unforeseeable disaster had thrown this pretty woman onto the streets? I had seen her before, here and on the sidewalk, her lips moving silently, her eyes fastened on the ground beneath. She was ill, no doubt about it, though I wondered if the illness had come before she moved to the streets or after. I nodded slightly. The woman turned her head to the magazine rack.

Across the table, one hand spread across the upper edge of my *New York Review,* a homeless man snored softly, his head cradled in his arms. I sighed. It was the beginning of the winter, when the homeless came to the library for warmth, a toilet, a place to wash. Not long from now, the smell of rotting backpacks, of plastic bags, of old and unwashed clothes and people, would come to be overwhelming. But none of the librarians objected to this seasonal takeover, nor did any of the patrons. We were bound together by guilt and frustration and an unutterable desire to feel the touch of another human being.

I pulled a pen and a pad of paper out of my purse and began to change my life. The cost would far exceed the paltry $136.50 I had so far calculated. So would the return.

THREE

Triage

A nd so I e-mailed it in. Right to *The New York Review of Books.* Along with my payment of $136.50. Oh gosh, what would they think, those smart people who worked for the *Review?* Would they even print the ad? Did they have rules about using the word *sex* in their ads? Would someone call me on the telephone and admonish me to rewrite in a manner appropriate to so august a journal? What the hell. What was done was done and could not be undone. I felt great. I felt terrific. I walked taller. I looked people in the eye, in the face, in the crotch, anywhere I felt like looking. Sometimes, it seemed to me, they looked back in a friendly manner. My secret—wanting sex with a man I liked—was no longer secret; it was no longer dirty, never had been really, was no longer just mine. I had broadcast an essential truth to the world at large, or small, given the readership of the *New York Review,* and I felt terrifically free and clean and, well, sort of proud. I wanted something and I had taken steps to get it. Yessiree. Or, how about this: I had taken control of my life. Oh yes, I had. We would see how long I could hold this tiger by its tail.

All the while, I went on living my regular life. I taught my seminar at the college. I traveled to high schools to observe and mentor beginning teachers. On Fridays I drove to Planned Parenthood, where I volunteered as an abortion escort. And, of course, there was prison. That was Wednesday, St. Mary's College was Tuesday and Thursday, Planned Parenthood Friday, and, oh yes, I sang in a chorale, that was Monday. Nobody knew that I had created a secret life. Secret Delight came to live inside me and I made it welcome. What would those sanctimonious antiabortion demonstrators think if they knew what I had done? Would they repaint their signs with me as their target? Go ahead, assholes, just leave these pregnant women alone. What would my students think? In my college class? In my prison class? And my friends? Would they remain my friends? I found myself smiling, thinking to myself as I walked down the street, stood in front of my students, brushed past the demonstrators—Have you any idea? Could you even imagine what I have done? Do you know that I am not at all what you think I am? That I am more? And I would chirp and warble very silently, Delight tickling me all the while. The world was fun. And so was I.

From the minute I sent off the ad I knew I would get an answer, probably even more than one, maybe even a lot, maybe as many as ten. But if I got none—and that was a possibility, too—the important part for me was that I did it, that I advertised myself without shame, without remorse, without a shade of embarrassment. So whatever the response, the best part was already done. I smiled a lot in the days before the ad appeared in the *Review* the first week of November. And then there it was: the personals people had not censored it; they had gone ahead and printed it just the way I wrote it. It stood out from all the rest.

On November 8, 1999, here they came—the dirty and the clean ones, the romantic and the mean ones—in a respectable *New York Review* manila envelope, twelve letters inside. My hands shook; my mouth went dry as I drew the packet out of the mailbox. I peered furtively over my shoulder, certain that my neighbors had developed X-ray eyes and would heap their castigations upon me at any moment. Oh, for heaven's sake, I told myself, if you were afraid of what the neighbors might think, you wouldn't have sent in the ad. The trouble was I was sort of afraid of what the neighbors/my mother/grandmother/first-grade teacher would think. Analysis had done a good job of cleaning me out, but shreds of need, like the need for approval, fragments of all the *should*s and *should-not*s, personified most terrifyingly by my grandmother, clung to the lining of my psyche. I brushed them away, grabbed the packet, and raced into my cottage.

I could hardly breathe. I began to do triage. As I read, I tossed each letter onto one of three piles: *yes, maybe,* and *no.* My hesitation vanished and I threw the letters as if I were tossing cards into a hat: a flick of the wrist, a wry smile, an arch of the eyebrow, like Robert Mitchum at his coolest. I took a nasty pleasure from zinging unsuitable letters onto the *no* pile. Oh, the power with glory not far behind. Still, the *no* pile was the smallest, this one on top: *"Call me at the office, Monday through Thurs., 9–5."* And gave a phone number.

Another *no* came from Giorgio: *"I'm 68 young and eager to have a relationship with healthy lady like you, and sex hungry."* Giorgio wrote from Leisure World in Utah.

Wilson's address—Gramercy Park in New York—was in his favor; not so *"I'm 72 and very horny."* I have never been fond of the word *horny.* It did its job when Shakespeare used it to designate a cuckold. But people didn't use it in that way anymore, and it had an ugly sound to it. Horns could hurt. I did wonder about Wilson's age: his seventy-two seemed so much older than my sixty-six, and with all these letters (and more and more to come) I could afford to be picky. I got uppity. Would Zeus notice?

Still, I decided, age alone was no basis for rejection. That's exactly the basis on which I have been rejected many times. The bank, given my age, refused my request for a loan when, in my first year of renting, I found a small house I wanted to buy. The loan I could get—based on my future earning power—would have been a very small one and the down payment would have had to be enormous. On the street, the eyes of the young and not so young slid by me. I look my age. Nobody but someone even older than I wants to look my age. Nobody wants to be my age. I am too close to death for younger people to want to pay attention to me. People think it a great compliment to say to me, "You certainly don't look your age." Well, what should my age look like? And if I did look my age, would I be unbearably ugly? Should I stay inside the rest of my life? Because I wasn't going to look better, not ever. So, really, was I going to do the same with the men who answered my ad? No. It would take more than the age of the writer for a letter to hit the *no* pile. So it wasn't Herb's *"Have Viagara, will travel"* that consigned him to the *no* pile; it was its brevity.

In the days to come, letters in their respectable manila envelopes packed my mailbox. Rob, age thirty-eight, sent a photograph of himself fully and frontally nude, save for a pair of sunglasses balanced on his nose. He was tall and naked and his penis stood erect. I hadn't seen a naked man in years, more than ten, and then I just peeked through my fingers. I turned the photograph over. He had included several three-by-five-inch cards on which he had printed, in blue ballpoint ink, a poem undeniably his own: *"Actually, old people make me sick/they really know how to shrink a dick/they're rude, obnoxious, pathetic, and gross/but the guts you displayed I dig the most/Your notice is actually rather romantic/ What is your strategy? (to make my pants frantic)."*

Larry, from Michigan, promised specific delights: *"If you were my wife I would give you oral sex several times per night, as well as kisses, hugs, fondling, stroking and intercourse (whichever way you like). I would suck your clitoris and rub my dick inside your cunt. I would do it during the night and in the morning and matinees.*" He signed his promises "*With the utmost respect.*" I relegated Larry to the oblivion of the *no*s.

Hal's letter, its typed messages single-spaced, jammed onto two pages, looked as nuts as Hal probably was: "*I'm writing you,*" he said, "*because I like sugar on my big ground mincemeat pie.*" And "*My hero is Little Black Sambo: I watch those tigers of ambition churn themselves into butter at the bottom of my tree. . . . I'll warn you of my politics: I like all rebels against tyranny, privilege, and intolerance who perish before tasting the poisonous fruit of victory and power: all weak peoples are apt to cherish a sense of superior virtue, corresponding to the crimes they have been powerless to commit.*" And on a personal note, "*A letter from you, and I'll spend more time with warm glaciers and cuddly icebergs.*" Hal proclaimed himself to be in his early seventies. That's right, I thought, you're right out of the early seventies and holding.

Carl lay in the *maybe* pile. His first sentence was in his favor: "*Your ad is highly enticing and your objective is complementary to mine.*" The third sentence was not: "*I'm a married white male . . .*" No, no, no. But then, "*During Viet Nam I served as a naval officer aboard ship in combat waters.*" Well, maybe. No, no, Jane, he's married.

I would answer all the letters in the *maybe* pile, explaining that, while I appreciated their efforts, I lived too far away to suggest a next step. "Alas"—I made sure to include the word *alas* in all the letters, confirming the portrait I had painted of myself as a well-read, articulate, essentially old-fashioned lady. Okay, so maybe not "lady," not with an ad like that. "Woman"—that's what I wanted to be and what I wasn't. My idea of being a woman required a man. I could be a person all by myself, I could be an adult, I could be a mother, and I was all of those.

And I suppose I could claim to have been a woman once upon a time since I had, after all, been married, though my marriage had not been one to enhance my womanliness. Finally, I am not a man so I must be a woman. Weak, very weak. I wanted to be a woman for real now. To be that, I needed a man who would fuck me.

Once, way back, when I was in my twenties, I sat in the No Name Bar in Sausalito drinking beer on a Saturday afternoon. Out of nowhere, a man neither young nor old passed by our table and said to me, "You're a beautiful woman." And he left. No one ever said that to me again, and never, but for that brief moment, would I ever feel it. The men I would know as my life continued might think I was beautiful or a woman or even both, but none of them would ever say it. And so I wasn't. But now, now, I was on my way to becoming a woman. It was too late for me to be beautiful, but, well, look at all these letters! All these men! One of them was sure to make me a woman. I squirmed into the cushions of my futon.

Here is a fragment of a poem by Ted Kooser called "Daddy Longlegs":

> . . . If mine,
> it would be the secret dream
> of walking alone across the floor of my life
> with an easy grace, and with love enough
> to live on at the center of myself.

Sometimes, I have been able to do this: to walk alone . . . *"with love enough/to live on at the center of myself."* I will say that walking alone and living at the center of myself is my desire, my goal, if you will. So what, exactly, was I doing sending messages in bottles to hundreds of men?

I wanted to be the woman I was never able to be, a woman

who delights in intimacy with a man, not fears it. I wanted to be touched physically and emotionally. I wanted to be rich—I was greedy—in the ways of the flesh. I wanted to get fat on the bounty of men. I wanted to unleash (honest, I did) my passion. These guys had no idea who they were going to get. And all the while, I knew that, in reaching out for a full life, I could not choose, would not get, only the good parts. A full life was just that, pleasure and pain, joy and despair. I knew that from the beginning. I just didn't know the form they would take.

The *yes* pile was the biggest. I was enchanted. These men knew how to write. They even knew how to spell, and I had no trouble tossing onto the big pile letters with sentences like *"There is a chance you live in Tupelo and suffer from a wasting disease. So please tell me."* Yes! And *"I have written poetry, built stone walls, edited books, dealt with ministers of government . . . am a free man, and reasonably comfortable financially."* Yes! I was tempted to say yes to Brad, *". . . a retired surgeon, working as a consultant in the city,"* but I couldn't imagine myself undressed in front of a forty-something man, no matter that he was *"looking for a connection (of several sorts) with an older woman."* I wrote Brad, declining on the basis of geography, a decision I would come to regret when not so many months hence I found myself in New York City, on a street not far from Brad's, crying into my mitten over a man whose letter had been a *yes* and to whom I had become a *no*.

The letter I answered first came from a woman. *"I'm a woman too, just turned 60 and have some dark moments about it. Seeing ads like yours (there aren't many) remind one that it's not over yet. Best of luck— I'm sure you'll find what you want, with that courage!"* I wrote back my thank-you, ending with *"Placing the ad didn't take much courage. It's the next step."* I had no idea what the next step would be.

The second letter I answered came from England. It was from Paul, age fifty. I flicked the letter toward the *no* pile—fifty was just too young, England too far—and then a sentence caught my eye: *"My partner died of cancer earlier this year. We had been together many years, and we had a wonderful, loving relationship. She was 15 years older than I and died at the age of 64. Many people did not approve of the age difference, but we had a full and energetic sex/love life which showed no signs of diminishing until she was too ill to enjoy such pleasures."* Paul had included two photographs of himself, one leaning against a very full bookcase gazing thoughtfully (and very attractively) into the camera. I felt his sadness and answered, *"I am sorry for your loss. From what you describe of your relationship, you were fortunate to have found each other. Those who disapproved were of course simply envious. May your life be rich again."* And in the way that I began to develop and refine as I wrote to one man after another, I threw in a tease. *"I plan to be in England next fall. . . . If you are still a free man, perhaps we can meet."*

What fun this all was. And so, except for those letters in the *yes* pile, I decided not to include my mailing address or my e-mail address or my phone number. I ended each letter with only my name. Seemed the sensible, the wise, thing to do. I would grow bolder in the weeks to come.

This triage was fun. I was having a party and, finally, every man present was paying attention to me! I picked up a long blue envelope with a famous name in the upper-left corner. This would be a definite *yes*. Whoops, a photograph. The fully erect penis belonging to the very famous name stared up at me. A self-portrait. Well, there it was again: a naked man or part of one. I still couldn't look very long. I read his note: *"Your message-in-a-bottle caught my eye in a pleasing way. . . . Much of what goes on in the world amuses me, and I tend toward the sardonic view while remaining appreciative of life's ironies and serendipities."* Well, he could write, no doubt about that. But I tossed Famous into the *no* pile, another decision I would come to regret. I had no idea that not many weeks hence I would recall the photo, not with disgust but with longing.

Now, in the first flush of triumph, I sat on my futon taller than ever before and considered the standards I had conceived during this first-round draft. They were rules gathered from my own experience and intelligence—I was feeling especially smart—that would guide me and those fortunate enough to become my lovers. Hubris, hubris, oh Jane, watch out. How come nobody who has hubris knows it? If you have hubris, are you automatically a hero? Are you automatically blind so that even in the end, somebody else has to tell you, like the chorus? If we did know, would we rid ourselves of it? Of course, if we did, there would be no stories, no plays, novels, poems; well, there would be poems—there are always poets and always will be— hubris is not big with poets. I was just at the beginning of my hubris, with more to come, so my rules came easily:

1. Political Affiliation
   Never sleep with a Republican even if he looks like John McCain. It would be sleeping with the enemy.

2. Personal Affiliation
   No married men. I was grown up now, not like in the early years of my marriage, when I thought this one little affair would enliven my stuporous married life. I was wrong; all I got was a stuporous affair. I was through lying in bed listening to guilty confessions, apologies, and self-recriminations from a married mess huddled on the other side of the bed.

3. Sexual Affiliation
   No Kinky Sex. Whatever that was.

I would break them all.

I held my glass aloft and toasted myself. "To me. Long may I wave." At the end of my first night of triumph—twelve letters, wow!—I dressed for bed: long-sleeved T-shirt, flannel pants elasticized at waist and ankle, truly a fetching sight. Oh god, what will I wear if . . . if . . . I opened my French doors to the cool, clear California air. It smelled of possibility.

In the weeks to come, I would receive six more packets, sixty-three letters in all.

FOUR

Oh, Danny Boy

I will be in town the weekend of December 2 on my way to Ireland.
Could we meet for lunch?
—DAN

I stood in front of my closet. Nothing looked right. All my clothes were old; almost all of them were either black or white and none of them included a skirt. Oh well, black and white is always safe; everybody wears black and white in San Francisco all the time: summer, winter, fall. I will not iron. I will not make this into a big deal.

But it was. I had not been on a date in forty-two years. My friends Alison and Scott, in 1983, had invited me to dinner "to meet a tennis friend of Scott's," who, as it happened, was single. I don't count that a date, though. I count it as just another disaster. Alison and Scott discreetly left the dinner table, leaving me and this man—divorced, male, terribly good-looking and younger than I—alone. "What do you do?" he asked.

"I am a teacher," I said. "An English teacher."

"My worst subject," he said. "I'm dyslexic."

"Oh," I said, "school must have been hard for you."

"Actually, no," he said. "Some girl always helped me, stole the tests ahead of time, wrote my papers for me. I did all right."

Conversation turned to hobbies. "I read a lot," I said before I could swallow it.

"My favorite thing to do," he said, "is to go to the Financial District in San Francisco around five o'clock and watch the girls come out of the office buildings. Great sight." He smiled, ruminating about his favorite thing. Not soon enough, in the silence that ensued, Scott and Alison returned, I said good night, and that was that. So that doesn't count. This one counted. It was going to be a date.

I DID NOT DATE in high school. The kids in my class, almost all thirty-two of us who would graduate, the largest class ever to finish twelfth grade, had been together since kindergarten. Many of our parents had gone to school together. In the upper-left corner of Ohio, where the earth was rich for farming, where cornfields provided the natural boundaries of town, where kids dropped out in tenth grade to help their fathers in the fields, this little town named Archbold, population 1,234, flourished during World War I, the Depression, World War II, the recession, and Ronald Reagan; it is healthy today.

Not so sturdy myself, I avoided all physical contact with boys. When everyone began to go steady, I didn't. My mother had a lot to do with this. In eighth grade Dick gave me his ID bracelet. That meant we were a couple, we were going steady, no matter that we never went anywhere, that we were never alone, that we never actually talked to each other. He liked me; that's why he gave his bracelet to my best friend to give to me. I took the bracelet, which meant I liked him, which is what my best friend went back and told him. At Christmastime, during gift exchange in social studies class, I gave him a picture of me beautifully wrapped; my mom did the classiest wrapping of anyone in town. Miss Nafziger, the teacher, Old Step-and-a-Half, we called her— she wore a brace that clanked when she walked—made everybody unwrap their presents and hold them up for everyone to see. Dick unwrapped the picture of me and everybody laughed. Everybody but Dick and me.

When I showed the bracelet to my mother, she scowled. "It's ridiculous," she said. "Before you know it, you'll want to wear lipstick. One day you'll have an accident because you're looking at yourself in the rearview mirror when you should be driving." My mother could see much farther into the future than I could, none of it, apparently, to be wished for if I intended to be a girl.

My mother had a horror of "silly things girls do." From my very beginning she fought to save me from girldom. She didn't like girls, thought them uninteresting, frivolous, useless. No daughter of hers would be a drum majorette—"Where did you get that baton? Get rid of it"—or a cheerleader—"I know what you girls are doing down in the basement," she would say in response to our "Yea, team!" "Keep it in the basement," she commanded. We did. When I was in my later teens, she would advise me, "If ever you're at a party, talk to the boys, the men. Conversation will be much more rewarding." It would take the women's movement, some thirty years in the future, along with my experience as an unaccompanied woman, to convince me that my mother had been wrong.

When I began menstruating, the first girl in sixth grade to do so, my mother sighed, looked heavenward, and took me to the bathroom, where she told me that I had gotten the Curse, that I would have it every month, so get used to it. She gave me a Kotex, showed me how to hook it to the sanitary belt that stretched over my belly and was a sickly beige and bumpy, and left the bathroom. When cramps accompanied my "time of the month," when I "fell off the roof," when "company came to call," my mother, clearly disgusted that her daughter would give in to woman's weakness, ordered me to get out of bed and walk. The pain is in your head, she said. Well, she was half right. In twelfth-grade physiology, I learned that female bleeding was a "sloughing off of the endometrium," that the reproductive cycle was playing itself out in my body, and I was truly surprised. It was not my mother who told me about conception and birth and all parts in between; it was a high school textbook—and Norma, my best friend, who lived on a farm.

"You should give that back," said my mother, pointing to Dick's ID bracelet. So I did. Only the teasing of my friends—girls all—would get me to shave my legs, and then not until tenth grade. By then—way before then—I had breasts to worry about. They were just so damn big. My mother's were a normal size though they drooped; she explained, when she caught me peeking, that in the twenties she had bound them, as was the style, so as to make girls look like boys; in my mother's case her breasts went with the rest of her athletic self. I wore blousy blouses, dresses full on top, my breasts never going with anything respectable. I never wore a sweater. Everyone would surely see how abnormal I was; my shame would be for all to see. My favorite article of clothing was a sweatshirt, size XL. I had six of them.

My mother was also a wonderful woman. She loved me and my sister, all of us, especially my brothers. My doctor father was too busy to have much of a hand in rearing us. But sometimes my mother insisted on his participation.

One summer evening, the summer before I was to leave home to go to college, my mother called upstairs where I was reading—I was always reading. "Put that book down and come down here," she called. "Your father is going to teach you to dance."

I pretended I wasn't there. I pretended that I was deaf, that I was dead. "Take off that sweatshirt"—my mother had X-ray vision, too—"put on a blouse and skirt and get down here."

I had never danced with a boy or with a man. My town and the surrounding farms and my school were heavily populated with Mennonites, Amish, religious folk who did not allow dancing, movies, recorded music, television when it was invented. Now, my family, not being Mennonites, owned a record player and a television set; when it was on, our hired girl, Amish born and bred, kept her back to it; she would pass through the living room backward. I was fourteen before the town got a movie theater, a huge change. And dancing? Once, during my junior year, Sue Ellen, who, with her family, had once lived in Toledo, a city far to the north, talked the principal into letting us use the gymnasium for a school dance. About twenty-four girls and one boy—Johnny—showed up. Johnny, it turned out, could jitterbug (he was adopted), and so could Sue Ellen of Toledo. So they danced with each other and the rest of us took early training in wallflowering. Dances in the high school gym faded soon thereafter. Incidentally, we did not have a senior prom; we had a senior banquet. No dancing. And I went with the only teenage gay (I had no concept of that yet) atheist (that either) in Ohio. He was also poor, something unusual in our little town. His front door didn't even have a porch, just a cement block for a step. He didn't have a father either, just a mother who hardly ever came outside and who was old when she did. At the banquet, we had a good time. We talked about theater arts and laughed at the couples who were going steady. After high school, my date moved to New York City, became a curator at the Metropolitan

Museum of Art, married, and had five sons. You just never know.

So here was my mother commanding me to dance with my father. I skulked into the library, where my father sat reading the newspaper. "He's easy to follow," said my mother. "He always does the same thing." What same thing? I watched as Mom put a Bing Crosby record on the turntable. "Blue Room": oh god, I was going to have to slow-dance with my father. How incestuous could this be? Fortunately, I did not know the word *incest* either, so instead of bolting, I stood forlornly in the middle of the room.

"Ed, pay attention," said my mother. "She needs to know how to do this."

Reluctantly, my father put aside his newspaper and stepped forward in dance position. He smiled, not much more at ease than I was. But my father loved music, particularly Bing Crosby's music, so he quickly found the rhythm and led me about the room.

"Excuse me, I'm sorry, whoops . . ."

"Relax," said my father.

"He's doing the same thing over and over," my mother called from the sidelines.

"Relax," said my father. "Just follow my lead."

"Put your hand up over his shoulder," my mother ordered. "Don't drag on his arm."

I couldn't. I stumbled over my own feet, stepped on my father's feet, dragged on his arm, until at last the record ended. My father breathed a sigh of relief, my mother just sighed, and I scurried back upstairs to my book.

But she wasn't finished preparing me for college. I had to learn how to play bridge. Every night after dinner, she and my father and my brother, three years younger than I, would gather at the bridge table in the living room. While I tried to shuffle cards and deal them gracefully, the way my mother did, my father read the newspaper. "Ed, put that paper down," my mother would say. And he would while he bid or played the hand. Otherwise, he was completely uninterested, oblivious to all but his newspaper. My parents were good bridge players. This must have been hell on them, for I never learned how to play bridge, though my brother got quite good; actually, I did learn how to play bridge—badly.

The next college prep course my mother gave me I aced. It was How to Mix a Drink. "Never, ever stir a drink with a spoon," my mother admonished as she got out the ingredients for the cocktail hour. "Remember: the spoon is the enemy of the highball." I nodded solemnly. "If you want to stir it," she went on, "use this." She held up her index finger. "It's nature's swizzle stick. Here." She held out the properly mixed scotch and soda. "Drink this." It tasted terrible. I scowled. "That's all right, honey," she said. "You'll get used to it. Like coffee." I didn't like that either. "Another thing," she said. "When you drink gin and tonic, always leave the lime in the glass when you mix the next one. That way you'll always know how many you've had." Oh gee, would I remember all this? I envisioned college as one big cocktail party that I would pass or fail depending on my bartending skills.

Well, she had done all she could. She sighed and said to me, on my final day at home, "I worry about you. You're too nice."

The next day my mother and father drove me to Ann Arbor. I would spend my sophomore year playing bridge; by my junior year I could drink right along with the best of them, which made dancing not quite so terrifying. But in the first semester of my freshman year, I did something my mother had never said a word about: kissing. I wasn't too nice after all. I was a girl.

———

NOW, HERE IT WAS, forty-eight years later, 1999, and I was going on a date. Just me and a man in a public place.

"Your choice," he had said when I phoned to accept his invitation.

The Zuni Café in San Francisco is cool. It is the best place in town for people watching, not that it's full of famous people but that the people who come here are interesting: sort of theatrical-looking, offbeat, European or punk or sometimes African, most times all mixed up. In fact, it's where Nicolas Cage used to hang out before he changed his jawline and ripped his abs. The Zuni makes me feel like I'm in another country where, though I am an obvious tourist, the natives are happy to see me. It also serves the best hamburger in town and the very best Caesar salad anywhere. So whatever else might happen, I figured I would get a good meal out of this.

I was early. I am always early; comes from being a teacher, I guess. So I waited for this man upstairs in the café, the Zuni being on three levels, our table-to-be on the third. I sat, my back to the wall, facing the entryway. Here he came.

Bantam rooster, I thought, as I watched him come toward me. His chest stuck out, his legs were shorter than mine and more bowed, and along the top of his head the gray fuzz of his hair made a perfect coxcomb. He strutted. I smiled and held out my hand. He ignored it and sat down.

"Haven't had a drink in two years," he said. "Coffee!" he called to the waiter. When it came, he clattered the cup in the saucer, and as he raised it to his lips, his hand shook so violently that the coffee splashed onto the white tablecloth. "Another cup!" he ordered. "So you're a teacher, are you?" Before I could answer, he said, "Me, too. Business math. Being sued got me sober."

"For what?" I asked.

"Sexual harassment," he said. "Of course they'd try to get

me on that. Natural to suspect an ex-priest of something that stupid. Sorry about the tablecloth." We both looked at the cloth around his place, wet through, the dark of the coffee spreading into the middle of the table. The waiter came forward, quickly and efficiently exchanged the stained cloth for a new one, and took our orders.

"My daughter understands me," he said. "Nobody else does." I believed him at once. "And Ireland," he remembered. "They know how to handle me in Ireland."

Not a rooster, I thought, a leprechaun. That's what he looks like. I had never been partial to leprechauns or to anything Irish, with the exceptions of G. B. Shaw, James Joyce, W. B. Yeats, and, lately, Roddy Doyle. I was certainly not warming to this man. I would try harder. I leaned forward and said, "Tell me what it's like when people don't understand you. Tell me what it's like to be sued. Did you really win?" I was genuinely curious and relieved: I was certainly not going to sleep with this man, not even see him again. I relaxed. If he could just hold his coffee.

His eyes brightened, dimmed when he spilled his third cup of coffee, and regained a bit o' glimmer as he launched into the telling of a tale in which he was the hero, the victim, the loser, the winner, the cleverest little guy in the entire college. "Actually," he said, "I think they just used the sexual harassment thing to try and get rid of me." I shuddered as he lifted a glass of water to his mouth with both hands. I imagined him holding his glass full of whiskey, Irish no doubt, in just that way, spilling a good bit but belting enough to calm his nerves, steady his hands for the next one.

"You know," he continued, "ever since this women's movement, some damn female has been out to get people like me. I'm just a guy who's friendly, a guy who'll pat you on the back or the fanny, maybe put an arm around your waist . . ." He reached across the table to grab my hand, which, ever so quickly, I tucked beneath the table, where I dug my nails into my palm. "Anyway, they paid me a huge amount of money to resign." He blushed unbecomingly. "It's what's taking me to Ireland."

I had had enough. But I didn't get up and leave. I could have. It wasn't that I cared what the other diners in the room thought of me; I certainly didn't care what Danny here thought of me. But I stayed. Days later, as I related this experience to my friend, she asked, "Why didn't you leave?" I answered, "I wanted to find out how it would turn out." I had no idea what I was in for.

"I've got a great sense of humor," Danny said. "Watch this."

He spun in his chair, began to jerk his head back and forth, looked at the waiter, who came forward, our hamburgers balanced on his arm, and said, in a loud voice shaking with desperation, "Who took my medication? I can't function without my medication!"

The hamburgers on the waiter's arm almost tumbled; the waiter said, "Oh, sir, I don't know . . ."

Danny rose from his chair, whirled around, and, arms and legs moving spasmodically about, addressed the entire room: "Who's got it? My medication! I had it when I came in! I gotta have it! I do crazy things without it!" He looked wildly about him and bounced across the floor to the window. The waiter, white-faced, put the hamburgers down and moved to stop Danny from leaping to his death. The diners at the other tables watched open-mouthed, wide-eyed, frozen in disbelief.

I moved quickly from embarrassment to anger and, just as Danny lifted his leg and placed it on the windowsill, I bellowed in my best and loudest teacher voice, "Sit down!" And he did. He turned from the window, came back to the table, and sat down. "See?" he said, a triumphant grin on his face. "I told you I've got a great sense of humor." The gray fuzz on the top of his head stood out in all directions, as if it had been electrified by its owner's performance. He turned and addressed the people at the table across the room. "This is our first date," he said. "How'm I doing?"

"Eat your hamburger," I ordered. "You're going to leave that waiter a very large tip."

"Boy, some people these days just don't know how to take a joke, know what I mean?" The men at the table across the room smiled their understanding. What was wrong with these people? The women looked at me in dismay and sympathy. Those men and those women didn't belong together. But, then, neither did we, this Danny so pleased with his cleverness and I so grimly angry.

I gulped the last of my hamburger—never let a good hamburger go to waste, and these were the days before *E. coli*—and signaled the waiter, still pale, for the check. I placed half the amount in front of Danny. "You're paying for your own lunch?" Danny asked.

"Yes, I am."

"That's classy," he said. "You're a classy woman."

"You are leaving the tip," I ordered.

Danny got out his wallet and pulled a few bills from the roll of money won from some exhausted junior college and intended now for Ireland. He placed three dollars on the table. "That's not enough," I said. Obediently, he placed dollar bills on the table, one on top of the other, until they made a sizable pile. "Keep going," I said and finally nodded. "That's enough." I added my tip to the pile and rose to leave.

As I passed the table of onlookers, I shook my head in sympathy at the young women who knew now, if they hadn't known before, that they were stuck with bozos. I never knew what happened to Danny, whether he sat there in the restaurant stuffing his harassment money back into his wallet, whether he chatted up the people at the surrounding tables, whether he trailed forlornly after me out of the restaurant. I suspect he left quite jauntily, having no audience to impress with his sense of humor, no fans, that is, until he returned to the land of his ancestors, where they understood him. I suspect he brushed our date away as just another failure of the Wrong Side of the Atlantic to appreciate him. Ah, the indomitability of the human spirit.

On the way home, I puzzled over this man. I think he lost his heart somewhere along the way of his life and never got it back. Maybe he thinks it's in Ireland. Oh, Ireland, here he comes, and just when you thought your troubles were over.

FIVE

The Fabulous Fifties

I left the safety of my little town for the mysteries of Ann Arbor confident that my bartending skills would see me through college. My first semester at the University of Michigan I spent kissing, and learning to talk dirty. Kissing came surprisingly easily, surprising in one whose high school friends called her (behind her back) the Ice Queen. Talking dirty took a little longer. My freshman roommate came from a Chicago suburb, a nice one. My swear word up to that time had been *fudge*. Hers was *fuck*. And she said it all the time. *Shit* was another word I had never uttered—I had hardly even heard it! Peggy used it frequently and as naturally as she used *fuck,* which was very natural. She taught me this ditty she and her high school friends had composed. It is sung to the tune of the radio jingle advertising Ajax, the foaming cleanser. Join me, won't you.

> *Boom boom boom penis (boom boom)*
> *The milky seminal (ba ba b-b-b bum bum)*
> *Floats the sperm right down the cunt (k-k-k-k-k-cunt)*
>
> *Aaaaand urine*
> *That yellow piss*

It's what you get
In a German kiss (k-k-k-k-k-k-kiss).

From that jingle I learned more about sex than I had in all my years up to that time. I sang it up and down the halls of the dormitory, delighted with my newfound crudeness and what I perceived as the introduction to wild sexual abandon. Peggy smoked Pall Malls, so I did that, too. The desk we shared— Peggy on one side, me on the other—was covered with cigarette ash; cigarette butts spilled onto it from the huge, rarely emptied, and always filthy ashtray. The curtains over the one window in our room, heavy with smoke, were always closed. Smoke trailed above our heads and settled into a permanent haze over our single converted to double by way of bunk beds. Our fingers turned yellow; our mouths and breaths reeked of stale, burned tobacco. Peggy loved that room, and so I did, too. About the only thing I didn't do that Peggy did was get elected to Phi Beta Kappa. I had to settle for smoking and swearing. It was enough. And, oh yes, I almost forgot. Peggy taught me to study. "Spark me, kid," she'd say in the early morning, and I would hold a match to her first cigarette. She did the same for me. We just lit up and hit the books. Some years later, Peggy told me, "You ask more of life than anyone I know." It was not a compliment, it was a warning. Phi Beta Kappa knew how to pick them.

Smoking and swearing lasted long past kissing. In college, one had dates. One went to mixers, one got fixed up by girlfriends with boys. And I was passing good-looking. Thanks once more to my mother, who daily cooked lean beef and supplied me with amphetamines, I had spent the previous six months dieting; except for my still-mammoth breasts, I looked okay. She had even had some of her classy clothes cut down to fit me, clothes she no longer wore. So, in my mother's suits and skirts, I went to beer parties and football games with boys. At the end of the second date—never on the first—I stood on the porch of my dorm and kissed Lance or Dave or Pete good night. I even did it open-mouthed like Dave taught me. "Not quite so wide," he said. I liked open-mouth kissing—French kissing, I learned it was. The boys seemed to enjoy it, too, once they got over worrying I might swallow their face. Then always the porch light would flicker, the sign from the housemother that the time to stop such goings-on had arrived. And then the porch light would come on and stay on, no environment for any kind of hanky-panky.

I would hurry up to my room and to Peggy, also returned from her date, and we would compare notes. The most important conversation we had, the most intimate I had ever had with anyone, was with Peggy. For we suffered from a similar handicap: large breasts, neither set perky. In the dark of our room, me on the top bunk, Peggy on the bottom, the bright tips of our cigarettes lighting up the night, we would wonder out loud about marriage. "What will we tell our husbands?" "Are you going to tell him before the wedding?" "What if he runs away?" Then we would laugh and pull the covers over our heads like the children we still were. "Do you ever let your date touch you there?" we asked each other. "Absolutely not," we answered.

The struggle to maintain my purity ended, with purity the victor, around December of that first semester. I had gained twenty pounds and looked not so good. My mother's clothes no longer fit, my breasts were even bigger, and I was ashamed of what I had done and of how I looked. The phone stopped ringing, and for the next three years, with a few exceptions, I remained dateless. One of the exceptions was Simon. He seemed to like me fat or not. He was Jewish, which appealed to me given my father's warnings that "There will be loud people in your classes who talk all the time and are pushy." My father's anti-Semitism appalled me; his feet turned to clay before my very eyes, and so it was with pride and a certain self-satisfaction that I sent home the photograph of Simon and me at the spring formal. He looked Jewish. He looked good. He was irreverent, and I liked that about him; he drove me all the way from Ann Arbor to Detroit to the burlesque. We drank beer, ate popcorn, and watched Tall, Tantalizing Tamara do things with a pole. She was beautiful. I wanted to be her. We went again, on Family Night. Popcorn was free and I think there was a donkey.

Simon wanted to kiss me and even more, and I didn't want him to. There must have been something wrong with him, I figured, if he liked me. By my junior year, I was a fashion embarrassment. I had taken to wearing the same pleated skirt, the same very big cardigan sweater, day after day. In the privacy of the sorority house, I wore khaki pants and—you guessed it—a sweatshirt. What was wrong with this tall, good-looking, Jewish, funny, nice boy that he liked me? I hated me, and gradually Simon grew discouraged and we became friends.

I had a lot of friends once word got around that I could hold my liquor. Peggy and I had pledged the same sorority—her grades got her in, my mother got me in—where she had pretty much given up dating in favor of studying. I had figured out how to get B's with very little work. In my free time, I saw every movie shown in Ann Arbor between 1951 and the year of my graduation, 1955. Now recall: my hometown had one movie theater and not even that until I was in eighth grade. Ann Arbor had three, plus the tiny one in the basement of Angell Hall where some cineast showed weird movies like Kafka's *The Metamorphosis,* one of the most powerful pieces of my education. So I didn't go to Angell Hall often. I stayed commercial and fell passionately in love with Marlon Brando in that motorcycle movie, *The Wild One.* I was the small-town girl in that movie, the one Marlon Brando saves from the bad motorcycle guys who are closing in on her to do unspeakable acts. He saved me eight times, the number of times I saw the movie. I also never missed a hockey game in four years—the team gave me an autographed stick, I caught a puck—and in between, I squeezed in a few baseball and basketball games. My fall was devoted, of course, to football games. Swim meets were always fun. If I couldn't sleep with boys, even kiss them, I could look at them. And catch their pucks. Ah, youth, ah, wilderness.

Weekend nights Peggy and I and others unaccompanied by boys to boring parties went to the movies with each other and wondered what Ginny and Judy did on the nights they climbed through the window after curfew. I, a beacon of rectitude, was elected to Standards Board. Standards Board determined the fates of wrongdoers. I must have been at my ugliest and not only physically when I voted to put Judy on probation for Staying Out All Night at a fraternity party. I watched, no doubt with a smug smile on my face, when Judy did as ordered and unpinned herself. No Delta Gamma for girls who flaunted their sexuality. Judy's breasts might be perky, but they didn't wear the DG anchor. Mine did.

My mother was a help here, too. We had never had a sex talk, really, like how one did it and why, if procreation wasn't on one's agenda. What advice she passed on to me had come while she and I changed the sheets on the beds once she determined I had learned to miter the corners properly. I was a senior in high school and the scandal in town was that Sally was pregnant. Sally was a senior, too, definitely a girl and a pretty one; she had a boyfriend named Alvin. They necked all over town. My mother decided to use Sally's unfortunate behavior to direct me in my life at the big university, where the freshman class was five times bigger than the entire town in which I grew up.

Pulling the bottom sheet tight, my mother said, "I hear Sally got herself in trouble."

I nodded. Sally was my friend.

"Whenever a girl gets pregnant outside of marriage, it's her fault." She straightened up to her full height of five feet nine inches and looked across the bed at me.

"It is?"

"It is." She continued, "Men have animal passions. It is the woman's duty to subdue them. If she fails, she may very well become pregnant. And she has only herself to blame."

I believed her. I believed everything my mother told me. She would never lie. She would never be mistaken. She would never be wrong. She was my mother.

On the other hand, I read books all the time. Not in English class, of course. In high school English class we had an anthology, so we read part of *Hamlet* and short stories by Saki and O. Henry. At the University of Michigan the faculty apparently assumed students had read all the famous works, so we were assigned the second and the third famous. I was, I figured, at least two years behind; it would take me most of my life to catch up on my reading, a most felicitous way to spend one's life.

The books I read while I was in high school came from the town library, where Sarah Levi steered me away from the adult shelves as long as she could. Eventually, at the library and in my grandmother's house, I came upon, I fell upon, what we now call bodice rippers. Frank G. Slaughter was my favorite, *Battle Surgeon* his best. The hero was a surgeon in battle in World War II. My dad was a surgeon, and during World War II he traveled to the county seat once a month to see if the draft board would call him up for duty. Every month he returned downhearted: the father of four and the only surgeon in three counties, he was essential to the homefront, which in fact wasn't all that beleaguered, most of its residents being Mennonites and so conscientious objectors. In *Battle Surgeon* the main character is terribly handsome, as was my father, and he wants this particular nurse. She is a good girl and resists; she is noble in wartime and gifted in her nursing, but one night, fresh from battlefield surgery, where the doctor and the nurse looked meaningfully at each other over their operating masks, the battle surgeon seizes her 'round the waist right when all the bombs are bursting and she feels the roughness of him pressing against her. He feels the mounds of her breasts (!) beneath her scrubs. Their hearts beat wildly and they kiss. Holy Toledo!

Then there was Frank Yerby. *Foxes of Harrow,* another winner (think Rex Harrison as the lead, which he was). The hero of this one is so enormously masculine, yet underneath his cavalier behavior so gentle, that no woman (Maureen O'Hara) could resist him. And she doesn't. She, like the battle nurse, is swept up, overpowered, overwhelmed by Manhood, and can't be held responsible for her passionate behavior.

One Christmas my grandmother, who lived across the street and belonged to the Literary Guild and read all of Taylor Caldwell's novels as fast as Ms. Caldwell could write them, gave my mother her very own copy of *Gone with the Wind* (so she would quit borrowing hers). At the tender age of sixteen, I read it. Sakes alive! Ashley, oh Ashley! Rhett, how could you? Scarlett, despite your first sentence, you were beautiful! You drove men wild with desire! And then, when he carried you up those stairs, and you did it, you did it against your will and only after you were married and you loved it. That's how sex ought to be!

There was no stopping me now.

Janice Meredith was a Revolutionary War romance, not nearly as torrid as *Gone with the Wind,* whose background of the Civil War far outshone *Janice*'s Revolutionary setting. Janice, too, saved an injured soldier, so she had to marry him, and she was

happy except that he was British, but what else could she do after she let him kiss her under the bridge? The very best of all,
though, was *The Sheik*. Ahhhh, *The Sheik*! I read *The Sheik* almost
as many times as my mother, though she never knew it. She
would send me to the library to get it and *Janice,* and I would
sneak it when she was paying attention to the younger kids in
my family or to my dad, who didn't read anything but medical
books in which my brother discovered photographs and draw-
ings of naked parts and showed them to me. *The Sheik,* a major
motion picture in 1921 starring Rudolph Valentino and Agnes
Ayres, beat *Gone with the Wind* all to heck when it came to sex.
Agnes played a smart-alecky, independent, rich English beauty
named Lady Diana Mayo, who travels to the desert to relieve the
boredom of her wealth-ridden life in rural England. She gets
kidnapped. She gets swooped up—by the sheik—carried to his
horse, put on the saddle right in front of the sheik, and trans-
ported far into the desert. All the way she can hear the pound-
ing of his heart and feel his burnoose pressing into her neck
and shoulders. And when they get there—to the sheik's silken
tent—he carries her not to his tent, but to her very own tent,
from which there is no escape being that it is the desert and all.
Then, one night he comes into the tent, her tent. "Why have
you brought me here?" Lady Diana demands. And the sheik
replies, "Are you not woman enough to know?" He kneels down
and covers her mouth with kisses. She resists, her little fists flail-
ing futilely against his brawny chest about to become nude. Finally, there is nothing for it but to succumb to his superior
strength and good looks, so succumb she does. They do it, she
likes it, and we're not even halfway through the book!

No wonder Miss Levi didn't want me reading this stuff. She
undoubtedly understood that Scarlett and Janice and Lady Diana were, in fact, raped, that these novels showed women who
enjoyed going limp, having it done to them against their will;

for, after all, what nice girl would do it willingly? That's what I learned, and although Miss Levi tried her best to keep me in the dark, she probably knew, too, that sex education begins at home.

In real life, my best friend's father was fire chief and roughly handsome. Her mother was delicately beautiful and played the violin. Life imitates art, don't you think?

So I went about my mother's business once I got to college, though I was dreadfully confused about what that business was. Still, the safe road is the high road. A few kisses, but more than that—no, no matter what Simon wanted. I subdued him, and me along with him. In fact, if I had been able to put two and two together, Simon, at six feet four inches and oh so fond of me, was the embodiment of all those fictional heroes. However, I was my mother's daughter, I was pretty sure, and I chose not to put anything together.

THESE WERE the fabulous fifties. In 1955 the pill was yet to be invented, *Roe* v. *Wade* was eighteen years away, but I was a twenty-two-year-old virgin living in San Francisco. ("I suppose you couldn't find anywhere farther away," my mother remarked acidly.) I fell in love.

I did not own a diaphragm. I had never heard of Planned Parenthood. And Jack made me come for the first time in my life, and I wanted him to do it again and again. And I loved him inside of me and I made myself not think about wanting this and him. And I hated condoms, which he wore most of the time; they were yucky, especially with all that gunk in them afterward. I had failed miserably at subduing his animal passions and, worse, I had to admit to having some of my own. I was on my way to hell. There was only one answer: we would marry.

Jack taught me oral sex. Not that he did it on me. Me going

down on him was what he taught. It was our form of birth control. It was better for him than having to pull out of me before he came. I loved giving him pleasure. I got right to it when I felt his insistent hand on the top of my head and listened to him groan as I swallowed his sperm, which I began to do regularly, after I forgot the Kleenex one night. For the first time in my life, I was powerful. Of course, I also knew I was a slut. So I didn't think about it. And I didn't think about what it might feel like if Jack reciprocated on me. I knew the words *blow job.* I knew boys got them. I had never heard of girls getting them, so they didn't because there was no such thing. I was Jack's to command. But I was the Keeper of the Flame.

In between times of lovemaking, and sometimes during, Jack got drunk. Sometimes he drank himself sick and threw up, more than once all over me, all over my sheets and pillow, and, as he leaned over the bed, into his shoes. This ought to have bothered me. He did it far too often, and once should have been enough for me to figure out that something was wrong. I knew that the young man I loved was not happy. But gosh, I honestly believed that I would make him happy and all things right once I became his wife. I had not the slightest doubt that, once we were married, his behavior would change.

What was going on here? What was going on here was that I wanted Jack to marry me so he could continue to fuck me. I loved Jack's lovemaking. He was sexy in a sloppy sort of way. To keep him in my bed or his bed or any bed at all with me in it, too, I tolerated vomit, long silences, slurred speech when speech came at all, and driving under the influence. I cleaned up after him, mixed his highballs, baked pies, knitted sweaters (I actually did all that) in the belief that surely he would see the light and that it would be at the end of the center aisle of the church. Poor Jack. Poor me.

After five years of this, one day the thought struck me that

Jack was getting tired of pulling out, that, despite the eloquence of my mouth and tongue, he was getting tired. I ought to get a diaphragm, that is, if I wanted to keep him, if I wanted him to marry me, which of course I did—why else would I be committing sin all over the place?

I turned to my sex guide, Mary McCarthy's *The Group*. The novel, a best-seller when it came out in 1954, concerned a group of college girls and their sex lives. My god, every one of them had one. And they were nice girls, too, from well-to-do families. They had gone to one of those fancy girls' schools in the East, which may have accounted for their being way, way ahead of Midwestern Me. But reading that novel I felt a rush of cool air. Sex was public. Mary McCarthy had made it so. Sex was not dirty. Unless nasty people had it. Happy and unhappy people had sex; sometimes the sex was wonderful, sometimes it wasn't. But definitely it was something that normal girls and boys did. And not always inside marriage. Maybe I wasn't so bad after all.

In the book one of the characters, Dottie, does what I ought to have done at the very beginning of my love affair with Jack. Dottie goes to a doctor to be fitted with a diaphragm. Surely, I thought, the doctor will castigate her—an unmarried woman—and very possibly refuse her request for contraception. No such worries plague Dottie, for she is here at the request of the young man she loves. "A female contraceptive, a plug," he tells her. "Get it from a doctor."

Jack had never been this forthright with me. Jack didn't talk much at all, actually, and never about making love to me. I suspect he felt guilty for turning me into a slut. In the novel, Dottie believes her lover must really like her, must love her, to want her to keep herself safe from his desire: he must want to make love to her terribly. Surely, this must be true of Jack, too. I thought that, if I had a diaphragm, if I could make it possible for Jack, free of messy condoms, to stay in me, not to have to pull out at the last minute, he would like sex with me instead of groaning at the last minute and throwing himself toward the other side of the bed and the box of Kleenex.

And, according to Mary McCarthy, getting fixed up was legal, pretty much. Doctors were allowed to prescribe contraceptives for the prevention or cure of disease. In my case, pregnancy would be a disease if I weren't married, the worst disease possible. Abortion was out of the question. When I was still in high school, I asked my mother what would happen if I got pregnant before I was married. "Don't any doctors [thinking of my doctor father] help?"

"No reputable physician would touch you," my mother answered, "and those who would are filthy and you would die from the infection."

That is what happened to one of my friends who returned from Europe pregnant by her Italian lover. She found an abortionist in New York and, sure enough, developed an infection that put her in the hospital. Her mother visited her there, looked down at her daughter, and said, "We will never speak of this again." I knew this was exactly what my mother would do.

Another friend, finding herself pregnant by her married boyfriend, journeyed to Mexico. She returned infected physically and emotionally. I spent long nights listening to her describe the horrors of the dirty table in the dirty room, of the pain with no anesthesia, of the humiliation when the abortionist held up the fetus and ordered her to "Look! Shame!" It was a boy, my friend said, before she killed it.

So, for better or for worse, babies and sex went together. Unless there were other ways of doing it. In the novel, Dottie's doctor—a woman!—tells Dottie, "Any techniques that give both partners pleasure are perfectly allowable and natural. There are no practices, oral or manual, that are wrong in lovemaking, as long as both partners enjoy them." My skin crawled. Could this doctor mean that oral sex, which I knew I practiced on Jack, went both ways—that a man might "go down" on me? God, no. I would never put a man through that. Think of the smell.

I didn't go to the doctor. I did not get fitted with a diaphragm. I just couldn't. If I had taken such a bold step I would have had to face the fact that I was having illicit sex, that I was enjoying it, and that I was a whore without the money. I was getting so good at pretending—most of the time I believed Jack was in love with me—that facing Science in the person of a doctor would blow my cover. Not far below the surface of my pretending was my guilty secret that if I did get pregnant, Jack would have to marry me. And way below even that lay my desire to get pregnant, to do the very thing my mother had warned me most fiercely about. Revenge, how sweet.

Besides, I knew from my reading that I would have to have a pelvic examination. I had never had one, but I had seen one happen. The summer of my sophomore year in college, I worked in my father's office as a receptionist for him and the two other doctors who made up his practice. One afternoon, Jeanine Monroe, a girl two years ahead of me in high school, came in for her pregnancy checkup. I did not know the law mandated that someone in addition to the doctor be present during a pelvic exam. My father did not explain this to me. He said, from the examining room, "Come in here." I do not remember my demur, but there must have been one because he said loudly, "Get in here and behave like an adult."

Jeanine Monroe used to sit in the back booth of the City Drugstore and smoke cigarettes—in high school! The boys would come in after basketball practice and stand around while Jeanine blew smoke rings and drank the cherry Cokes they bought her. She would look up from under her long eyelashes, through the veil of smoke, and sometimes she would smile at the boys, sometimes she just looked back at them. I admired her tremendously. The boys on the team—Babe and Paul and Guy and Roger, the crushes of every girl in school including me—rocked back and forth on their heels and punched each other out of the way so they could squeeze into the booth with Jeanine.

Pretty soon something would happen, like Rutheda Dimke, wearing something see-through and flimsy and tacky, would come in—she was secretary at the ladder factory—and buy something from Ray Klopfenstein, the owner of the store and father of the adopted boy who could dance, Johnny. All conversation in the store would stop, the boys would shush each other, and Jeanine would pause in her smoking while we listened to hear what Rutheda would order. If she asked Ray for a box of Kotex, it meant that she had her period and couldn't meet him upstairs in the attic of the store for their affair. The attic of the City Drug was where Stinky Burkholder did it to Lauretta Riegsecker, too, and had to go to the army. Everybody in the store, everybody in town, knew what was going on and didn't really blame Ray. Ray's wife, Louella, was not the world's greatest-looking woman. We did, of course, blame Rutheda; we were scandalized by her. No wonder she wasn't married. The City Drug absolutely teemed with sex.

Only a few short years later, in my father's office, there I was in the examining room, Jeanine, now properly married and pregnant, on the table. I stood, my back against the wall, my eyes on the ceiling, while my father put his fingers into Jeanine. It lasted forever. I thought I would be sick. I don't know if this was my father's idea of sex education or if he was just grossly insensitive, probably both.

And now, in my own real twenty-two-year life as a sex person in need of a diaphragm, a doctor—of course, he would be male—would put his finger right up me. The picture in my mind of me lying on an examining table, legs spread, while some strange man peered into my very self terrified me. Sex was dark; it belonged to the night, to the back booth of the City Drug, to the backseat of a car, to a blanket on the ground after midnight. Sex was furtive, dangerous, secret, forbidden, and therefore very exciting. Besides all that, look what happens to Dottie in the book: she gets her diaphragm, calls her lover, aptly named Dick, who is not at home and is never at home to her ever again. That's what you get when you go crazy outside of marriage.

So no diaphragm for me, and I continued to feel guilty as the times Jack and I made love grew fewer and fewer. I continued also to repress any thinking about what we were doing. I just waited for Jack to come round and marry me. Marriage would keep me from being a nymphomaniac.

When Jack betrayed me with another girl, when I found them in his bed, our bed, I forgave him. So he disappeared. He ran away. He fled. My sexual neediness, my desires, my requests, everything my mother had told me was improper—unless they belonged to men—had done this, had driven away forever the man who might have married me and made me respectable. So once again, I gave up on sex, tucked it way down deep, out of sight, out of mind. Until my biological clock, the phrase having yet to be born, began to chime.

Jack had done something terribly important for me besides introducing me to the thrill of the orgasm. Wordless though he usually was, he said near what would be the end of our affair, "Why don't you do something for yourself?" What was he talking about? Doing for myself meant getting married, having children, and making everybody happy the way all my friends were doing. What would doing something for myself be? What had I ever liked doing? The answer came quickly. I had liked going to school. I had liked getting taught by smart people, all men, of course. And so I went back to find them. To the University of California at Berkeley. I have Jack to thank for starting me off on what would be the happiest time of my life. Until now, of course.

SIX

My Very Own Jew

*I grew up a Jew in a neighborhood peopled by Polish foundry workers
whose children, in packs, would surround me shouting, "Christ
killer!" Until I would go berserk and drive them away, large and
small, by the fearsomeness of my rage and fear.*

—JONAH

I stood at the corner of College and Ashby, one of the busiest
intersections of Berkeley, and listened intently to my friend
Sandy. I love this corner. Almost always it is crowded with people walking and talking, young and old, homeless and not. It is a
university corner and has a vitality I find in no other city, with
the possible exceptions of Florence, Oxford, Ann Arbor, Cam-
bridge, and I could go on. Be patient while I outgrow an adolescent addiction to hyperbole.

Thanksgiving, not far away, will empty Berkeley of many of
its young—about thirty thousand—but now, the air sang with
the energy of people of all ages busy with ideas and each other.
I stepped back from the curb as an old BMW roared around the
corner, heedless of those who might be waiting to cross. Always
interesting, Berkeley is not always friendly.

Sandy's voice, its Chicago accent outperforming all the noises of the street, says, "This Jonah guy's coming when? This weekend? You've got to be kidding me!" I smile shyly. Sandy says, "Condoms! Have you got condoms?" A passing couple looks at us and smiles. I put my head down and my hand up to one side of my face. "You don't!" Sandy yells. "Your generation never thinks of things like that. That's why I'm talking to you." Today, Sandy looks like Margaret O'Brien in *Meet Me in St. Louis* dressed for Halloween. Sandy's clothes are big, long, wide on her slim little body. The top is green, the pants some shade of magenta. The sleeves fall over her wrists, the hems of her pants cover her shoes. Even without the voice, Sandy is someone people notice. The more excited she gets, the more she flaps. She is a sail whose sheets no one can catch. She is three sheets to the wind without a need for alcohol to put her there.

"Let's have a cup of tea." I point at the café across the street. I am regretting sharing my joyful secret. But I had had to. Keeping the deliciousness all to myself was more than I could manage. As the days passed since I had answered the first letters, tension had mounted. Sometimes, inside my own silence, I felt terror and desire wrapped in a ball, starting somewhere in my middle, rising into my chest, then dropping suddenly to the parts of me I wasn't used to feeling at all. It might really happen, a man might really touch me. Sometimes, I thought I might faint. So I had told a few friends, one of them Sandy, this young woman with the pink-tipped hair.

Sandy is on a roll. She throws her hands into the air. Birds dart away. "My generation? Condoms are just part of everyday life. They're de rigueur. We wouldn't think of having sex without some kind of protection." She softens and puts her hand on my shoulder. "But sweetie, I know. I know guys your age, they go way back, they go back to the time when they didn't use anything, or if they did, it was the girl who was supposed to provide the protection, a diaphragm, something like that. STDs? Never heard of 'em." I refrain from lecturing her on syphilis and the generations it had ravaged before penicillin. Let her rant. It is too late to stop her or the people who slow to hear her. I hear titters.

Sandy and I met at a nearby exercise studio where we are regulars. Like her, I am a fervent exerciser. Now. Not always. In the past I had subscribed to Mark Twain's "Whenever I feel the urge to exercise, I lie down until it passes." And so I grew fat.

In 1983, I turned fifty. I weighed 234 pounds. My son was a runaway living on the streets of Berkeley. I was polishing off a goodly amount of scotch each evening. I was living in a house I couldn't afford, and I was working sixty hours a week. I had not had sex in fifteen years, save with myself, an act grown increasingly unappealing with each ten pounds I added to my five-foot-three-inch frame. Paradoxically, I was a successful teacher of English in a California public high school. I was good at one thing. I was a helluva teacher. Teaching saved me from becoming a full-time drunk but not from becoming an obese, middle-aged, unhappy, distraught, frantic woman. I was bound for an early death.

At my fiftieth birthday party, one of my friends—in what surely he meant as a friendly, not a hostile, gesture—took many photographs of the people gathered to celebrate this important birthday, of the lavish buffet, the fully stocked bar, the hors d'oeuvres, the gifts, and of me. What he did was a kind of intervention. Nobody knew how to tell me I was out of control. So Rob did this: he put those photographs, carefully selected so that I was in every one of them, into an album, and a few days later, he gave the album to me. There I was, multiple images of me on every single page for pages and pages. Dreadful, absolutely dreadful. My color was high, like my blood pressure, which is to say, my cheeks were flushed; my chins rolled over the collar of my dress. (Yes, I had found a dress at the store for large women, which is where I shopped when absolute necessity made me do it; otherwise, I went to school to teach in one of three muumuus a friend had run up on her sewing machine.) My front self stuck out, way out, my breasts were enormous of course—surely you know by now—and I looked awful. So I never looked anywhere that might show my reflection—not in a mirror, not into a store window, and never into the faces of people I saw coming toward me on the street; their quick glances, their quicker turning away, telling me everything I did not want to know.

Still, public humiliations were there to remind me. One day, I took my son, then about seven, to the little train up in Tilden Park. The little train is a miniature train in which kids and their parents may ride along a miniature track through the leafiness of the park. My son and I sat in one of the cars, my bulk over-flowing its sides. Behind us sat a child who could talk and sing and who did. About me. "Lady, lady," he chanted singsong over and over, "fat old lady." It was the longest ride of my life. My son laughed—what else could he do? I was devastated. When I got the courage to face the facts of my obesity, I would realize that, in the four years since leaving my husband, I had gained seventy pounds. I was safe from men, to be sure, but not from children and other living things.

I was also not safe from illness. In my forties I began to get sick every so often and then regularly. At least once a year, during the Christmas holidays usually, I could count on a severe bronchitis attacking my lungs and staying there for months. I lost time from school, went to school sick, and was exhausted well into spring. I continued to smoke. When school ended in June, and I was able to force myself to look back on my year, I had to admit that it had been lousy: half of it I had spent dragging myself to school, half of it getting ready to drag myself there. And I am not accounting here—you can figure this out for yourself—for the quality of my mothering.

Then came the year the bronchitis turned into pneumonia. I coughed blood and I got scared. So, put it all together— my health, my appearance, my all-too-soon-to-be-orphaned son—and I changed my life.

At Alta Bates hospital in Berkeley, with the help of a nutritionist, a psychologist, an exercise physiologist, many aerobics teachers—every one of them heroic, every one of them memorable—I lost weight, one hundred pounds of it. My goals were three: (1) run the Bay to Breakers (seven miles through San Francisco to the Pacific Ocean, a hundred thousand people dressed in serious running shorts, dressed in costumes to shock and amuse, or dressed in nothing at all; (2) fit into 501 Levi's; and (3) go to the Black and White Ball (a benefit for the symphony in the middle of San Francisco, when all of the Civic Center—the enormous plaza bordered by the opera house, the symphony hall, City Hall, the library—becomes a dance floor where jazz bands and polka bands and rock bands and the San Francisco Symphony play music while men in black and white tuxedos and women in black and white ball gowns dance into the wee hours of the morning). It is the most romantic event in the city. In May I ran my first Bay to Breakers, and I ran three after that. I am wearing 501's as I write this. The ball? Two out of three's not bad.

One year later, in March 1984, I weighed 122 pounds. On my fifty-first birthday a friend took pictures of me. I looked awful: no color, scrawny, caved in everywhere. So I put back some. More or less, I've kept the weight off, though not without the help of Diet Center, Weight Watchers, and my own fear of being fat.

At the center of all this obsessiveness was the exercise studio. I was like Ben in *Death of a Salesman,* who boasted, "I went into the jungle and when I came out—by God—I was rich!" Me? I went into the gym and when I came out—by God—I was thin! You can never be too rich or too thin, right? Wrong. You can be either or both. But I have yet to meet a woman who thinks she's just right. Anyway, here's the gym:

In the eighties high-impact aerobic exercise was all the rage, even among serious-minded students of exercise and its benefits. Coaches at the university began requiring some of their athletes to enroll in aerobics classes as a way to develop balance and coordination. Physicians and counselors of addicts recommended aerobic exercise as a substitute for addiction, as a way to get high without benefit of illegal substances. Classes were full. Newspapers carried stories of exercisers who turned violent when someone took their space on the floor.

When I entered the studio for the very first time, at 234 pounds, dressed in the only exercise clothes that would fit— sweatpants and sweatshirt—one of the instructors barred the way to the floor. "Hi," she said, her smile chock-full of teeth, "I'm Debi. And I'm sorry, but we'll have to see your doctor's written permission before you can take classes here."

She was little and cute, bouncy as all get-out, perky even. She was no match for my girth. I swept her aside and walked to the middle of the floor. "Start the music," I ordered. She did.

On my way home from the studio, I stopped at an athletic-shoe store. Inside, a young man asked me if he could help. "I want a pair of running shoes," I said. "For whom?" he inquired. (Salespersons in Berkeley talk like that.) "For me," I said. He looked doubtful. "How often do you plan to run?" he asked. "Every day." The look on his face said, Humor her, she'll be dead in a week.

But I wasn't. I began to run from mailbox to mailbox. In the beginning weeks, I made it to the second mailbox. Before long,

I wasn't counting mailboxes anymore, and not long after that, I began to run races. Uphill, downhill, far and near.

I discovered my body. It stretched, it bent, it bowed, it jumped and jiggled and reached and stepped and moved—to rhythm, to the commands—"Suck it in! Breathe! Pull it in! Inhale! Exhale!" I came alive.

One evening I found myself in the front row of the studio, only inches from the mirror that covered the entire front wall, the only place left on the crowded floor. Usually, I got to class early to claim my spot in the back row. This particular evening—I went to class after school so was sometimes late—I found myself next to a gigantic young man who could only be a linebacker. On my other side was a tall young man, well over six feet, heavily muscled, whom I had noticed before, who seemed to spend most of his day at the studio, taking two, three, and more aerobics classes. Later, I learned from one of the instructors that he had been sent by his drug counselor, that he was sweating out drugs and alcohol and using his time in a way that would keep him out of the hospital and out of jail. In between classes, outside, at the curb, he smoked furiously, one cigarette after another.

"It's Raining Men" roared through the studio, and we began to move to its insistent beat. On my left, the man's long blond hair swung from side to side as the music pumped its way into our bodies. On the other side of me the linebacker pounded his legs into the floor. For a brief moment, I feared I might be crushed between them. Then we caught the rhythm—"Back two, three, four; up two, three, four; pick up those knees!" I looked at the three of us in the mirror, waving our hands, raising our knees, and I knew that at age fifty-two, I could keep up with these boys who were no more than twenty. We grinned at each other in the mirror as the sweat streamed down our faces, and congratulated ourselves silently when the Weather Girls brought things to an end with "Hallelujah" and "Amen."

Eventually, the young men disappeared; I stayed on and am there to this day. High-impact aerobics was followed by low-impact, safer for the joints. Things calmed down at the studio. Now, the regulars meet at 6:45 in the morning to exchange a bit of talk and to sweat against the coming of the new day. The times are different; people have calmed down; the energy is underground; the world seems to have grown up, not an altogether felicitous change. Given the seriousness—nay, the humorlessness—of the new century, I find Sandy especially precious.

"What about oral sex?" Sandy peers intently through her green-rimmed harlequin glasses, the scarlet spikes of her hair piercing the early morning fog. "Are you listening, Jane?" Now the passersby have definitely slowed. A crowd is about to gather. "AIDS," Sandy shouts. She is impatient, like a teacher who has had to ask the same question too many times. "Can you get AIDS from oral sex? Do you know, Jane?" She reins herself in and says, as if speaking to a slow-minded child, "Do you plan on having oral sex?" Her patience is at an end. "Oral sex, are you going to do it or not?" A woman smiles as she passes. She nods yes.

"Listen," says Sandy, "I've got to go. I'm due at my therapist." She hugs me. "Don't worry. You'll do fine. Me, I'm crazy, I know it, everybody knows it. Don't listen to me." And then, from the middle of the street, which she is crossing against the light, she turns and calls to me, "Call the San Francisco Hotline. Promise me!" I nod fervently, eager to do whatever I can to get Sandy out of traffic.

I hurry home to call the San Francisco Hotline. Because, of course, I plan on having oral sex. At least, I hope I will have oral sex. And I plan on giving some. In the dimness of my memory, I am good at both.

The young man on the other end of the hotline has a gentle, soothing voice. The possibility of contracting AIDS from oral sex is higher than had been thought in earlier times. My heart sinks. But the percentage is still low: up from 3 to perhaps 8 percent of the time the disease is contracted by way of oral sex. There should be little to fear, he tells me, as long as there are no cuts or sores on either the genital area or in the mouth. Of course, there won't be. The young man advises me that, if I do not know my partner intimately, I will do well to ask him for his sexual history. Okay, I will do whatever anybody tells me to. I will write Jonah at once. I will ask him, casually—good lord, how would that go: "Oh and by the way, I was just wondering, uh . . . " Jonah—this stranger—will be here within a week.

My e-mail to him borders on hysteria: *"How could I have been so naïve? This friend of mine says men of my generation don't give a flying fig for STDs!"* and at my teasing best, of which I am not altogether proud, I add, *"If I can't kiss you all over, then cancel your travel plans because long walks on the beach will simply not do."* I hate coy.

Jonah answers at once, declaring that he has been tested twice for AIDS, both times with negative results. His doctor has recently given him a clean bill of health. He ends with *"Listen to a lot of classical music and we'll be fine. Love and kisses, Jonah."* What a guy.

Jonah had arrived in packet number 1. I moved him immediately to the *yes* pile when I read, *"When I returned from my tea plantation in Sri Lanka, I went straight to the Breadloaf Conference in Vermont."* We wrote daily, sometimes more than once. He wanted to know about me. Where had I grown up? When had I first heard classical music? What was it? Where was I when I heard it? This was utterly seductive. No man, save for my analyst, whose job it was to ask me about myself, had ever been interested in me and the things, like music and books, that were important to me. I wrote to Jonah my memory of hearing, for the first time and only by an accident of radio waves, Rachmaninoff's First Piano Concerto in my bedroom upstairs in the northwest corner of my house in the wintertime of my little Ohio town. In return, Jonah wrote about hearing Rachmaninoff in his boardinghouse in New York while he was a graduate student at Columbia. Omigod, Columbia! He got better and better. Every single thing he told me about himself added to the picture I had of the ideal man, a man who wanted to know me, a man who was a Jew and for whom I could be a shiksa. Philip Roth would understand. Of course, in Roth's fiction, the coming together of Jew and shiksa spells disaster. Oh well, what does he know?

Jonah and I exchanged photographs. Mine had been taken by my son the previous Thanksgiving from far enough away that the lines in my face and the drooping of my parts were not visible. It was taken after I began to receive the answers to my ad and before I had met anyone face-to-face. In the photograph I am damn near radiant. I felt radiant. Where the hell did I put the negative of that picture? I'll never look like that again, and Jonah and a few others have the only evidence that I did.

In his photograph Jonah looked Mephistophelian in his pointed black beard and reddish hair. He looked absolutely foreign. He looked terribly exciting. And then, for no reason I could decipher, he stopped writing. A long, to me very long, silence ensued. I returned his photograph without a message. Later, he would tell me that receiving the photograph sans words had determined for him that he would fly across the country to sleep with me. *"I have no intention of sleeping alone,"* he wrote. The last letter before he boarded the plane ended with *"Let joy be unconfined."*

My friends who knew about all this—Bess, Celia, Jean—were

through cautioning me. They had said all the right things— "How do you know this guy's not crazy?" "What if you hate him?" "You're not going to let him stay with you, are you?" I convinced them that I had taken their concerns under advisement, that no matter what, I was going to do this unless something from Jonah made me decide otherwise, that I was perfectly capable of taking care of myself. So they decided to enjoy my ride.

I had given a lot of thought—hours and hours, waking and sleeping—to this visit. As soon as he had announced that he was coming all the way from Virginia, before I had even invited him, my mind went not to *no* but to details. I did not want to put him up in my tiny cottage. I wanted somewhere both more private and more public. I wanted somewhere neutral, a place we could decide if, really, we liked each other enough to take the next step. Jonah had written, in reply to my apprehensions, *"You and I have made a kind of unconventional contract. I will do my best to hold up my end—pun intended—and I hope your conflicts will not interfere with your will to hold up your end."* I wrote back, most assertively, *"I have entered into no contract and reserve the right to change my mind right up to and including the first moment of intimacy."* By god, I was in control and planned to remain that way.

Jonah wrote that he promised to *"send you on your way to being as sexually capable as my third wife was when we divorced."* Hmmm. He wrote that he was bringing his favorite wine and champagne and *"a few little extras to keep things interesting."* I flashed on the French movie *Romance,* where the girl finds herself with a sadomasochist. And likes it. Ah, those French. Thanks to them, I at least knew what the equipment looked like.

The night before his arrival I got tipsy on my own wine and went for a walk. Everybody should walk the world drunk. Or in love. Or both. People smiled. People were pretty, they moved sweetly, spoke softly, and no one seemed to mind when I drifted from one side of the sidewalk to the other. It was not the last time I would turn to wine to escape the terror of what might happen and the pain of what did.

The Claremont is a Berkeley landmark. It was built, rather it was begun to be built, in 1906, finished in 1915, added to since. It is beautiful. White, gabled, a gold-tipped tower at its center, it rambles along a hillside overlooking San Francisco Bay. It is expensive. This is where I decided Jonah and I would spend two, maybe even three, nights. We'd see after that. I couldn't afford one night, let alone two or three, but what the hell, I was going to do this right. And then the most extraordinary things began to happen: my friend Celia took great delight in all these goings-on. My age, she was and is feisty, funny, and friendly. The day before Jonah was to arrive, Celia beckoned me to her car outside our exercise studio. "Here," she said, "take this." She handed me an envelope. Inside was a card into which she had written, "Your shenanigans have given me such joy I want to be a small part of them." There sat a check for $250. "You can't afford the Claremont," she said. "Have fun."

When I got home, on the steps of my cottage was a package from Ann Arbor, Michigan, the home of my friend Bess. Inside the package was a beautiful bag from Pierre Deux and inside the bag was the most gorgeous nightgown I had ever seen: satin with lace trim on the neck and hem. I put it on. I looked at Celia's check. I would cash it. In the mirror, I looked at myself in the nightgown. I took it off. Not yet. Someday, but not yet.

I HAD MODELED for my friend Jean, who lived a few blocks away, what I had discovered in Macy's, where I was trying to answer the question What shall I wear? I pulled it out of the bag, held it up, and breathed a sigh of relief when Jean said, "Perfect." It was a red, very red, silk shirt. Underneath were red-white-and-blue striped pajama shorts. "Will you need them, do you think?" she asked, shaking her head no.

And so I had taken care of everything. Tomorrow morning, on my way to the airport, I would drop off at the Claremont the picnic I had put together from the finest delis of Berkeley: pâté, Brie, a baguette, olives, grapes, those little chicken legs, a bottle of champagne. I had requested from the hotel that there be in the room a refrigerator and a CD player for the music I was bringing—Rachmaninoff and Bruch's Violin Concerto, the piece Jonah had said was the very most romantic music ever composed. I of course went out and bought it. I had bought champagne glasses, too. They were pretty and tinkled when tapped lightly together. Things were going to be perfect if I had anything to do with them. If they weren't, it wouldn't be my fault.

At the airport—I am early—I walk resolutely to the gate. Here it is December and it is supposed to be at least cool! Instead, it is hot and I am dressed as if it were December in Minnesota. I wear what I will wear for future meetings with strange men: trousers and a very big sweater—a wool turtleneck tunic—on top. I will hide my body as long as possible; I am not, after all, a trollop. What I am is hot. Sweat rolls down my back, forming a little puddle somewhere below. I stride on, resolute, the back of my sweater sticking to me, my stomach in little to big knots that feel like billiard balls crashing into each other as they roll around my guts. But I am sure I look confident, in control. In fact, I have no idea how I look. If I walk the way I feel, I will crash into walls, people, benches, anything in the way of my veering. My head swims. My mouth is dry. What the hell am I doing?

Passengers begin to file off the plane. Can this be Jonah? He is carrying a wooden box, rectangular, big enough for whips and chains and manacles and masks. But no, he walks on by. And then I see him.

Pick up your feet. The man coming toward me is a leached-out version of the Jonah in the photograph. His color is gone; his hair is gone and, My god, I think, this man is old. He carries a duffel bag perfect for leather straps and handcuffs and lots of keys. It looks heavy; I can almost hear it clank. This is going to be disastrous. Then I remember what he had written in response to my tale of discovering classical music: *"When I was a graduate fellow in psychology at Columbia, years ago, the house where I stayed had its radio tuned to New York's radio station WQXR, which played classical—and some jazz—all day long. The signature melody of the morning wake-up program was exactly the piano concerto you first heard— the one that stole your musical virginity, so to speak. It made a lifelong romantic of me—which ain't necessarily good."* I breathe more easily. Would an aficionado of S and M write wonderful stuff like this? Of course, I had never actually seen a person I knew to be a fan of S and M. They could be all around.

He scuffs his way toward me and, as he draws even, I say, "Jonah?" His sidelong glance is both shy and shrewd, like Shylock's. It asks the question, Am I going to get away with this? And then he says, "Jane? You're prettier than your picture." Okay, this is going to work.

On the long walk from the airport to the car, Jonah shifts the heavy bag from one hand to the other. Proud of my well-exercised suitcase muscles (known officially as triceps), and being a good deal younger, I offer to carry the bag. "No, no," he says. "I'm fine." Of course, he doesn't want me discovering the paraphernalia right here in a public place. I lead the way and suddenly, I feel Jonah's hand on my butt. This is going to be good. So what if he does have a few small articles of torture? I can at least have the courtesy of listening while he explains what he will do with these things if I let him, which of course I won't, and besides, we will be in a public hotel and oh how I wished I hadn't asked for a room "very private."

In the car, Jonah asks, "What kind of car is this? Pretty fancy." I explain that I had bought it secondhand, that I had had the car for eight years. "Goes with your clothes," he says. "Nice. I especially like your pants." He slides his hand between my legs and runs it up and down the inside of my thigh. The car swerves, Jonah removes his hand and says, "Did you notice I'm not wearing my seatbelt?" "Put it on," I order. He doesn't, and his grin returns him to his photograph. And then he says, "I am a perfect gentleman until I get behind closed doors." The car swerves again, a tiny swerve, just enough for the car coming toward us to honk. People are so hostile these days.

I turn into the driveway of the Claremont and Jonah says, "I don't feel comfortable in places I don't belong." What is this about?

I say, "You belong wherever you are."

He follows me meekly to the desk, where I had reserved the room in his name. There, that ought to make him feel comfortable, especially when he sees I've already paid for it.

In the hallway on the way to the room, following the bellboy, whose ass is quite good, Jonah cups my left buttock, which, it seems to me, is settling even lower on my frame than when I got up this morning. I flash on a day of yore when one of my gay friends whispered the ultimate compliment to me: "We think you've got a great ass." Not too round, it had been firm and high, dammit, I had had a firm ass. Oh, what the hell, whatever he is doing feels good. I walk a little slower.

The bellboy unlocks the room, carries our bags inside, and cracks open the tiny window, which offers, according to my request, a view of San Francisco Bay. It offers a sliver of a view of San Francisco Bay. I look around the room: no refrigerator, no

CD player, and where is my picnic? I watch as Jonah tips the bellboy: one dollar.

We are alone. I walk to the phone. I list the errors of this room and demand my picnic. Within minutes—thank god, I can stall a bit longer—there comes a knock at the door. A very apologetic man, official-looking, leads us to the other end of the hotel and opens the door to a suite where there is everything—a sweeping view of San Francisco across the bay— and more, my picnic. "I think you'll like these arrangements," the man says. "Enjoy your stay."

And now we are alone. Jonah backs me up to the bed, his hand on my breast, his mouth not at all too red or too wet or too dry. He kisses me and I fall away into desire. I am lying next to a real person, a man who seems to like the way I feel. He is warm and hard in places, soft in others, smooth and rough. I touch him, run my hands up and down the whole of him. He touches me. I squirm. He laughs and dives south. He's not old at all. I come in minutes, probably seconds. Then it is his turn. "Talk dirty," he commands.

"I don't know how," I say.

"I'll teach you," he says. "Say 'cunt.' "

I don't want to, and I don't like his language, which does indeed qualify as "talking dirty." "Say 'fucking cunt,' " he says. "Are you? Are you a fucking cunt?"

"Shut up," I say.

He does and plunges into me. I like it. I love that part of sex, when the man first enters me. I know, I'm supposed to be complete, to be whole in and of myself, but truly, I love getting filled up. I do have, after all, this open space. And all that feminist stuff about sex being violence has never been true for me, though probably it's just that I never had enough to know. "Don't stop," I order Jonah. He doesn't. "Come in me," I say. He does.

Well, how about that. Kind of military, wouldn't you say: commands and obedience, mission completed in a minimal time period, thank you sir. I will not have another orgasm with this man Jonah. But I don't know that yet and so I will try because I think I ought to. I think that, in order to have successful sex—the right kind of sex—the woman has to have an orgasm in her vagina. I am just about as dumb as I was forty years ago when I read Doris Lessing's *The Golden Notebook* and, for the first time, saw the word *orgasm* and heard a character say "tampon" and "menstruating." In it her two women, "free" women, complain that men "get erections when they're with a woman they don't care anything about, but we don't have an orgasm unless we love him." Well, I don't want to believe that; I want to get an erection and have an orgasm just for the sheer pleasure of it. It seems to me logical and right that I be like a man in this regard. Plus, there is this G spot. It's in the vagina and I'm supposed to have one. In the seventies I had heard the word *clitoris* for the first time and was directed by women in the articles they were writing to forget the vagina and go for the sure thing. That was a relief, though I remembered, when I was married, having an orgasm in what I'm pretty sure was my vagina, so when Shere Hite came out with this G spot, I had to admit that I probably had had one. Isn't that what dildos go after? (That is not a rhetorical question.)

Well, right now, I have a real, live dildo, so if I do everything right, this man is going to hit my G spot (a carnival game on the midway in which the object is to ring my bell) and the world will rock. If I do it right. So Jonah is page one of the test booklet. Here is the scoring: simultaneous orgasm, 1,500 points (perfect score); vaginal orgasm, 1,200; clitoral but he does it, 1,000; clitoral but I do it, 700; he comes but I don't, 500; nobody comes, 0–10. (The 10 is if both of us try.) Jonah certainly seems without problems in this area, at least so far as his pleasure is concerned, so we're pretty well assured of 500 points, enough to get us into the next round. Right now, he is the only one here who seems not only willing but eager to keep trying. I am filled almost to the brim with pleasure when he does. I have never been crazy about tests, but this one . . . I agree with President Bush: testing should occur regularly.

Hours later, or probably an hour later, I stand at the window looking out at all of San Francisco Bay. The sun is going down behind the Golden Gate Bridge. The red silk nightshirt, which, thinking about it now, reflects the brilliance of the sunset, I am sure, slides along my body just as Jonah had and will again. "Jonah," I ask, "what do you have in your bag?"

He laughs and opens his bag. "I brought some special things just as I said I would." He pulls out a bottle of champagne. "The rest is more of the same, one for each night."

"I was afraid, you said, you implied . . ."

He laughs again. "Just wanted to keep you on edge."

"That's not funny," I say.

"Yes, it is," and he bites into a chicken leg.

At the end of the second day, which is much like the first, except that Jonah doesn't go down on me again and so I never come but that's okay, I put what remains of our picnic on the table in the living room of the suite and put Rachmaninoff on the CD player. Jonah opens the second bottle of champagne—it is Spanish sparkling wine, "Cheap," Jonah says—and I turn to get the champagne flutes. I can't find them.

"Shall I call housekeeping and complain now or wait until morning?" I ask.

"Might as well strike while the iron is hot," Jonah says.

I am furious. I can't believe a hotel as reputable as this one is would include thieves on its staff. The woman on the other end of the phone promises to check her supplies carefully. "In the meantime, would you like us to send up two of ours?" And they do. Promptly.

The next day we rest. We take walks. I hardly notice his shuffle. Jonah tells me about the plants growing along the way. He holds buds and petals in his hands and shows me parts of them, gives them names I have never heard before. It is while he holds the buds and leaves that I notice the skin on his hands stretched between the joints: it is pulled tight and smooth until it looks glassy, almost transparent, like the skin I see on old people. How old is this man and does it matter? Arm in arm, we walk down the streets of my neighborhood and I want to call to people, Look! Look at me! I am a normal woman! Here is a man who is touching me! Aren't I the most enviable woman you know? Don't you wish you were me? Didn't I do right to run an ad and sleep with a man I hardly knew? Don't you wish you had done it? Be happy for me, please. What keeps me silent and humble is the knowledge that I didn't get it right yet: I didn't have a vaginal orgasm. Jesus, sometimes I wonder about myself.

Jonah is a masterful storyteller. He tells stories about hard times in Sri Lanka, about his three children, grown now, his three ex-wives, gone now, his work with UNESCO, that, too, in the past. He tells jokes, not one-liners, story jokes that go on and on and are wonderful in his telling of them. Sometimes they are so long I guess the ending before he gets there and he laughs as he swings into the punchline. "You're the best audience I've ever had," he says. "You are a wonderful listener." I bask.

On the evening of the third day—Celia's check had been used up long before—Jonah pours champagne into the hotel's flutes; the glorious second movement of the Bruch warms the room. I smile at Jonah across the table. "How old are you, really?"

"I told you in my e-mail," he says.

"You said in your e-mail you were some years my senior. How many years senior?"

"A few."

"You look older than your photograph. I think you misled me, Jonah."

"I never lied." He looks down at the olive pits and chicken bones on his plate.

"How old are you?"

He looks past me, out the window where once again the sun is going down on the Golden Gate Bridge like I wish Jonah would on me and maybe would if I weren't too shy to ask. "I'm eighty-two. But I never lied."

That night, in bed, I get wet. I can feel the dampness in my red-white-and-blue shorts. I reach over for Jonah. He is lying on his back, eyes wide open. He says, "I do not desire you." And he rolls onto his side away from me.

It is the longest night I can remember. I lie on the edge of the bed, sick with humiliation, begging the morning to come. What had I done? Why didn't he want me? Jonah sleeps, still as death, the sheets pulled up under his chin.

In the morning, as I brush my teeth, I decide what to do. From the bedroom I hear Jonah say, "Do you want me to leave?"

"Yes," I say, and hand him the phone number of his airline.

We are silent almost all the way to the airport. Finally, I say, "Since I must look at this as a learning situation, do you have any thoughts about this debacle?"

Jonah looks straight ahead and says, "Get yourself some K-Y jelly. You get dry before I can get in and I can't keep it up long enough for you to get wet." What do you know, a test I didn't even know I was taking; no wonder I flunked.

My hands on the steering wheel are steady, the car moves ahead in a straight line, and I tell a joke. "There is this house of prostitution. The new owner decides he will put some class into the place. So he hires professionals. On the first floor he puts telephone operators." (This is a very old joke.) "On the second he puts secretaries. On the top floor he puts teachers." My voice is admirably steady and uninflected. It oozes with bitterness. "After about a month, the owner looks at his books and realizes that the first two floors are losing money. The third floor, the one with the teachers, is making money hand over fist. He decides to listen at the keyhole to find out what is going on." Jonah stares into traffic, still without his seatbelt. I resist the urge to unlock the door and push him out. I continue with my joke. "On the first floor, where the telephone operators are, he hears, 'I'm sorry, your three minutes are up.' Well, he thinks, that explains that. On the second, where the secretaries are, he hears, 'Sorry, it's time for my coffee break.' Okay, now I understand, he thinks. So he goes to the third floor, where the teachers are busy making money. He leans against the keyhole and hears, 'We're going to do this until we get it right.' "

At the drop-off, Jonah gets out, pulls his bag, now empty, or so I believe, from the backseat, leans into the car, and says, "I hope you get what you're looking for. You deserve it."

I wish I could quote a witty rejoinder here, something like "Fuck you." But I can't. I was too angry, too confused, too humiliated, to put anything into words. What was I looking for?

Back home, I call the hotel and release some of my anger onto housekeeping. Where the hell were those flutes? I want to know. When the woman assures me they have looked everywhere to no avail, I say, "I would like to be paid for those flutes. I would like you to replace them."

The rest of the day passes like molasses on cement. Exhausted, I thank whatever it is that brings eight P.M. around. Thank goodness I can go to sleep and tomorrow everything will be, will be . . . I open my bag and throw everything into the laundry basket: my red nightshirt, my pajama pants. Wait a minute, where are my pajama pants? I plow through my underwear, my socks, throw my shoes on the floor. No pants. Where on earth? Probably tangled at the bottom of the bed. I call housekeeping. No pants, no red-white-and-blue shorties.

And then it hits me. Housekeeping hadn't taken the flutes. Jonah had. And he had taken my pajama pants. No one else could have, no one else would have. I race for my purse—money is all there. What could he have wanted, this liar, this thief, this eighty-two-year-old man who had brought me back to life, sort of? Eventually, certainly not then, I would feel flattered. In his way, he wanted to remember his adventure to the other side of the country, to a woman he had courted across the ether, in a place too rich for his blood. I hope that's right.

A long time later, months later, when I was able to think about Jonah and me without cringing, without crying, I considered the matter of age and passion and desire. Jonah, I'd bet anything, wondered if he still could; I was a way of finding out. More than that, like me, he was looking for a place for his passion. The world has little use for us: we are old, what business have we with passion? So we found each other and who would know? Who would care? Old people, they should be dry. But we weren't.

Not at all philosophical that first night, I sit on my futon swathed in my big old pajamas and think about my ad: So, is it answered? Did I have a lot of sex with a man I like? Kind of, sort of, maybe. But I got rejected. No matter what he stole, he didn't want me. I got dry, I got ugly, I got whatever I got to make him not desire me. "I don't desire you," he said. Oh god, I hurt. It would take me a long time before I could imagine that Jonah, too, hurt. What Jonah was saying, I believe, was just that: he no longer desired me. I hadn't done wrong; neither had he. For more than two whole days, he had desired me and done wonderfully well by me. I suspect that is why, despite my imperious demands for his sexual history, my insistence on being in control, he flew three thousand miles—he wanted to find out about himself. Sexual partners for older men are no doubt as scarce as they are for older women. And here was my ad, blatantly, boldly calling for sex. If he had told me by e-mail of his real age, would I have urged him to come all this way? Would I have met his plane if he had? No, I would not have. I am ashamed.

But I would not get philosophical for a long time. That night, I think only of myself. I open the bottle of wine I bought in the week before Jonah's arrival. Perhaps, I had hoped, we would get along so well we might spend an hour or so in my very own cottage. He might like me not so rich as the Claremont suggested I was. Face facts. He doesn't desire me.

I drink the whole bottle.

SEVEN

Back to the Couch

You'd think I would have quit. Heavy losses in the first two rounds. Low test scores. Injuries painful though not fatal. I am, however, an equal opportunity woman. One Catholic, one Jew, how about an Episcopalian or a Muslim or—now, this was appealing—an atheist. But first, to the outpatient wing for a binding up of wounds. Back to the couch. Back to Dr. V.

During the five years I spent redesigning myself on Dr. V's couch, I did what analysands are supposed to do. (Debate over this is current.) I transferred my feelings for my father to my doctor, thereby gaining the opportunity of (forcibly) examining those emotions and coming to some kind of rational assessment of them. While I did this to good effect, I went beyond and fell in love with Dr. V. At least, I think that's what I did. And, if I thought I did, then I did. People who say "Oh, you just think you're in love" don't know what they're talking about.

Dr. V was perfect for me. (Are you laughing?) He understood me. (Now you're laughing.) He was like me (sort of), well, gosh, we had similar interests! Bach, for instance. And, more obscure, Trollope. I learned this not because Dr. V told me but—well, listen.

Dr. V's office is a small, brown-shingle cottage at the end of his own personal driveway, not unlike a primrose path. Inside is a small waiting room, a bathroom, and the inner office. The walls of the inner office are lined with books. On the table are beautiful miniatures from Africa or South America or Alaska, or Albuquerque, what do I know? Freud's desk held artifacts, too, ancient, small, intriguing, though not so colorful as these. In both offices, they sat where the doctors could see them. I think they helped keep the doctors from strangling their patients or just plain falling asleep.

In the room is a fireplace. One time, during the cold of winter, the heat stopped, and Dr. V lit a fire in the fireplace. From the couch I watched this sexiest of all men (him), wearing a herringbone jacket with leather elbow patches, urging sticks of wood (me) to blazing light (him and me). Now, I ask you.

During another fifty-minute hour I am lying on that damn couch, which looks pretty much like Freud's, and groaning about a passage from Trollope's *Miss MacKenzie*. In the passage Miss MacKenzie is lamenting the passing of her good looks. She is getting old. She is forty. I, age sixty, am wailing. And Dr. V says this amazing thing: "I think you're forgetting how that scene ends. It ends with Miss MacKenzie seeing her image in a mirror and kissing her reflection." Oh god, of course, he is right. But imagine! I held my breath. Trollope's novels, certainly this one, are long. How could anyone recall the end of a particular scene? We were meant to be, Dr. V and me. (Bear with me, dear reader, especially if you are Dr. V.)

So, of course, this man, this doctor, this scholar, this lover of music and literature, was perfect for me. Plus, he was Jewish! And I was pretty sure he read the *New York Review*. The only problem was, he wouldn't cooperate. Finally, I had to accept the fact that he was my doctor. Period. Goddamn professionalism gets in the way all the time. At the end of the five years I was still in love with this man who had had the good timing to get a divorce himself during my tenure as his patient. I was sure it was because of me. (I blush as I write this.) But he wouldn't come across even figuratively. Finally, I realized that analysis had done all it could for me—a lot—and that staying on would only prolong my misery over unrequited passion.

One year later, I wrote that ad for him. One year posttherapy and I wasn't cured. After I sent the ad in to the *New York Review,* I wrote in my journal, "I'm still looking for the likes of you." And now I was going back. Because I didn't know where else to go, what else to do, and I hurt something awful.

So I am lying on the couch—again—feeling like a failure and I am telling him about the ad and I tell him about getting sixty-three responses and suddenly I hear these strangled sounds from behind me, from Dr. V in his chair behind my head. He is laughing! "Forgive me," he stammers. "Of course, I read the ad. I suspected it came from you. Trollope was the signal. I wondered how things turned out. And now"—he's practically hiccuping with laughter—"I just can't remember when I've enjoyed a story more." He laughs out loud. And so do I. Right there, we become friends.

Love is a tyrant, isn't it. It keeps you in thrall, it makes you do things you would never do in your right mind, go places you don't especially want to go. It screws up your thinking, not to mention your stomach. "Love is a universal migraine," wrote Auden. He's right. It was so liberating not to be in love anymore.

Except I was, almost, again, on my way to servitude and vulnerability and excitement and passion. With Robert. Fickle, that's me.

Dr. V had helped me get free of my mother, my grandmother, my own self, whom I had kept a stranger all those years. He had seen me through exactly that traumatic experience the critics of psychoanalysis rail against: recovered memory. A bad rap, recovered memory syndrome. While I was in analysis, the *New York Review* was full of articles outlining the misuses of psychoanalysis, the abuses perpetrated by its practitioners, the duplicity of Freud himself. I read the *New York Review*. I knew by reputation some of the writers of those articles. Their credentials were impeccable. I was scared to death. What would this Svengali, this Rasputin, lead me into? What would Dr. V do to me?

Still, it came. One day, after my session, I was driving home thinking, as I always did after my fifty minutes, about what had transpired in Dr. V's office. I had been talking about my mother, about her Victorian view of sex, about the sadness of my grandmother's marriage, about the silence that surrounded everything sexual. Sex did not exist in my upbringing. But I had come to understand during my thrice-weekly sessions that sex, talked about or not, encouraged or not, hidden or apparent, went on in some form in the life of every man, woman, and child. "What," I wondered idly, "did Werner do about sex?"

Werner was our hired man, my mother's and my grandmother's. Werner was retarded, a thin man of indeterminate age, his face lined with years, or was it pain, who rode his bicycle uptown on errands for my family, sort of a town character. He chopped wood, moved furniture, washed the cars, fed my father's horse, cut the lawn, shoveled snow, all those things a retarded man could do, all those things my mother, father, and grandmother were too busy or not quite strong enough to do. He spoke very little, never carried on a real conversation. In his back pocket, in a brown paper bag, he carried peanut clusters with vanilla or maple centers purchased from the City Drug. When I was little, five or six, not long after my brother was born, I followed Werner around on his errands, his jobs. Sometimes, he offered me a peanut cluster. He lived in a little room in the attic of my grandmother's house.

On Dr. V's couch, I began to remember Werner's room, the rocking chair, the little window that looked out over the main street below and across the street to my house, where my mother was. I liked Werner's room. It was more my size. And then I began to remember images: Werner's striped OshKosh overalls, the fly which was level with my eyes when he stood facing me, and, after endless sessions of agony on Dr. V's couch, Werner's penis emerging. It was like a faucet; he showed me how to pump it up and down and how to drink from it. On the couch in Dr. V's office, I threw my hands over my eyes and sobbed. Dr. V never said a word. Then we went to work.

I am, if you haven't already figured it out, a cliché. Here I was, a victim of sexual abuse discovering it all on a doctor's couch, recovering my memory, repressed as hell, falling in love with my analyst. Well, you have to start somewhere.

Here's what I came to understand: I was probably repulsed and fascinated, curious and frightened, by the experience. I do not recall there being more than one such incident, though I do recall tiptoeing upstairs to Werner's room when he moved to a room over my grandmother's garage. I remember that. I remember being terrified on those stairs that Werner would be at the top, and feeling relieved or disappointed or both when he wasn't.

Sixty years later, I learned that little girls have erotic feelings, too. I learned that my memories and perceptions were true, that they did not arise solely from fantasy or from reading the *New York Review*. I learned to trust myself. I understood that it was not the experience that had a lasting effect on me. It was the silence. For I told no one. And in 1939 in a little Ohio town where everybody knew everybody, where everyone looked after everyone, no one, not my parents, not my grandparents, not the neighbors, wondered where this little girl went, where I might be going, as I followed Werner across the street and through the back door of my grandmother's house. No one wondered what Werner might do for sex. No one wondered about sex. Even so, somewhere in all that silence, they had taught me that sex was forbidden. It was bad. I had done a bad thing. So I kept ever so quiet. Werner worked for our family for the next thirty-five years.

Repression became a way of life for me. Pretending, lying to myself, mainly not thinking: I got so good at pretending that by the time I was having sex—with Jack; with Tom, my husband-to-be—I could convince myself of just about anything, even that I wasn't having sex, that I was just going camping or resting in a park at midnight on a blanket with a friend. I was a pro at not thinking. But, oh god, how I needed to feel. And I couldn't, all blocked up like that.

I tried, though.

In 1962, my third year of teaching high school English, I was terribly busy. My passion had all these places to go, all these kids to use it up; there were all these books to be read and loved again. I was tired all the time, but I was happy. So why did I begin to go out at night alone? I was twenty-nine years old, on my way to being an old maid.

I sat at a table near the window of Little Joe's café in North Beach in San Francisco. My school was far away, my little rented house just across the Bay Bridge. In the back of the café six or eight young men played pool. A few couples occupied nearby tables, but for a popular place, it was pretty empty for a Friday night. I had come here many times, in the beginning with my friends, then occasionally alone after my friends and roommates married and scattered to the four corners of the universe, dragging babies and basinettes behind them. By now, I knew the bartender and the cook at Little Joe's. I ordered a beer and a Hangtown fry.

He stood at the bar and he was alone. I went to the bar and

ordered another beer. He was tall. He looked down at me, smiled, and introduced himself. His name was Tom. He was from Cleveland. He was a graduate student at Berkeley. In math. My dad would approve. Tom was a sports fan. My mother would approve. Perfect.

The following weekend we went camping. We never left the tent. On Sunday evening we left the campground exhausted and the next weekend we went again.

After a few months, I decided I must be in love with Tom; how else could I excuse my behavior? Tom naked was something else: he had those wonderful muscles over his hips that Greek statues have—think Michelangelo's David. He looked a lot like most of Art History 101. Though I saw myself as the ancient carving, the squat, rotund Venus of Willendorf, I began to feel less embarrassed about my body. Lying down I wasn't so short and stubby. Lying down became my favorite position. Lying on top of me was Tom's. We were a perfect match.

Back in Ohio, my mother had given up on me. "I just tell everybody who asks, 'Oh, we've given up on Jane. We don't think she'll ever get married.'" To my sister she said, "I worry about this camping Jane and that boy are doing. I'm afraid of what might be going on there." My sister replied, "She's twenty-nine years old. I hope something's going on."

Far away in California, clinging to the vestiges of what I knew was my duty, I should have jumped at the chance when, in December 1963, just before my thirtieth birthday, Tom proposed. I should have been relieved, elated, even grateful, but I knew I didn't love this man; lots of times I didn't even like him. He made me ashamed when he snapped his fingers at me when he caught me gnawing a fingernail. He made me afraid when he drove my car pell-mell and helter-skelter across lanes, within inches of other vehicles, through yellow lights, asserting all the while that if there were an accident, it wouldn't be his fault, he hadn't broken any laws. He made me angry when he turned all discussions into arguments and he humiliated me when he demanded in front of the other bridge players that I explain exactly why I had bid four clubs and led with a heart. He was not nice to me, and beneath my desperation I knew I didn't want to marry him. But ahead of me lay a future so empty save for my mother's disapproval, so dark, so lonely, I said to Tom, "May I have time to think about it?" He gave me a peck on the cheek, said, "Sure, take all the time you want," and trotted off to his rooming house full of graduate students just like him.

Not long after, I missed my period for the first time in my life. I went to the doctor for my first pelvic examination and the test that would determine my future. I was pregnant. I called Tom. He came right over. I said, "I've thought it over and I would very much like to marry you." He would make it all right. He would explain everything to my mother. We would be happy. Everybody would be happy. I was happy. I was going to have a baby. I burst into tears.

"I'm pregnant," I sobbed. "I'm so sorry, I really am."

Tom looked at me very seriously and said, "I suppose the wedding ought to be sooner than later."

We were married that summer, me in a dress that hid the bulge in my tummy, Tom in a suit I bought for him at Brooks Brothers. My father flew out for the ceremony. My mother was not well enough to make the trip. The reception took place in the driveway in front of my house in Berkeley. The weather was unseasonably hot. I do not know what disaster befell the men, but the high heels of the women sank into the tar, and for an uncomfortable time we were stuck.

ON MY HONEYMOON, my untimely pregnancy returned me to my virgin state: no sex, no lovemaking; I was bleeding, I was an untouchable. My son no more than a pea pod inside me, I spotted all across the country as Tom and I drove to the Midwest to visit our parents. I began to bleed in Lovelock, Nevada, site of our first married and fully chaste night together, continued intermittently all the way across the country, and stopped right after I told my parents I was pregnant. Andy was born just fine six months later.

Archbold seemed the same. My parents seemed the same. It was I who was different. I could feel my mother's eyes on me throughout dinner. She and Tom talked enthusiastically about the Cleveland Browns' chances for the upcoming season. My father, whom I had consulted about the spotting, watched me as I stuffed my mouth with baked potato running with butter, beef tenderloin pink and juicy, and fresh peas from my grandmother's garden. My mother looked at me disapprovingly. I swallowed and said, "I suppose you're wondering about my expanded waistline."

"Expanded everything," my mother said.

"I'm going to have a baby," I exclaimed proudly. Somehow, I thought having a baby was terrific. I was happy. I was married and I was pregnant, something my mother had always wanted for me, just not in that order. Why was my mother folding her napkin and pushing her chair away from the table?

Her eyes blazed. "It doesn't mean you have to get fat. What will I tell people?" She left the room.

Late that night, Tom slipped into bed beside me. "Where have you been?" I asked.

"Talking to your mother. She summoned me."

The queen bee, I thought. Tom wasn't the first of my boyfriends to choose my mother. Frank, when he left me, had said, "It's really your mother I've fallen in love with." What the hell, I, too, loved my mother more than I loved me. So did my father.

"What did you talk about?" I asked Tom.

"I didn't talk much at all. She did most of the talking."

"What did she say?"

"She apologized."

"Apologized for what?"

"For you. For your behavior." The way he said it, I knew that my mother had won. He believed her. He hated being caught by a girl, now his wife, who had trapped him. And now he would have to tell this to his own mother; he would somehow have to defend this pregnant stranger to his Catholic mother and convince her that his life was not ruined. "Did you ever love me?" he wanted to know.

"I love you now," I said. And I did. I was pregnant and, until the baby came, he was all I had. I loved him desperately.

The next morning, we packed up and bid good-bye. My mother never spoke to me again. Of course, she would have; of course she would have fallen in love with my beautiful son. She would have held him and, when he got older, played catch with him and shown him how to hold a tennis racket. And she would have talked to me, her firstborn child, about how to be a good mother and how to stop his crying and how to tell colic from whatever else kept him up all night and how not to feel guilty when I had to go back to work when he was so very very little. She would have talked to me; she would have made everything all right. But my mother died four months after Andy was born. No one knew she was so sick, not my doctor father, not even the surgeons at the Cleveland Clinic, where they operated on her heart, a successful operation, they told us. "I'm going to die, aren't I?" she said to my father. "Of course not," he said. "The prognosis is good." At six o'clock the following morning she died, all alone. How could I have let her die alone? How could she leave me so alone? What would become of us without her?

EIGHT

A Woman of Many Parts

My mother was a remarkable woman. She was, as these pages have shown, Victorian in her view of sex. In all other ways, she was ahead of her time, outside of her time, and fascinating to all who knew her.

I disappointed my mother terribly. I had done the very worst she could imagine. How could her daughter have allowed this to happen when, all the years of her growing up, they were not just mother and daughter but best friends? It was a betrayal my mother would never get over.

In the days of our friendship, when I was fifteen, before my sexuality made me an alien, my mother introduced me to New York. At fifteen I was as awkward an adolescent as an over-weight, acneified girl could be. My mother, all by herself, put the two of us on the train and off we went. I think she had it in mind to let the city she and my father loved shake some of the hayseed from my hair. I suspect she was beginning to worry about my ever being suitable enough to attract the kind of boy she planned for me to marry. She had never been to New York without my father; there was a certain desperation to this trip. Whatever her motives, she introduced me to the city with which I would have a lifelong love affair.

My mother was tall—five feet, nine inches—with long arms and legs. Her nose had been broken on the basketball floor where she played center for her high school team. It had healed into something handsomely Roman. She moved elegantly, gracefully, with a golfer's easy stride. When I saw Glenn Close on the screen in *The Natural,* I caught my breath. My mother was just that beautiful.

My father used to joke, "I married your mother so I'd have time to beat her at something." A fine athlete himself, he never did. She was happiest on the tennis court or the golf course. She played like a man. She was beautiful to watch. When we moved into the house in Archbold that was built for us, right across the street from my paternal grandparents (now, there's a story), my dad bought the lot in back of the house and had a tennis court made, the first tennis court in all of Fulton County. It was 1938; people came from some distance and slowed their cars almost to a stall to see this remarkable sight: a woman, the wife of the town doctor, dressed in shorts, slamming the ball back across the net every time and every bit as hard as what her husband returned to her. Trophies decorated the mantel over our fireplace.

When television came to our town, she watched hockey, baseball, and football. On football Sundays she would stick a pot roast in the oven around ten A.M., put the oven on low, and say, "This will be ready around two; don't bother me." And she would position herself to watch football on, almost all the time, a snowy screen.

She listened to baseball on the radio. From her childhood on, the Detroit Tigers were her team. In the basement of our house, my mother sat before the mangle, ironing the sheets and pillowcases she had laundered and bleached and blued and fed through the wringer and hung on the line in the backyard to dry but not quite, just damp enough to send through the mangle without burning. On one corner of the mangle sat her bottle of

Coke, which she bought by the case. On the other corner, perched on its ashtray, a Lucky Strike sent its smoke spiraling into the air. My mother was an ironing fool. Sheets, dish towels, my brothers' T-shirts, my father's shirts and shorts: nothing escaped the mangle. On the shelf nearby sat the radio. The ball game was on, the Tigers were playing. My mother was a happy woman.

The Detroit Lions were her football team. She hated the Cleveland Browns with a passion. "The only team in the country where the quarterback doesn't call his own plays," she would remind us in scathing tones. When a Cleveland player was injured and lay writhing on the turf, she would say, "I hope it's nothing minor." We learned to hate the Browns, too. And Ohio State. The Red Wings were her hockey team. During hockey season she showed by example how to hate most of Canada.

Some of the finest times she and I had together were listening on the radio to Indiana high school basketball, especially the tournaments. My mother taught me how to score those games, showed me how to signify baskets attempted, baskets missed, made, one point or two. Together, we followed teams right through to the finals, which were broadcast from courtside far away in Indiana. The reception was often crackly, so we had to lean in to the radio and listen through the scratchiness for what was happening. Then we would come out of our huddle to mark our score sheets. During halftime, we talked about who would foul out.

At dusk, on warm spring and summer evenings, we sat on our front steps and watched the cars go by. As dark came on, she taught me how to identify the makes of the cars by the spread of their headlights: Oldsmobiles wide, Pontiacs narrow. In between cars she would point out the bus carrying Seventh-Day Adventists. "They don't eat meat," she said. "That's why they're so pasty." She passed judgment: "Well, they can't go into the army, but they can drive their cars like a bat out of hell." She was referring to Mennonite boys, conscientious objectors during the war, who were unfortunate enough to drive their cars past my mother's scrutiny.

During the war, she taught me how to knit. She knitted sweaters and scarves for Bundles for Britain while I sat beside her and knitted long chains. She was a nurses' aide at the hospital. She ordered chocolate and cigarettes from the black market in Chicago. They came wrapped in plain brown paper, and my mother put them in a drawer we were forbidden to touch.

She taught me how to fold towels properly and how to miter the corners of sheets. She taught me to dislike cooking, cheerleaders, bell peppers, bowling, and Spanish. She taught me the pleasure of lying on my stomach in the springtime in search of four-leaf clovers. She told me that Loretta Young got her face lifted in Grand Rapids, Michigan, and that Spencer Tracy would never marry Katharine Hepburn because he was Catholic. She told me that Negroes wore suits of a special kind of blue called electric. She taught me not to mind when my grandmother said mean things to me. She showed me where to find wild violets.

Our mother died too young, at fifty-five, and for the last ten years of her life, she was unable to play tennis or golf or anything else. For a while, it was thought that her allergies to ragweed and wild mustard were what made her breathing difficult, but gradually, she was exhausted, struggling for breath during the winter months, too. Trips to and from University Hospital in Ann Arbor showed lungs black from tar, and soon emphysema emptied her of the energy so natural to her her whole life. She must have been furious. A couple of years ago my sister, who grew into a fine athlete herself, said to me, "Write something about Mom." I did and, because my sister and I are both teachers, titled it "The Very Best Teacher in the Whole Wide

World." I hand it off to you. It is about my mother's finest gift to me.

THE VERY BEST TEACHER IN THE
WHOLE WIDE WORLD

In my mother's kitchen, I learned Latin. In an early memory I am ten, my brother eight, and it is 1943. Far away across the seas bombs are bursting, but here, in northernmost Ohio, my brother and I are bored. We are hanging around our mother in the late afternoon, as she prepares dinner. "There's nothing to do," we complain. "Well then," our mother says, "mildew and boohoo." We stamp our feet then, and screw up our faces; she is no help at all, no matter that she explains to us that her mother, our faraway grandmother, advised her and her sisters to do the same—mildew and boohoo—when they complained. "Manufacture something," she says then. "What's manufacture?" my brother wants to know. "It's from the Latin, *facio*." Our mother looks up from the sink where she is peeling potatoes and out the window, across the fields, far away to the University of Michigan, where she once captained the field hockey team and majored in classics. "It means 'to do, to make, to build . . . *facio, feci, factum*: to make or do.' " Her feet begin to scuff the floor: "Mildew, boohoo, to make or do, it's from the Latin and it's for you." And she picks my brother up way high, tucks him under her arm, and shuffles off to Buffalo right there in her Ohio kitchen while her children shriek with delight at the wondrousness of this person who belongs to them.

I am too big by then to dance with my mother high above the floor, and so I stop their silliness by asking, "What's the other part of that word, 'man-you' something?" It works. My brother sticks his tongue out at me as my mother swings him back to earth. "It's Latin," she says. "It's from the Latin *manus* meaning hand. *Manus,* one hand, *mani,* more than one hand. Manufacture, to make by hand."

That settled, she returns to her chores. "Time to set the table," she says. Happily, we move to do her bidding. "Can you speak more languages?" I want to know. "Fork goes on the left, turn the blade of the knife toward the plate, and yes, I know Greek and a smattering of French."

Our mother is so smart! She knows smatterings and everything! How ever did she get that way?

When I reached ninth grade, I signed up to take Latin. Mrs. Bourquin, our teacher, taught me to conjugate and decline with the best of them. But it wasn't the same. Mrs. Bourquin did her job just fine, but she never got that faraway look my mother got. She never danced to the language. "Latin is a dead language," she told us. She told us that at least once a week. She would tell us that in all different ways though her frown remained the same. "Nobody speaks Latin," she would say, rescuing her handkerchief from deep within the bosom of her dress (not bosom*s* I would argue later, to the delight of the snickering boys who took wood shop). Mrs. Bourquin was tendentious. From the Latin *teneo,* meaning to hold. *Teneo, tenere, tenavi, tenatus,* to hold. To hold to one view, to be biased. That was Mrs. Bourquin all right. Maybe to her Latin was dead, but it wasn't to me, not as long as my mother scuffed her way across the kitchen linoleum, conjugating as she went. *"Amo, amas, amat"* (step tap, step tap, step tap), "I love my daughter a lot. *Amamus, amatis, amant"* (step tap, step tap, step tap), "the boys for her will pant." "Mo-ther!"

Just before our father came home was quiz time. "All right, now, pay attention," she said. She took two tall glasses out of the cupboard. "These glasses are for——?" "These glasses are for a libation," I answered as I tore the iceberg lettuce into the bowl. "Libation, from the Latin *libo,* meaning to drink. *Libo, libare, libavi, libatus,* to drink." My feet were beginning to tickle. "Correct. And when will we drink it? Quarter those tomatoes, don't slice them." "Before dinner." My right foot slid behind my left. "Correct. So what do we call this drink your father and I will have before dinner?" "A preprandial libation. *Pre* meaning before, *prandial* meaning meal, *preprandial,* before the meal." (Rock, step, ball change.) "Correct," said my mother. "You get an A." And we would do a buck and wing into the pantry.

At school, I got an A in Latin I and in Latin II, and that was the end of my formal training in the language my teacher could never convince me was dead. At home, we all spoke Latin. My father, the doctor, dissected for us the language of his profession, proclaiming the beauty of its specificity as he went: "The suffix *-itis!*" he would call down the length of the dinner table. "It means?" "Inflammation!" we would call back.

"Tonsillitis?" "Inflammation of the tonsils." "You get an A," he would exclaim, "especially you," and he would pass his hand over the forehead of our youngest sister, who always had an *-itis* of something.

Every once in a while, I caught my mother and father smiling at each other from their opposite ends of the table. They were pleased with their children, we knew that. They gave us A's all the time. Many years later, I understood that my mother and father were pleased with each other; in their very secret way, they were dancing together to a language that would keep us a family long after we tapped our way out of the warmth of that Ohio kitchen, long after the light went out.

As you will recall, I ended the family idyll by getting pregnant before I got married. So the last part of the piece I've given you is wishful thinking.

My mother would have loved my son, her first grandson. She was, after all, partial to boys.

NINE

San Quentin State Prison

Luck and Joy and Grief and I
Set off together into the world of existence.
Luck lay down and Joy ran off,
But Grief and I go wandering on.

—A Persian poem, author unknown

With two strikeouts under my belt, I decide to postpone actual meetings for a while, maybe even forever. I am, however, a slow learner and eventually will step up to the plate once again. In the meantime, I have a life, a rather busy life, in fact. Monday, I sing, Tuesday and Thursday, I teach. On Wednesday, I drive across the bridge to prison.

San Quentin State Prison is a formidable monument to society's failure. It is California's oldest prison and houses 6,000 men. Of these, 634 men live on Death Row. In years past, inmates were allowed to apply for Pell Grants, and with that money they paid for teachers from a nearby community college to come to the prison. In his second term President Clinton signed a bill with a rider prohibiting Pell Grants for the incarcerated. So, under the direction of Naomi, champion of lost causes, who has talked this program into being, we teach for free. We and our teaching assistants are from U.C. Berkeley, U.C. Davis, and St. Mary's College. We will give grades even though, in the beginning, there is no apparatus in place for credits earned. In a very real way, this is a fantasy college. The instructors teach courses they are not allowed to teach in their day-to-day lives; thus, Naomi, who in her day job is director of Religious Studies at Davis, teaches Eastern philosophy; John, a professor of history at Berkeley, teaches Shakespeare; I, normally in the School of Education, teach writing; Sue, who has put aside her Ph.D. in chemistry in order to rear her children, teaches science. My class, the class I made up, the class that will combine the best elements of all the courses I have ever taught, is called English 234: Reading, Writing and Telling Stories. It turns out a winner. But, like every course I have ever taught, I will learn the most, so that, while my students learn to read stories, write stories, and tell stories, I learn about love and sex and language behind prison walls and the lives my students live there.

> Let us go then, you and I,
> When the evening is spread out against the sky
> Like a patient etherised upon a table.
> —T. S. Eliot

San Quentin stretches along the eastern shore of California's Marin County. It looks out onto San Francisco Bay, where, not far away, Alcatraz sits in splendid isolation on its very own island, now a federal park and a popular tourist site. San Quentin, while offering one of the world's most beautiful views of sky and sea and San Francisco itself, is a working prison; tourists need not apply.

In the winter, the wind whips in from the bay. Every night

we come here the rain lashes us as we make our way along the chain-link fence from the main gate, where we have been wanded and our briefcases searched, to the second gate, where again we sign in, open our briefcases, show our brown cards, and proceed. I am cold and wet, my yellow raincoat is in my closet at home. We are forbidden to wear yellow, that being the color of the inmates' slickers, and, we are told, we might be mistaken for an inmate and shot. We are not allowed to wear blue, that being the color of the inmates' trousers and shirts. We are warned not to run.

A large sign on the wall of this second guardhouse informs us that we have entered a No-Hostage Zone, which means that if one or more of us are taken prisoner, the corrections officers (guards) will not negotiate our safe return. We have been ordered to wear whistles around our necks. We are required to display them in such a way as to be visible at all times to the corrections officers.

Once we are cleared, the guard signals another officer high up in a glass-enclosed cage to open the iron gate. We hold our brown cards high and shudder—we never get used to it—as the gate opens with a deep, resounding clang. The sound is like nothing we have ever heard: it pierces our bodies, slams our heads, a chain mail of sound. One more door—not so tall and not so wide but heavy, heavy steel—and we enter the courtyard of the prison itself.

On our left is a building marked over its door "Adjustment Center." The corrections officer has told us that some men who enter San Quentin are not ready for life on the Row, and so spend some time here. From my students, I will learn another name for this center: the Hole. It is where some of my students, Hectare, for one, will spend some of their time. It is solitary confinement. "Don't expect him back anytime soon," my students say of Hectare.

Behind the Adjustment Center, Death Row rises high above the rest of the prison. The lights are on all night and all day.

Everything I have ever heard about prison is true. And I haven't heard the half of it.

Tonight the storm has made us late. Our students are supposed to be on the six o'clock movement, ticketed to Education. Sometimes they are late because, as a student explains, "Feeding was late because counting was late, and counting was late because there were too many orange men." Orange men are new arrivals who await the classification that will determine whether they stay at San Quentin or go elsewhere; they wear orange jumpsuits. But, at least, tonight is not lockdown. Lockdown means just that: nobody goes anywhere—inmates must remain in their cells, outsiders stay out. It means that something dangerous has happened in the prison: a killing; weapons discovered. Whatever it is, lockdown means the other teachers and I will have to go back across the bay and wait for another night.

Tonight, no lockdown and our students are not late. Because they are not allowed to go into the classrooms without us, they huddle against our classroom building, heads bent against the weather, yellow slickers shiny with rain. They greet us with "Afraid you weren't going to make it," and "Thanks for coming." They are glad to see us. Likewise. It has been a long and arduous journey.

Most of the men in my class are housed on North Block, the unit with the highest security next to Death Row (which we have been instructed by prison officials to call Condemned Row). The men on the Row could, if I consented, take my writing class by videotape. But I do not consent; too much of what will be valuable to my students will come to them by way of interaction, live-action learning, if you will. My students are long-time inhabitants of San Quentin. Those who don't come from North Block come from the Ranch (minimum security), or

H Unit (medium security). A few, a very few, will be released during my five-year tenure at the prison.

Frederick is different. There is at San Quentin a special housing unit for cross-dressers, preop transsexuals, flamboyantly gay men. It is called Dorm 5 and, I am told, is a special kind of hell. Frederick comes from there. Frederick is unlike any student, any man, any person, I have ever encountered, in or out of prison. In common parlance, he is flaming. He flaunts his gayness: he does not walk, he sashays; he does not stroll, he minces; he does not sit, he flounces. His wrists are limp, his nails are long, his hips rhumba to a rhythm heard only by him. Each week he sports a new hairstyle: marcelled, dyed blond; crew, dyed black; spikes, dyed platinum. He is African-American. He is, in this classroom, utterly alone.

When I ask the men to read their writing to a partner, Frederick doesn't have one. When I ask the men to move into their response groups, Frederick doesn't have one. When Frederick chooses a chair in which he will sit for this evening's class, men move away from him. But Frederick stays with it. He does not withdraw, as he did from his basic composition course the previous semester, claiming sexual harassment. Frederick does his work, keeps to himself, and seems content, more or less, to have me for a partner and a group. No one in the class says a word to Frederick or about him. He is an island unto himself. He bears up admirably.

Early in the semester, my mind on my day job back across the bay, I assigned for the following week's reading one of my favorite short stories, included in our text, *The Best American Short Stories, 1994,* donated by good people at Houghton Mifflin. It is Carolyn Ferrell's "Proper Library." The story is memorable for its gorgeous rendering of black dialect in the voice of Lorrie, a fourteen-year-old boy growing up in the projects. It is funny, sad, and full of love. To my mind, that is reason enough to assign it as reading to my students, who, as the semester continues, will reveal themselves as funny, sad, and full of love. All this is not quite clear at this point; I am certain only that the story will speak for itself to these men who have signed up for this course in an attempt to escape the boredom and the brutality of prison life if only for three hours a week. On the other side of the wall, a history class murmurs forward; on the opposite side, math with its occasional outburst of frustration. Along our wall, the radiator hisses and clanks.

And so on this night, in the few minutes before class is to begin, I scan "Proper Library." One thing I can count on: my students have done their homework, they have read this story. Tonight, the men seem unusually reluctant to take their seats. Then I see it, there, in the second paragraph, the phrase "fucking in the butt." I forgot: Lorrie, one of the most lovable and most loving characters in all literature, is gay. Where is Frederick?

Quietly, most of the students take their seats in what Mike has named Our Circle of Kings Plus One, the One being me. From the group of four standing near the door, D.C. says, "We think, given our environment here . . . uh . . ." He stares at the floor from his six-foot-seven-inch height. Homer continues for him: "We do not think this story is appropriate reading material for us, in . . . uh . . . these circumstances."

From my seat in the circle, one eye on the door should Frederick come in late, and because I have no idea on earth what ought to be said, I repeat the title "Proper Library" and open my book. Outside the floor-to-ceiling window of our classroom the wind howls in from San Francisco Bay and slaps the winter rain against the bulletproof glass. Inside is not very cozy either. I say to the reluctant learners at the door, "Are you saying we can't talk about it?"

From his seat, Barney says, "We can talk about it, analyze it, we just can't allow ourselves to feel about it." With this, everybody, finally, is sitting in the circle and nobody, absolutely nobody, likes this story.

Marcellus takes us through: "I'm reading along about all this food in this paragraph and I get to . . ."—he won't say "fucking in the butt" but continues—"and I say, Whoa! What's that doing there?" A few chuckles. Marcellus reads from the story: " 'Boston cream pie and pancakes, roast turkey'—and I'm loving this story and then . . . that." More laughter. "And then, a couple more pages and his mother says, 'If that boy puts his thing on you, cut it off.' And I got it! This kid's a faggot!"

Cameron jumps in: "Yeah! Up to then I'm right with the story, but no way, no how, am I going to get with this boy." All heads nod in agreement. Barney will write in his Reader Response that he is "unable to identify emotionally with the subject."

The chair outside the circle, the one in the back corner, the one Frederick would sit in were he here, is empty. I breathe a bit easier. "Turn to page one hundred fourteen," I say. I read aloud a paragraph in which this boy, Lorrie, this "faggot," is thinking about his biology teacher, on whom he has a crush: *"Love is a pie and I am lucky enough to have almost every flavor in mine. . . . And Mr. D'Angelo, do you know . . . I would give anything if you ask me to sit on your lap and ask me to bite into your ear so that it tingles like the bell that rips me in and out of your class. I would give anything. Love is a pie. Didn't you know that? Mr. D'Angelo, I am in silent love in a loud body. So don't turn away. Sweat."* I look around the circle at my murderers and rapists and thieves and addicts, some all of the above, and repeat, *"I am in silent love in a loud body."* And then I say to the students, "If I could write language like that, I would consider myself a most fortunate writer."

David bursts out with, "But that's just plain everyday language!"

"That's the beauty of it," says Fatim.

"What's this kid doing under the bridge anyway?" Homer wants to know.

"He's meeting with this Rakeem dude," answers D.C.

I read aloud: *"He traveled me to a quiet place where his hands were the oars and I drifted off to sleep."*

"But he don't stay there," says Marcellus. "He goes back to study his words for that big citywide test."

"So he got a choice," says Fatim. "He don't have to be no faggot."

Now we're talking. I say, "From what I know and from what I read in this story, this boy is by his very nature homosexual, gay from birth."

"I don't know about that," says David, "being born gay." Others nod in agreement.

Later, on the drive home, it will come to me that these men must be desperate to hang on to their heterosexuality, their manhood, no matter if in their present circumstances they are somebody's "wife" or "gal boy" or "old lady." They need to believe that prison has forced them to behave in ways they would never choose, that they are not faggots by birth, no matter what. They must believe that Lorrie has a choice and that if they, here in this prison, could get out from under this bridge, they would return easily and naturally to their essential straightness. "That Lorrie," says Marcellus, "he don't have to go to that bridge."

I will not argue. I am a happy teacher. Our talk, our language, and the language of Carolyn Ferrell has tempered the anger, the depression so integral to prison life. For now anyway.

And Frederick? Frederick did his homework. He stayed home.

ONE NIGHT, the discussion turns to letter-writing and whether they do it, and, if so, to whom. Those who write letters—almost everybody—write to their children. Virgil is too young to have children. Virgil doesn't write to anybody.

Virgil is housed on the Ranch, minimum security, located on the northwest corner of the prison grounds far across the yard. During this semester, the authorities will disallow prisoners on the Ranch from coming to the main compound where we are, something about weapons smuggling. So, while we don't know it, Virgil's time in my class is limited.

Virgil is in his early twenties, his hostility barely disguised. One evening, everyone is writing warm-ups where I say, "Give me a color. . . . Give me a kind of weather. . . . Give me a body part. . . . Let's write." Then we see what we come up with in seven or eight minutes. Then we read our stuff aloud. Normally, I write with them. Tonight, I wander about, pausing here and there, looking over one shoulder or another. I get to Virgil, lean over to peek at his writing, and inadvertently brush his shoulder. Virgil whirls on me, eyes blazing, half rises, catches himself. It is only me. He remembers where he is, sits down, and returns to his writing. From then on, I am careful to keep a distance between the two of us.

Of all the men I will teach in the five years I am at the prison, Virgil is the only one I could identify with any certainty as a victim of rape, not because he has told me but because he is so wary of being touched; in the beginning, he refuses to join a writing group here in class; by choice, he sits alone and apart—on the other side of the room from Frederick, need I add. None of the men I will teach seems like a rapist, though no doubt some of them are or have been. But the men have been in prison a very long time and most of them will remain in prison even longer. So I must conclude that they have made some kind of sexual life for themselves, some of them willingly (though in prison how can anything be said to be done willingly), some by force. In our class discussions, however, we never get any closer than "Proper Library" to talking about sex and choice and force and acquiescence. At least, not directly. Homer tells me, "I'm leaving here a whole man no matter what." In the meantime, our class is a safe place, a time-out.

There is the oblique, however. As the weeks go by, Virgil relaxes, so that by the time our discussion turns to letter-writing, he is an intelligent and eager participant. I bring to class Emily Dickinson's poem that begins, "All the letters I can write . . ."

> All the letters I can write
> Are not fair as this—
> Syllables of Velvet—
> Sentences of Plush,
> Depths of Ruby, undrained,
> Hid, Lip, for Thee—
> Play it were a Humming Bird—
> And just sipped—me—

"This is highly sexual," says Virgil.

"It is?"

"Look at the words," he says. "This poem isn't about no letter."

"Read it again," says Barney.

I do. Clearly, Virgil is right and I feel my face grow warm.

"You read it, Virgil," says D.C. Virgil reads and we glow from the heat.

"That Emily, she something," says Marcellus.

Virgil beams.

"*I am in silent love in a loud body,*" says Lorrie in Ferrell's story. The bodies of my students are loud. They are proud of getting ripped, of being buff as the result of working out on exercise equipment. Underneath their tattoos Eddie's biceps bulge, D.C.'s shoulders strain at the fabric of his prison shirt. During my tenure at the prison, the authorities see fit to remove all exercise equipment. Eddie explains: "They don't want physically fit killers on their watch." The mood grows somber, bodies less loud. But there is silent love.

Lionel has a large and loving family on the outside. His wife comes to visit and, when she can, brings their sons, the youngest just five, born after a conjugal weekend in the trailer provided by the prison. (Conjugal visits—"boneyards"—for lifers, like the exercise equipment, have since been excised by the prison authorities.)

Tonight Lionel sits at my desk, waiting for me to comment on the writing he has given me. Much of what he writes, stories with an Afrocentric plot and setting, is for his youngest boy. "Lionel," I say, "this is good. Where did it come from?"

Lionel takes scraps of paper from his shirt pocket. "From some of the warm-ups you have us do."

I am looking, however, at a well-developed piece of writing. "How did you know how to make this into a full piece?"

Lionel, always the shyest, the sweetest, the gentlest student in class, who never, ever looks at me, stares now at the floor and says, "Well, I did that, that writing, here in class, and then I read it to my cellie and he told me to add things and make some changes and I did." He shifts in his chair and murmurs, "Should I make some more? What do you think?"

"I think you should listen to your cellie. He's a smart guy."

Lionel ducks his head, then looks straight at me and smiles. "Yeah, my cellie, I'm lucky."

I smile back. Lionel loves this man, his cellie, who knows how, just that they are lucky to be penned up in a six-foot-by-eight-foot cell with each other.

AND THEN there is me. The teacher. Who is a woman. "Were you afraid to come here?" David asks one night near the end of class. "Yeah," says Homer, "did they tell you we were terrible, desperate men who'd do anything to get out of here?" He laughs. "What're you laughing at?" says D.C. "We are terrible, desperate men who'd do anything to get out of here." David insists, "So, were you scared?" Without thinking, I say, "No, I used to teach high school." We all laugh.

By mid-semester, we laugh a lot, Steve, a longtime resident of North Block, being the exception, having forgotten how to laugh if he ever knew how. One night Steve's face is wildly contorted. "Are you all right?" I ask, fearing some illness has struck all of a sudden. "I'm practicing to smile," he explains, "in case I come across something funny. It's a goal." He is very serious about his goals and by the end of the semester he will be able to twist his mouth into what he insists is a smile. "Now, that was funny," he will say about something in a story that is not funny at all. He is most serious about seeing to it that I am treated right. One of the requirements of this course is that the students submit a story or an article or a poem, something they have written, to a publication. They scour my copies of *Writer's Market* for addresses. It is simpler for them to give their pieces to me since buying manila envelopes, if they are available, is more than their seventeen-cents-an-hour income can handle. Yet for me to pay for postage on that envelope and the SASE they will include will get very expensive, given that I have already bought the envelopes themselves. So I ask, "If at all possible, could you provide stamps? Any number will do." Steve says, "No problem." The rest of the class looks puzzled. He rises from his chair, puts his fists on his hips, and addresses the men, "She's not paying for any stamps."

On the night the students hand me their pieces, complete with cover letters and SASEs, Steve takes from his pockets, from all his pockets, postage stamps. Some are crumpled, some torn at the edges, some pristine, all of them beautiful. "Here," he says. I thank him and all the rest of the men, who nod a you're-welcome.

What happened was this: from the top tiers to the bottom and all along each row of North Block, all night long the men exchanged cigarettes for stamps, cigarettes for money to buy stamps. "It was mighty quiet up there last night," Marcellus tells me. Steve, I think, is smiling.

As silently, as safely as they can, in their very loud bodies, the men love me. "Did you see what I did?" asks Mike. "I took my shoe off. You took your shoe off, so I did, too." "Why did you cut your hair?" asks Homer, visibly distressed. "My wife cut her hair once. I got used to it, though. I liked it finally." Homer has not seen his wife for fifteen years. "I hate this fucking place!" yells Willie one night. Steve rears from his chair: "None of that, none of that! There's a lady present!" "Sorry," says Willie, "forgot myself." Now, part of their gallantry comes from their desire to keep this class and the other classes in which they are enrolled going. They know that if one man gets out of line, if propriety is breached to any degree whatsoever, the prison authorities will shut down the program. My students do not want that. So, while I might enjoy a fantasy involving my own irresistibility, I know whence their courtliness springs. And yet, for all that, they love me, and what they love me for the very most is that I have brought them language. It is a gift they thought to have lost forever.

One night, in the classroom next to us, a young woman, a guest lecturer, talks and talks and talks. Virgil asks, "What's she doing over there?" He brings his hands together in front of his chest and pushes them against each other. "She's procrasti— No, it's . . . She's prevar—. Oh!" He raises his fists into the air. "I used to be a walking thesaurus! Now I can't remember anything!" "She's pontificating," I offer. "That's it! Like the pope!" Virgil brings his hands to his sides. "It's frustrating," he says.

"I'm afraid I'll lose it all in here." I lie: "When you need your language, it will come back to you."

On another night, Homer says, "Shit." And then, "Sorry, I forgot." He explains, "You gotta understand, Professor." (I am not a professor, but they want me to be one so I am.) "All we hear is the language in the yard. And that's pretty . . . bad. It's very simple language, if you know what I mean." He smiles apologetically and ducks his head. "So when we come in here, we're supposed to understand what you say and . . . and . . . it takes a little while. But we can do it, we can." Nods all around.

So I read to them. I read them Charles Dickens, from *Great Expectations:*

"A fearful man, all in coarse grey, with a great iron on his leg. A man with no hat, and with broken shoes, and with an old rag tied round his head. A man who had been soaked in water, and smothered in mud, and lamed by stones, and cut by flints, and stung by nettles, and torn by briars; who limped and shivered, and glared, and growled; and whose teeth chattered in his head, as he seized me by the chin."

"Tell me about this man," I say.

"He's a convict in the woods."

"He's miserable."

"Down and out."

"Read some more."

I do.

On yet another night, Kareem asks about metaphor. "My history professor [a young man, a doctoral candidate at Berkeley who has grown a beard to offset his youthful beauty] says Nietzsche uses metaphor. Maybe that's why I'm having trouble understanding him."

I write on the board, "My father is a bear."

"Oh," says Kareem, "I been using metaphors all my life. I just didn't know it."

Another night I refer to our assigned story's point of view as "omniscient." Heads go up, eyes light up. "Write that on the board," they command. I do, break it into *omni* and *scientia,* explain.

"Like *science,*" yells Dan. *"To know!"* They scribble furiously into their notebooks.

"Omnivorous," I write. "What's that?"

"Carnivorous, only different."

"Like *omni, omni, everything,* eating everything!" We are on a roll.

"Omniscient?" I ask.

"Knowing everything!" It's very noisy in here.

"You are so smart," I say. But they are not finished.

Marcellus shouts, *"Omnipotent!* All-powerful! Like God!"

"Write it on the board!" I do, they write in their notebooks, our classroom is abuzz with happiness.

It is the word *empathy* that brings down the house. I have written it on the board. It's what they're after in the stories they are writing. They look puzzled. I explain. They are enrapt.

But now an argument breaks out. "You can't have empathy with me," says Kareem, "because you don't know my troubles."

"Yes, I can," answers Mike. "I can feel right with you," he insists.

Kareem is stubborn. "You don't have children," he says to Mike. "Unless you got children, you can't know my troubles so you can't have empathy." They lean forward from their chairs into the middle of our circle, like two wrestlers who have found language irrelevant.

I interrupt. "Yes, Mike can," I say. "He can feel right with you."

Suddenly Steve, silent until now, speaks: "That was my problem, that was me. I didn't have empathy my whole life. I didn't care about anybody's feelings—didn't matter to me if anybody got hurt. Then a couple of years ago, when we used to have a really fine librarian here, he gave me this book. It was *Les Misérables*. How do you say it?" I tell him. He repeats the title. "That book changed my life. It gave me feelings, it gave me empathy. Who wrote that book, now?"

"Victor Hugo," I say.

Steve repeats softly, *"Les Misérables* by Victor Hugo." He is wrapping up this gift and holding it close. It is his forever.

And in their writing, listen to David:

> My first engine was an International Harvester DT4656, an inline six-cylinder diesel engine. . . . She was like my first girlfriend. Once you've been down deep into an engine all the way down to the pistons and have held them in your hands, and have . . . cleaned every single part and assembled every piece with care hoping it will be a success and last forever, it's like an intimate relationship. If the engine runs well and doesn't blow up, well then that relationship was a success, and you don't want to give the truck back to the owner, he won't know how to take care of her. Seeing my trucks rolling down the highway . . . is like seeing old girlfriends. You remember the long, intimate nights together, like women you really love but don't own and can't hold on to, you wish the trucks well and send them on their way.

As for me, their teacher, I have never been loved by so many for so good a reason.

FREDERICK'S WRITING IS different from the other students'. While almost everyone works on short stories or poems or articles, Frederick is writing a novel. It is about two best friends, Harriet and Evelyn, who spend their days happily in the dressing room of a large department store trying on clothes.

Their clothes are the work of a very imaginative writer: they have peplums, ruffles, polka dots mixed with stripes—the women giggle over their daring—and push-up bras that send them laughing so hard the manager comes to call.

During our conference, I ask Frederick what the conflict is in his novel. "Is it the manager?" "Oh, no," says Frederick, "he gets a real kick out of Harriet especially." He thinks for a moment. "There isn't no conflict."

I explain that, to make the story move ahead, a conflict is very helpful, that most novels have conflicts. "Problems?" I ask. "Do Harriet and Evelyn have any problems?"

"No," he says. "They're having too good a time."

"What will happen next?"

"They go home to their men and try on their new clothes."

"Are the men upset with all the money they spent?"

"No, they like their ladies to look good." He looks into the future. "Then they go out. To dance."

Next.

THE LAST NIGHT of this class, Reading, Writing and Telling Stories, is devoted to storytelling. This is a major part of their final exam. Each man will tell the class a story that he has written or read or heard. Over the course of the semester, the students and I have developed criteria for good storytelling. They will use these criteria to score the storytelling of their classmates; scores are from 1 (low) to 5 (high). The men have been given opportunities to practice their stories in front of the class. "No way am I going to practice," says Lionel. "This is gonna be a one-shot deal." I can't blame him; I practiced telling my story and they gave me a 4. "What do you mean, I got a four!" I exclaim. "I'm the teacher!" "Just being honest with you, that's all."

I am a nervous wreck. Will they do it? What if they don't?

Tonight's guests—a professional storyteller, my two teaching assistants, the director of the education program at the prison—
all of them invited with permission of the students—add to the
seriousness of the task ahead. The room is full. So is the moon.

Things go well. Lionel tells the story he has written for his
son; Willie tells a story of how he learned to read in Jamaica;
Barney tells a shaggy-dog story he heard growing up in Minnesota. Steve reads a diatribe against unjust and illegal intimi-
dation, the object of his fury the policeman in *Les Misérables*
named Javert. And now it is Frederick's turn.

Tonight Frederick's hair is a burnished gold, no waves, just a
bronze cap; his nails shine out beyond his fingertips; we can see
that, while his wardrobe is limited to his prison blues like all the
rest of the men in the room, he has taken special care for this
special night. He sashays up to the front of the room. "Excuse
me," he says in a lisp I hope we have all gotten used to, "I'll be
right back." He leaves the room. Where has he gone? Will he return? He'd better or he'll get shot.

Suddenly, the door flies open and in he comes, pelvic thrusts
worthy of Tempest Storm, Gypsy Rose Lee, the entire Golden
Age of Strippers. To a drumbeat felt only by Frederick, he
swivels his hips stage left, stage right, extends his right arm,
palm-side up, and beckons to his audience with fiery red nails.
"Ooooo," he says. Center stage now, he leans forward, shaking
his little booty, and says, "Hi there, boys and girl!" He puts his
fingers to his lips and giggles. "I've got a story for you tonight.
But first, I want to get us all in the mood. I want us all to sing a
little song. Ready?"

Oh, god. What if somebody can't stand it anymore and just
lets Frederick have it? Where is the whistle I'm supposed to use
in case of emergency? I peek through my fingers. Every single
person in this room is rigid with wonder (let's hope that's what it

is). Many of them stare open-mouthed. Frederick takes this as a sign of encouragement and begins to lead us in song. "Eensy, beensy spider went up a water spout," he sings. With a roll of his hips, he beckons and says, "Come on now, everybody. Sing out."

The deus ex machina comes in the form of my teaching assistant, Josh, who is a graduate student in sociology at the University of California at Berkeley, who deserves to get his Ph.D. now without any further effort on his part, and who will, without question, go to heaven if he so chooses. The men like Josh; Josh begins to sing. Some of the men join in. I join in. Frederick says, "Okay, now, from the top," and before we know it, we are all singing, sort of. Steve is having trouble making his mouth move, having learned only how to smile, not to sing; Cameron, always afraid a bipolar swing will strike, sings worriedly as only Cameron can; and Willie, in his Jamaican accent and his rolling bass, outdoes us all in volume and enthusiasm. Frederick is having a ball.

At the end of the song, he prances back and forth across the room and says, "And now I'm going to tell you a story. Once upon a time, there were three bears." In Frederick's version, Mama Bear wears a cute little ruffled apron with navy polka dots, and whenever she talks, especially when she says, "Someone's been . . . " her little behind sticks out and her hips wiggle back and forth and she giggles up and down the scale. And when Mama Bear says, "Oh, my," which she does three times, her manicure sparkles as her hands flex and point, flex and point. At the end, Frederick says, "And now I'm going to tell you another story, about three little pigs."

"Sit down, Fred," says Marcellus.

"Yeah, quit while you're ahead," says Cameron.

Frederick takes his seat. He is delighted when the class

awards him a 3. He rises from his chair, says, "Thank you all," and curtsies.

At the end of the previous week's conference, Frederick whispered to me, "I know one thing. When I get out of this place, I'm going straight."

The miracle of language.

TEN

The New Millennium: In Which I Turn Sixty-Seven

We are never so defenceless against suffering as when we love,
never so forlornly unhappy as when we have lost our
love-object or its love.

—SIGMUND FREUD, in *Civilization and Its Discontents*

Spread your legs, sweetie.

—ROBERT

Near the end of my mother's life, confined to her bed by the illness that would kill her, unable to perform her wifely duties, she suggested to my father that he find someone, another woman, who might provide him comfort. He refused. My parents loved each other very much. Neither of them, though they loved me very much, would have understood or accepted or—god forbid—encouraged my search for someone who might provide me comfort. My mother would have been appalled, my father more confused than ever over his daughter's life. They would both think, though they might never say it, You reap what you sow. Or, in contemporary, though less interesting, language, Behavior has consequences. Or, if we turn once more to science, For every action there is an equal and opposite reaction. And, one of maybe two absolutes I hold to, everyone is 100 percent responsible for what happens to him or her. The exception to this, of course, is children. Well, I knew all that. I knew when I went into this thing that I could get hurt. I knew I could get beaten up every which way, slapped around on both coasts, mugged, assaulted all across the country, suffer injuries from which I would never recover. I could even die. I knew, when I decided to fill my life fully, I could not choose only the good parts. And I did it anyway. I did not begin this adventure seeking a husband, a long-term relationship (what an ugly bunch of sounds), a partner. I liked where I lived and, for the most part, the life I lived there. It just didn't have any touching in it. I would see what would happen. I would act with little consideration for the reaction. I would sow; who knew what I would reap. But I had felt a little dying happening to me for too long. I suppose placing the ad was my way of raging against that. I sure as hell wasn't going to go gentle into that good night. Fuck, fuck against the dying of the light.

Foreplay never entered my mind. True, in my ad in the *New York Review,* I had offered the possibility of conversation about Trollope as a prelude to sex, but more or less as a courtesy to men who might be shy. For myself, I was ready to hop to it after a bit of touching in all the right places, so I was unprepared for what happened, for the seduction that would come so powerfully in the form of e-mail on my screen and letters in my mailbox; I could not have predicted that Trollope would be so easily forgotten. A warning or an observation, take it for what you will. One ought not to fall in love with someone by way of their writing. One must be especially careful if the writing is good, for then one assumes the writer is good, funny, clever, profound, sensitive, smart, wise, loving, and true. It is unfair to the writer and dangerous to the reader to hold the writer to the standards of his writing, for in his writing, the writer is his best self; in person, he is a person, and we all know what that means. Well, not all of us. If you have been to as many readings as I have where a terribly attractive man, a writer, sits gracefully in a chair, one arm thrown over the back, one corduroyed leg draped gracefully over the other, on occasion so bold as to wear a tweed jacket with leather patches on the elbow, you will have found yourself in an audience composed of—need I tell you—women. Oh, here and there some man—is he gay?—listens intently. Don't look at the faces of these women; if you are a woman, you will be embarrassed for your entire sex; if you are a man, you will feel contempt. The questions they ask: Where do you get your ideas? Do you write in the morning? Or my favorite, How important to your writing is your dream life? Jesus. Those aren't even the questions. The real question is, How do I get into your pants? You want mine? Here. Think Tom Stoppard: to die for. Richard Ford: yummy. I don't go to these things anymore; why torture myself? What right do we have to peer at and slather over a man who spends most of his life alone making language the rest of us never even attempt? Read Kafka's "A Hunger Artist." Go to the zoo; the odds are fairer there. If you have to go to these readings, buy the book. It's the least you can do. Finally, writers and composers and painters and poets are in love with their art, so, while they might foster your illusions of loving and working side by side, they most often remain faithful to what they create, leaving not as much room for you as you deserve. Good luck.

GIVEN THE TERRAIN I was covering, landmines everywhere, it was only a matter of time before I stepped on one. Why did I think I wouldn't? His name was Robert. He was a wonderful writer. I fell in love.

In the beginning, when I was performing triage on all those letters, Robert was a weak *maybe*. On the inside of a notecard in a fine and legible hand he wrote very little to intrigue me. He was seventy-two and, lest I think him, in his words, a couch potato (dorky), he had hiked the Grand Canyon the previous summer (doubtful). However, he was a professor (retired), formerly on the medical faculty at Michigan, and you know what a sucker I am for academic credentials. He had had two marriages, twenty years each, and was divorced. And he had written the magic words "I would like to know you better." So on a cold and rainy Wednesday in early December 1999, I called the number he had written at the bottom of his note. He didn't remember me (memory gone), then did and seemed pleased (lonely). His voice was thin and wavery.

We talked disjointedly about nothing, and finally, just to get him off the line, I promised to call him in a few days. That's that, I thought, and for the first, but not the last, time wiped my hands clean of him. A week later, he called. "You said you would call," he said, clearly disappointed. I felt awful. I had promised and I hadn't, I apologized, and we began to talk. He sounded much stronger, not at all old, lonely, and sick, and in the end we exchanged e-mail addresses. I was in for it now.

Who would have thought the old man to have so much e-mail in him? The rollercoaster was about to leave. I hurried aboard. If that goddamn amusement park had had one of those measurement lines kids have to be taller than in order to ride, the one I needed was some kind of line that measured experience and toughness. I wouldn't have come halfway up. Somebody shoulda sent me home. Somebody shoulda told me to come back when I was older. Like one hundred.

Between early December and mid-January, Robert and I

will write almost two hundred pages of e-mail to each other. I will stop eating and start drinking. I will lose ten pounds. I will learn the joys of phone sex. He writes, *"If you were to call me at night, you needn't worry about waking me."* I call. I wake him up. His voice is warm and slow from sleep. It slides over my body just as his hands will, and from this very beginning I feel wrapped up, soothed, and very, very warm. "What are you wearing?" he whispers. "Just a minute," I answer, "nothing." His voice strokes me into orgasm.

From him I will hear, for the first time in my life, "I adore you." For the first time ever, a man will call me "sweetie." But I am not completely gone. I send him a warning, Friar Laurence's to Romeo: *"These violent delights have violent ends/And in their triumph die, like fire and powder,/Which, as they kiss, consume. . . . Therefore love moderately: long love doth so;/Too swift arrives as tardy as too slow."* We are behaving like teenagers, I tell him. Of course, that's part of the fun of it; for me, I never got to behave like a teenager when I was one; for Robert, I will learn that falling in love with me and the expression of that will become an embarrassment, something he'd prefer to forget, like his adolescence. But I don't know that he is such a grown-up, not yet. So when I worry about the haste with which we are progressing and suggest we keep an eye on how others might see the two of us up all night talking on the phone, at the computer most of the day talking, talking to each other, telling each other things that I, at least, had never told anyone, he writes to me *". . . last night on television I happened upon an interview with an attractive woman of about 40 who had rowed a boat across the Atlantic twice. I'll bet her mother and friends would have tried to dissuade her."* Isn't that elegant? Robert's e-mails were one elegant sentence after another, but do I think I should have listened to the warnings of my dead mother and grandmother and my living, sensible friends? No. Robert describes me thus: *"Your ad presented a woman who knows her mind and is clear about what she wants and will plunge ahead with a real sense of adventure."* Yup, that's me. I will row my boat all the way across the United States of America, and more than twice.

By Christmas we are in love. Jesus, I can hardly stand to write that. Even now, as I write with all the hindsight in the world, I'm not sorry. I'm not apologetic, not even embarrassed. A little defensive, maybe, but not in the least regretful. Right off the bat I got what I wanted: "sex with a man I like," and love from someone who would let me love him back. How could anyone wish any of that had never happened? Falling in love is wonderful, just like the song says. And when the other person falls in love, too, and it's with you, it's beyond compare. How many times have you fallen in love? Three for me, this time being the third. I loved being in the moment of love: I laughed easily, cried easily, tingled all over, danced alone in the moonlight (my neighbors were on sabbatical) to Stravinsky's "Rite of Spring" and Croce's "Bad, Bad Leroy Brown," with Madonna's "Sooner or Later" for variety. Every so often I felt beautiful. I was lucky. I got the glass that was all the way full. It ranneth over, and, alas, so thirsty was I, I never ever felt the warning waters lapping at my ankles, so I damn near drowned. *"I think I am falling in love with you,"* he wrote, and then that he had and now that he did. He could have told me also that he had buried several bodies beneath his apartment building, was stewing the corpse of his latest conquest, looked forward to flaying his date for the evening. Would have made no difference to me. I was in love. How young I was then, sixty-six.

"What are your fantasies?" I tell him everything. I tell him of my secret fascination with the beginning of *The Story of O,* in which O, in the backseat of a taxi along with her lover, does his bidding: "You have too many clothes on," he says. "Unfasten your stockings . . ." Near their destination, he unbuttons her blouse, "groping for the shoulder straps of her brassiere, which he snips with a small penknife. . . . Now, beneath her blouse which he has buttoned back up, her breasts are naked and free, as is the rest of her body, from waist to knee." I find that first chapter immensely stimulating. The rest of the book I don't like; as you no doubt know, the lover hands her over to humiliation and despair; in the end, she's supposed to like sadomasochism. Nonsense. But this stuff in the taxi. There was this movie, the first scene in a taxi. Tom Berenger, I think, and a beautiful woman are in the backseat of a taxi and, as I recall, they make love and they don't even know each other. This taxi thing weakens my knees. I send to Robert Elise Paschen's poem "Taxi." It goes, "Why don't we cruise/Times Square at noon/ enjoy the jam/I'm not immune/to your deft charm/in one stalled car/I'd like to take/you as you are." He likes it. I tell him I get squishy when I read that chapter in *O* and when I read his letters. He writes that he loves the taste and smell of squishy, that he could get lost between my legs. Jesus. And he tells me that he will meet me at the airport on January 18 and that we will take a cab home to his apartment.

In Robert's photograph he is not as appealing as he is in his e-mail. He looks kind of like a ferret: close-together, heavy-lidded dark eyes in a broad brow, full upper lip, more teeth than his mouth can hold. Only days after our meeting I will find his face endlessly fascinating, eternally sexy, and sometimes, when he looks at me, full of love. The photograph of me I have sent him is that picture my son took in which the lines in my face don't show, the pouch of my stomach is hidden beneath my sweater, the white of my hair is quite possibly blond. In the picture I am confident. When I emerge from the plane at JFK, I am not, but I have no trouble spotting him. I walk toward him and he looks over my head and behind me at the remaining passengers. "Robert?" I say. Startled, he looks down at me and says, "Oh, hi, sweetie, I didn't recognize you. You don't look at all like your picture." Does my heart sink? Nah, well, maybe a little, just briefly. In the taxi he takes me in his arms and kisses me. In the rearview mirror, the driver's eyes open wider and wider. New York, New York, a helluva town.

Back in December, on the telephone, he had said, "What would you like to do in New York? You can have anything you want."

On another morning, he called and said, "I am sitting in front of my computer with the seating chart of the Metropolitan Opera on my screen. Where would you like to sit for *Madame Butterfly*?"

"In your lap."

He laughed. "Good, that'll save me the price of a ticket."

And so he would show me New York: the opera, the ballet, the theater, the Frick, the Metropolitan, the Guggenheim. The whole city was mine, a gift from Robert, who, like me, had loved New York his whole life.

Yet I am not entirely trusting either in Robert or in me or in the circumstances that brought us together and would call for us to share his studio apartment. I write to Caroline, my wonderful, beautiful, successful thirty-three-year-old niece, who lives in Midtown. I tell her everything: about the ad, the multiple responses, Robert, my planned trip. She is enchanted, delighted. "Come stay with me if you want to or need to," she says. She is my backup, my back door, my escape hatch. She is also my friend, whose generosity I will count on in the months to come and whose patience and tolerance I will test to the limits. Not yet, but soon.

Robert is an elegant man: tall, slim, deliberate in his gestures, thoughtful in his speech. Retired from medicine, he writes novels with medicine as the background. He is working on his fifth. From his desk in the apartment we share, he turns to me and says, "I would be grateful if you could bring yourself to read my current manuscript and give me your opinion." I do, and I like the book, and I offer a few comments, some questions. "You might be my ideal reader," he says. "Tell me about your own writing." He listens, and not just politely either, as I tell him about my work at the college and the writing class at the prison, about my teaching in high school. He looks at me, he takes me seriously, he thinks I am smart. Of course I love him. How can I not?

When Robert's painful back (pain radiating from his lower back into the left leg, L-4, L-5 disk, I silently diagnose, candidate for laminectomy) allows for it, we go out. Wherever we are we talk. In bed and out of bed. In the kitchen and in the bathroom. In the elevator and in the cab and on Broadway at Steve's bookstand. Immune to the cold, oblivious to the snow whirling about, we stand in front of the tables full of books and talk. "Have you read Margaret Atwood?" "I'm not as fond of her as you seem to be. Now, Updike, look, here's his new one." "Updike should win the Nobel Prize." "So should Philip Roth." "What's your favorite Roth novel?" *"Sabbath's Theater."* I gasp. "The Id run amok!" Sometimes, we buy some of Steve's books and add them to the piles that climb the walls of Robert's apartment. (That's what walls are for: to hold up books.) At home we talk about books some more and music and politics and movies and about men and women: "Is there something particular to women," says Robert, "that causes them to make the bed?" I am doing this. I am making the bed. I have clambered across Robert's enormous mattress and stand, wedged against the window, which looks out onto Central Park. I tug at the sheet, look down at the floor, and wish for a Dustbuster.

"Yes," I answer. "It's an example of evolutionary adaptive behavior. It's called feathering your nest."

At his desk, Robert laughs.

"Does the female in all species do the feathering?" I ask. I love this part; I love looking into his mind, which is cool and clear as glass.

"I'm sure there are species in which both male and female prepare the nests. The males of our species, apparently, have discarded the making of beds, knowing the task will be done by the females." He moves his long fingers slowly along his chin and gazes at the computer screen, where the most recent chapter of his novel awaits his full attention.

"Does that mean the male no longer cares about preparing a place for the young?"

Robert rises from his chair and walks over to where I am smoothing the comforter. "In our case," he says, "yes. In our case we no longer have to prepare for anyone but ourselves. Stop doing that." He pulls me onto the bed. "Why are you wearing so many clothes?"

Afterward, I kneel on the mattress and watch the snow fall on New York. It is a fairyland.

When Robert's back hurts him too much, when the pain worsens with walking, I leave him to rest and go out alone. I find my library, the New York Society Library, around the corner from the Metropolitan. My card from my San Francisco library, the Mechanics' Institute, is honored at once, and I am to this day forever grateful for the respite both libraries have given me. In January, the New York library is warm, the librarians welcoming, the card catalog on-line, okay, but also in drawers that slide silently out and in, those beautiful small oak drawers with gold handles. Upstairs, where I spend most of my time, every journal I have ever admired—*The Paris Review,* the *Sewanee Review, Partisan Review, The American Scholar*—lies on tabletops waiting for me. I devour them and fall sound asleep in the big chair with a slipcover right out of my grandmother's living room. I am home.

IN BETWEEN TIMES came Walter and Sidney and a little bit of Graham, though of Graham there is no such thing as "a little bit." John, who lives in rural New England, would have to wait. Robert enjoys my peregrinations immensely. He has not a jealous bone in his body, and while I sort of wish he did, I am also fully aware of how fortunate I am. "Robert," I say after a brief conversation with Walter, "I feel kind of like a hooker working out of my pimp's apartment." He laughs and reminds me once again that he flourished in the openness of his second marriage. Okay, if you say so. This is something I will never understand, but Robert has not a drop of duplicity—oh, no, not a one, okay one—in him. He tells the truth as he sees it, hard as it may be for some to hear. So Walter, here I come.

Walter is a professor of sociology at the New School. He had sent a photograph of himself teaching a class. In it he leans against a stool and gestures with his right hand. He has a beard. He is tall. Best of all, it is clear he likes what he is doing, that is, teaching. "When you get to town," he wrote, "call me." So I did. "Come to my office at one," he says.

"Okay," I say, and I think, Hot dog, I've never been to the New School. This will be fun. I hop on the bus and off I go.

It is cold in New York in January. I am wearing the red knit cap with "NY" stitched on it in white that I bought from a street vendor, Robert's down jacket, which comes to my knees, underneath it my warmest, baggiest sweater—yes, that one—wool pants, and my hiking boots. These are my magic boots. They are scuffed at the toes and run-down at the heels, but in them I can walk the world. Together with my boots and my sweater, which covers me from chin to knee, I am without question a vision of loveliness.

The School of Social Research looks exactly the way it should—like a great big old house that would have fallen down if smart people hadn't saved it with paint and nails and cement in the foundation to hold it up for the next generation. Walter's office is on the main floor of the school.

Walter's office *is* the main floor. Walter, I am suspecting, is an important guy. My mouth is lined with chalk.

He sits behind his desk, gestures at the chair in front of it where I am to sit. He eyes me with that skim-and-scan sociology people do so fast. I am beginning to get warm. "Tell me about your work in prison," he says. This is my favorite subject, one I have no trouble talking about, so I tell him. He smiles sort of an approving smile—I say "sort of" because New Yorkers don't actually smile—and he says, "My field is the rehabilitation of chronic offenders. I often do consulting in Berkeley."

"Uh-huh," I say.

He says, "Take off your coat. It's warm in here."

I do. He calls to his secretary to close the door. His voice is really loud. If I were a chronic offender I would be rehabilitated right away.

From behind his desk, he skims and scans me, though slower this time, and stops right where my sweater, whipped against my chest by this damn New York static electricity, clings like an Ace bandage.

Walter says, "You have lovely breasts, more than ample, I would guess."

Right then and there I decide not to throw my hands over my whole entire torso. This is an interesting man, I remind myself, a smart one. I say, "I have become interested lately in male sexuality, especially as the male grows older. What must it be like to lose one's potency, especially when one may have defined oneself in terms of sexual prowess?" I can't believe it's me. "How is it with you?" Wow.

Walter leans forward in his chair and says, "The urge has not lessened. The decline of potency does not spell the end of pleasure." Oh, Robert, did you hear that? Pay attention! Seeing me mop my brow, Walter says, "It's warm in here for you, isn't it? Take off your sweater."

I don't.

Walter says, "I'm a voyeur."

Oh.

I could never take this sweater off even if I wanted to, which I don't. My entire torso is drenched; rivulets of sweat course along the streambed of my body, dampening the elastic waistband of my cotton Fruit of the Looms, running down the cleft between my buttocks; he might drown if he came too close. Suddenly, I have a little vision of what might happen if I did take off my sweater. Keep going, Walter might say, and if I did, like, remove my bra, well, if he's a voyeur, maybe just the stripping would be enough; maybe, well, I could maybe be like the strippers who so fascinated my father, only then what? What would Walter be doing while I was taking off my clothes? Would he do it behind his desk, or would he come out to where . . . and . . . like, do me right in the chair? Pop goes the vision. I pull my sweater down over my knees.

Walter sighs. "Next time I'm in Berkeley, I'll call you."

"Mmmglpd."

The interview at an end, Walter rises from his chair and, reaching for something next to his desk, pulls out a crutch, like Tiny Tim's in *A Christmas Carol,* and, with it under his arm, swings himself out into the room next to where I sit, face-to-face with his empty pant leg. I say, "Wow! What happened to your leg!" The sensitivity of my exclamation overwhelms us both. He never called. Apparently, rehabilitation of me was hopeless.

Back home, with Robert, we laughed together. But it was not

idle curiosity that had caused me to question Walter about aging and sexuality. It was that Robert was flagging. His back hurt, pain radiating down his leg. And, a member of AA, he was drinking. It was the end of Week One. If I had not given up clarity of mind in favor of romantic ooze, if I had let in the light of reason just for a bit, I could have prepared myself for what surely would come. I would have known that Robert's affections for me were diminishing. But no, no, I did not want this to end. I wanted to be in love and with him, with this man who paid every kind of attention to me, who touched me as no man ever had. I could not bear, would not bear, his falling out of love with me or, what eventually I came to understand, his loving me on e-mail but never, not from the first sight of me at the airport, in real person. I couldn't bear to be ugly again, oh, Robert, don't make me ugly. So I pretended I wasn't. And I made myself believe that Robert's back pain prohibited his lovemaking. And that his drinking was just, was . . . was . . . his problem, nothing to do with me. I was stupid with need. And so I stayed and crept ever closer to my side, the far side, the window side, the cold side, of the bed.

In Robert's apartment is a huge walk-in closet. It is in there I become acquainted with Sidney. Sidney, *"a senior member of a well-regarded investment firm,"* is sick. He has a terrible cold—"I seem to get this every January"—and so cannot meet me in person. "But perhaps we can get to know each other a bit by telephone." He does indeed sound sick, but being sick does not prevent him from talking for what seems like hours on the telephone to me.

Our letters have confirmed a mutual love for musical comedy. Sidney, in his youth, performed in musical comedy. We have a horror of Lloyd Webber and the tuneless monstrosities that sully the stages of Broadway. *Cats* we loathe. We love *Won-*

derful Town, Kiss Me, Kate, Bloomer Girl, all of Rodgers and Hart, and anything by Sondheim.

It is hot in Robert's closet. I tell this to Sidney. "It's time to come out of the closet," he says, laughing himself into a raspy cough.

And I get tired of standing. "Wait," I say, "I'm going to pull a chair in." Robert chuckles softly from the couch, where he is finishing the crossword puzzle he promised we would do together.

I pull a chair from the kitchen into the closet and seat myself. "Come out of the closet," Sidney says again.

I can't. It is the only place in the apartment that affords any kind of privacy, and I don't want Robert to hear me burbling over Nanette Fabray and Ethel Merman and Jerome Kern and all the music I ever loved. Besides, I was having fun with this clogged-up man who started liking me when I told him I came from Ohio. Sidney had never been to Ohio. Sidney had never been west of Pennsylvania. Sidney did not fly, had no interest in doing so, had lived his whole life in New York City. He thought I was the cat's meow. "Are you Ruth or Eileen in *Wonderful Town?*" he wanted to know. Ruth and Eileen were sisters who came to New York from Ohio and sang to us the very wonderful "Why oh why oh why oh, why did I ever leave Ohio."

"Sidney," I ask somewhere near the end of the first hour, "why are you talking to me? Why aren't you talking to all these sophisticated, beautiful women I see on the streets of New York?"

"In my experience, New York women carry a lot of baggage," he answers. "The edges are sharp."

"I'm Eileen," I say, referring to the younger of the sisters— sweet, unsophisticated, and beautiful—and figuring I would never meet this man Sidney in person.

"I can tell from your voice you probably are. Tell me, my dear, have you plans to visit our fair city again?"

He talked like that and got away with it. He had this sexy New York accent that did not include the letter *r*. In months to come, he would say "darling" just right. Now, I whisper into the phone, "I don't know. It will depend on my host."

"I understand," he says. "If you do return, give me a call either here or at my office."

Well, my goodness, another reason to come back.

In the week ahead, Robert's interest in sex continued to be replaced by the pain in his back and leg. Tylenol with codeine and an occasional scotch helped a bit, but not enough for him to satisfy what in me had not abated: my need to be wanted and my desire to be touched. I had never had sex like what Robert did for me. I wanted more. In the movies, at the opera, the ballet, sitting next to him, I wanted to slide to the floor. Touch me; I will him to touch me. I wear a skirt, a long skirt with a long slit up the side. Put your hand through the slit, I beg silently, it goes all the way up, all the way down. Touch me, Robert, and sometimes, in the dark of the theater, he does. Back home he says, Spread your legs, sweetie, and he stays forever at what has become the very center of me. You are a lovely pink, he says. Did you know that? I am all cunt, I tell him. Yes, you are, and he strokes me until I am wild and finally calm.

Every afternoon at four he called Sylvia. He had never lied to me about Sylvia. In his first letter, he told me that he had been companions with a woman for almost two years, that they did not live together, that increasingly their interests did not match, their tempers flared. But, he warned, he was not ready to make a break. "And so I will have to scheme when we're in New York together. She will e-mail me and occasionally call. And I will have to be loving. You will have to hear me tell her that I love her." And so every afternoon at four Robert would sit at his desk along the outer wall of the walk-in closet. Who was I kidding that the man I was in love with could talk affectionately to a woman and I not mind? It was not possible for me to sit comfortably on the couch and work the puzzle. Where was I to go? Where could I hide?

The bathroom. Every afternoon at four I went to the bathroom. I turned on the water in the sink full blast and sat on the toilet until I heard Robert call, "You can come out now, sweetie." I began to scrub the bathroom. On hands and knees in the corners behind the bowl, in the bowl, the tub, the walls, the sink. On the toilet I tried and tried, harder and harder, to rid myself of the shit that had accumulated and now impacted me until I thought I would burst. Finally, I did burst. I felt a rip, a dreadful tear, inside me, and when I looked into the bowl, the water was red with my blood.

It is Super Bowl Sunday, the day of contests among advertisers. Neither of us caring especially who wins, Madison Avenue or the NFL, Robert invites me to the Allstate Bar and Grill on West Seventy-second, just around the corner and up the street. It is a wonderful place, old, two steps down from the street, all but hidden. Inside is all old wood and working people along with a table of New York women who look as if they carry a lot of baggage with sharp edges. Robert drinks martinis, I scotch on the rocks. We talk very little. I recall that in the first days of my visit, dressed in my long skirt with the slit, a red cashmere sweater, ready for the opera, I said to Robert, "How do I look?"

"You look like someone I could love," he said.

After two weeks of unimagined intimacy, it is clear that he doesn't.

Next morning, in the cab that takes me to JFK, I look down at my hands. I am bleeding from every cuticle.

ELEVEN

Higher Education

What I want is to show students that they have the strength to cope with all the truth they perceive. . . . I want to show students that they are strong enough to deal with complexity and paradox without denying its existence.

—STEPHEN BOOTH, Distinguished Teaching Award,
University of California at Berkeley

Q: What do you teach?
A: Sustained ambiguity.

—JANE JUSKA, award for Best Field Trips,
Ygnacio Valley High

T hanks to Robert and New York and falling in love and not being fallen in love with, I have missed the beginning of the spring semester. Not for the first time, I am grateful to my profession for being so forgiving and at the same time so demanding. It requires of me my absolute and undivided attention. It compels me to ignore everything else in my life, to put my needs and wants and demands and cries for attention aside and

pay attention to those who might just possibly be more important than I.

The students I teach at St. Mary's College are going to be
high school and middle school teachers. For this I love them before I even meet them. What in the world would possess a man
or woman to choose to enter the teaching profession at this
time in our century? A number of my students over these past
years are older; that is, they have left careers in sales, computers,
journalism, the military. We want to make a difference, they say.
Larry, formerly a commercial real estate developer in San Francisco, tells us that all the years he was making big money, he
missed history. He said he found himself sneaking off to read
books until one day he quit developing real estate and came
here to learn to teach. Paula spent two years in Kosovo with the
Peace Corps. "I didn't know enough about teaching English,"
she said. "I want to learn to do that well. Then I'm going back."
She hesitates. "Unless my fiancé wants to go back to Vietnam,
then I'll go there." My job is to prepare them for life in the
classroom. I do the best I can. We read scholarly articles on
gender discrimination, financing, vouchers. They write papers. I
read them. In addition, I tell them some of what I learned in my
thirty-three years with kids. Now, please understand: I do not
offer a lecture on sex in the classroom, but gradually, over the
course of the semester, in response to my students' questions
and concerns, which mount as they assume the responsibilities
of classroom teaching, the following makes itself known: there
is a lot of sex in the classroom. High school and middle school
and no doubt school from the very beginning is larded with
sex, and no teacher or vice principal or superintendent or president of the world can insist that kids leave sex at the doorway
and expect that it will happen.

My mother tried to convince me not to become a teacher by

telling me that students really notice what the teacher wears. I, of course, decided not to become a teacher because what my mother was really saying was that kids look at your body. They look at their own bodies and the bodies of one another, their natural curiosity dampened by rules as they grow up. So I was twenty-seven years old before I got so bored with being a medical secretary that I didn't care who looked at my body. My mother's response, when I told her I was going back to school to get a credential, was, "Oh, Jane, we hoped for better things from you." She herself had been a teacher for one year until my father-to-be rescued her.

In the classroom kids bump against each other by mistake and by design. Boys punch each other, shove each other, fall into each other, in a kind of homoerotic working out of their own identity. Girls, more and more, do this overt physical stuff, too; in our liberation, behaving like boys was the way to express that we were up from slavery. Thus, girls began to curse and did it loudly inside and outside the classroom; they began to fist-fight, and there was no greater treat for the student body at large than a noontime ruckus between girls. "Girl fight!" someone would yell, and everybody would come running and quickly form a circle around the combatants to protect them from anyone like a teacher or an administrator who might try to break up the fight. Girls use fingernails, so often girls' fights are bloodier than boys'. The fights are always about boys.

The overt sexuality of girls, apparent in what passed for fashion, was something everyone—teacher and student alike—had to adapt to once the hippie era, featuring suggestively sexy neck-to-ankle cover-ups, was over. Dress codes never worked for very long: the school couldn't send half the student body home because of infractions of a rule like "No spaghetti straps." In many classrooms, beginning in the eighties and continuing up to my retirement in 1993, the chairs were arranged in a horseshoe. Girls sat, some unaware, some fully aware, that their teeny skirts had slid way, way up, that their legs sprawled, one hither and one yon, providing visual access to anyone—boys, girls, teachers—to parts of them better saved for another venue. Teachers, most of us, learned to gaze deeply into the mascaraed lash extenders of our girls, hoping that life as we knew it might be happening somewhere in there. Of course, some of the girls who sat splayed were very much aware of what they were doing and found this kind of play far more interesting than Huck and Jim, and, for sure, Hamlet and Ophelia. In the faculty lounge, we teachers used to entertain ourselves by imagining the perfect couple, who, copulating in front of the class, would hold the attention of our kids for more than one minute. Madonna and one of them? Keanu Reeves and Cher? *Eeeuw!* We never found the perfect couple, but I'm thinking right this very minute, How about Britney Spears and Ricky Martin? Britney and Madonna? Ricky and . . . Ricky.

For several years now, girls have featured their breasts. Even the most modest among them wear stretch tops, breasts peeping or spilling out of the V necks, the more daring wrapping their breasts in a bandeau that covers the nipples but not much else. Currently, it is the fashion for girls to present to the world at large their naked torsos—a wide swath of skin extending from just below the breasts to somewhere below the navel, which may or may not be pierced. Naked in their middles, girls often wear on their feet Doc Martens, heavy, black, dangerous-looking boots or shoes, steel-toed being the absolute finest. The message? "Look—you can't help it—but touch and I'll kick you in the balls." My sympathies these days lie with the boys. A story about Knute Rockne has it that he forbade his players to have sex during the season. His advice to them was "Wear corduroy pants and walk fast." Too bad corduroy is out.

Teachers are not immune to any of this. We have all heard

of affairs between students and teachers. But those unhappy arrangements are few. Occasionally, one hears of a teacher behaving outrageously, like one of my colleagues who strode up and down in front of the classroom and said to his students, "Look at me and tell me if I had sex last night." The problem for the teacher arose when the kids turned a deaf ear and a blind eye: they didn't care. This guy was a joke.

Another colleague decided to come out to his classes. He videotaped himself delivering an impassioned speech to his first-period kids; he played the tape for all four of his remaining classes. He wanted to get fired. He wanted to take his case to the Supreme Court. He wanted to be somebody. The kids cut him off at the pass. They just shrugged and, at home that evening, when asked what had gone on at school that day, they shrugged some more and said, "Nothing." Kids are cool.

Not so dramatic, there is nonetheless between all students and their teachers a subtle exchange, not all of it intellectual. Of course. Everybody's sexual. The problem is that sex is not supposed to be addressed in the classroom. It's a no-no; teachers can get in trouble acknowledging it unless it occurs in literature—*Romeo and Juliet* is pretty safe because it's Shakespeare, and so is *The Scarlet Letter* because nobody actually reads it—and then the classroom discussion of what goes on in those books had better be short. Too bad, because the classroom is exactly the place to mount a serious, rational discussion of an inflammatory subject. Where else can kids learn to douse the flames of hyperemotionality with reason? It is said that adult society wants us (teachers) to teach kids to think. I have serious doubts about this, since adult society perpetuates all kinds of impendimenta to thinking (standardized testing comes to mind). One barrier in place long before I became a teacher and after I stopped being a teacher was the taboo against sex as a topic for discussion in the classroom. An unfortunate prohibition, because it's easier and faster and more effective to teach kids to think if they are interested in what we ask them to think about. Sex beats out isosceles triangles every time.

And of course, teachers are sexual persons, too; some of them are even sexy. I am remembering this cute-as-a-bug history teacher standing before her class eating an apple and drinking the coffee her TA has brought her. He stands just to her right, drinking coffee, too, his reward for having gone off campus to where the latte is. She looks over and winks, his other reward. She is wearing a gray University of California at Santa Barbara sweatshirt, which sets off her blond hair, Levi's that fit, boy do they, and Reeboks. She is darling. And she plays it for all it's worth. Her darlingness, her sexuality, if you will, is part of her teaching. Kids pay attention to her because they like to look at her, because she flirts with them and they with her. Somewhere amongst all this, history gets learned.

I am not immune. In my early days of high school teaching, I became enamored of an ass belonging to a sixteen-year-old named Ben Jones. I was so entranced, I would get to school early and hang out casually in the hall down which I knew Ben would pass on his way to first period. I tee-heed and tittered when Ben became a student in my class; he took advantage of me and handed in his homework late or not at all. He knew that I would forgive his absences because I would be so glad to see him (or his ass). He just had his way with me, though he still got a C.

I will pass quickly over the time I ordered a particularly shrill ninth-grade boy never to speak again "until your testicles drop." He was silent until one fine spring day he entered the classroom and boomed, "Hi there, Mrs. Juska." He had become a man. I didn't get fired for that; however, over the years, I got more subtle in my classroom management techniques. In my last years of teaching high school, I used my sex or, must I say, gender, the kids not believing that sex visited the human female after forty. *Eeeuw!* Sitting in my chair in the open part of the horseshoe, I would command quiet and the attention of every one of my all-too-many ninth-graders by looking at them, just looking at them, and then, since there was always one miscreant who remained unmesmerized by my hypnotic stare, I would say, "If you don't stop talking, I'm going to come over there and kiss you." Then, if he (it was always a "he") didn't shut up, I would rise from my chair, glorious in all my sixty years, and move toward him. Hands and arms crossed over his face as if to ward off the devil herself, the poor kid would promise never, ever to talk again. After that, all I had to do to bring order out of chaos was purse my lips.

Another gimmick they don't teach in education school is this: Look at the kid who's misbehaving and mouth the words "I love you." Now, he probably won't see this because he is misbehaving flagrantly for the benefit of his buddies around him, but those sitting near him will see what I am saying and will punch him and poke him and roar with laughter at his expense. If the criminal is a girl, all I need to say is, "Will you get this class quiet?" and she will yell out something like "Shut the fuck up!" Everybody's quiet, thank you very much, let's learn something.

None of this works on juniors and seniors or if you, the teacher, are under fifty. The danger is that upperclassmen will respond to your threat to kiss them with "Hey, hey, hey, let's get it on!" I know; it happened. I underline this when I am with my teachers-to-be. "Wait till you get tenure," I add.

Superior in wisdom and experience as you are, sometimes the kids will strike first. If, as a teacher, you see a kid poke or nudge his friend sitting next to him, you know something's about to happen, probably with you as the target. One morning, once everyone got quiet, this boy—I have repressed his name—

said, no, wait, he raised his hand, which should have been my first clue—and said with all the sweetness of a snake, "Mrs. Juska, what was it like before fire?" I looked directly back at him and said, "Cold like your heart." Pause. "And dark like your mind." The friend jabbed the kid in the shoulder and chortled, "She got you, she got you." It's great to be victorious over fourteen-year-olds.

In my graduate seminar, questions arise eventually about offering personal information. Kids are naturally curious about the person in front of them posing as a teacher, so isn't it okay to share? The answer is, if you do or don't, you must know why. Will your answer to "Are you married?" or "Do you have any kids?" help learning occur? Usually, the answer is no. But sometimes, every so often, you can make their curiosity and your personal life part of a classroom negotiation. For example, there's the elbow, the signal to Watch This, and the kid says to me, "Hey, Mrs. Juska, did you ever do drugs?" *Snicker, snicker.* Now, the answer, as you know, is yes; but the question is, will telling them a little story about my twenty-five years of drug-taking lead to learning? Maybe. So if I want to risk it, I say, "Yes, actually, I did. I started when I was about your age." Oh, well, eyes pop, their attention is all mine, but no, no, I say, "We've got work to do; maybe, if it gets done quickly and well, I'll tell you the rest. We'll see." *Scurry, scurry.* Sometimes I tell them about the amphetamines and the tranquilizers and the laws that came down on people like me in 1970 and what it was like when I woke up that first morning without a pill to pop. Sometimes I don't. But whatever I tell them comes from the question in the back of my mind: How can I use this to get them to learn? I am ruthless.

Sometimes, though, I explain to my student teachers, you just lose it, like when a kid blurted out, "Why is this class so boring?" and I answered, "Because you're in it."

Juniors and seniors are more savvy and much bolder. To wit: fifth period came after lunch. In my fifth-period class, a class of juniors, were two lovers: Brian and Maxi. Brian was putting in his time until the Marines would agree to take him once he developed his upper body and came regularly to class, the Marines having insisted on both. Maxi was just Maxi. They came to class almost every day late, having spent the lunch hour in Brian's empty apartment, having themselves a nooner. Every day, they entered class, arms around each other, sat down in chairs next to each other, sometimes in the same chair, and entwined. Legs, arms, lips, amazing. The rest of us were open-mouthed, some in amazement, some in lust. I would order Brian and Maxi to cease and desist, and they would—for five minutes—then back at it. Finally, I said to them, "This isn't fair to the rest of us. How do you think we feel sitting here without our significant other?" This they understood; they paused momentarily and looked around at the rest of us in sympathy. "So I don't think you can sit together," I said. "You are just magnets, you are." They understood this, too. "You, Brian," I said, "stay where you are, and you, Maxi, sit over there." I knew I would not be able to move Brian, he being majorly buff by then, if he chose not to be moved. Maxi, on the other hand . . . She moved. From that time on, they did not touch each other. They sat across the room from each other and talked with their tongues. Out, around, in, mouth way open, halfway closed, eyes slits, heads back, Maxi's throat arched like some damn bird in heat. Brian and Maxi taught the rest of us that sex is not to be denied.

See why I miss all this?

I tell all my college students this stuff. They are learning to be teachers and are interested in real-life school. I tell them especially my notion, shared by others more notable than I, that controversial issues belong in the classroom. I tell them why and I tell them that they must be very, very careful, that perhaps they will need to wait until they get tenure before they risk losing their jobs over teaching kids to think.

I tell them about Discussion Day in my high school classes. What do we want kids to do? I ask. Read, write, listen, and talk. All these are vehicles for thinking, but we don't need to broadcast that. So, on Fridays or Tuesdays or on whatever day kids choose, we have Discussion Day. We have worked out the procedures for making Discussion Day work: no obscenities; no hitting; no name-calling; no getting out of your seat. Ten minutes before the end of class, we write about what we talked about. The last is mine, can you tell? The topics for discussion will come from the kids. They are free to put a slip of paper with a topic on it into the Discussion Basket right up until Discussion Day. We have agreed that no topic will be censored and that everything said in our class stays in our class. My college students are seeing that this is risky business. "You let them talk about anything they want?" asks one of my future teachers. "I encourage it," I say.

I wish I had done some kind of statistical count of the topics so that I could tell you exactly what proportion concerned sex. It was high. Here is ninth grade: The student designated to draw from the basket holds up the piece of paper and reads, "Condoms." Incidentally, I am not in this. At first, I moderate; as the year goes on, students moderate. Progress. At first, "Condoms" is greeted with silence. And then Jeremy says—Jeremy is bold—"My brother said if you use twelve condoms you're safe." Well, this does it. "Seven," says Cal. "Are you guys nuts?" says Sue, and begins to form the word "asshole" when a stern glance from the moderator silences her. Now, it's very hard for me, middle-aged demi-virgin that I am, not to interject information here. But I don't. Information is not what this is all about. Still, maybe I can take Jeremy aside . . . Next topic: "Penis." Oh, god. "Girls have a penis, too," says Mike. "Huh-uh," says

Amy. Ought I not to intervene? "Yes, they do," says Mike, "it's just real little." That pretty much does it for that. We proceed to the next, "Milk."

In my senior class, the topic is "Breasts." Those with large breasts say nothing, those with small are equally silent. No boy makes a sound. Finally, Shannon, medium breasts, says, "What I hate is when a teacher is talking to you and his eyes drift down . . . and I try to make eye contact . . ." "You mean there's more than one teacher?" asks Brad. "Oh, yeah," says Jennifer. "Since seventh grade," says Laurie. We are quiet all of us, the boys embarrassed for their sex, me embarrassed for my profession, the girls embarrassed for us all. The next topic is "Shit." "I vote we skip this," says Rob. He draws again. "Cafeteria food." We exhale.

Why is the saying "Sex rears its ugly head"? Sex isn't ugly, it's just sex. But rear it did, and this time I did not escape unscarred. In the mid-seventies, at my high school, I taught an elective course called Women in Literature. It was a first for the school, a first for me, a first for the kids—thirty-two "women" and two boys. It was great fun. To supplement the curriculum, which included *Jane Eyre, Pride and Prejudice,* and Kate Chopin's *The Awakening,* I ordered *Ms.* magazine to be delivered to the school library. One day one of the "women" in the class took *Ms.* magazine home with her. Her mother found it. It had sex ads in the back and a story with the word *fuck* in it and not just once either. She stormed into my principal's office, dirty magazine in hand. My principal ordered it removed from the library. He summoned me to his office.

Thoreau says somewhere that in every man's life there is a line beyond which he will not go. When I read that all those years ago, I wondered to myself if a line would appear in my life and if I would refuse to go beyond it. This was the line.

For now, things had gotten way out of hand. A group of

moms, all of them from an organization that wanted to change the name of our district, Mount Diablo, to Valley of the Kings, got busy. They demanded that *Ms.* be removed from all libraries in all eight high schools. A special school-board meeting was called. I went. So did four hundred other people. One after another, people from the audience went to the microphone and spoke ardently against children being exposed to the filth wrought by that dreadful woman, Gloria Steinem. At the end of the meeting, the board voted unanimously to rid the schools of *Ms.* Meeting adjourned. On her way out, one of the board members muttered to herself, "We're going to get the pants sued off us." Yes, indeedy.

So the chairman of our history department, two parents, two students, and I sued. The ACLU handled the case and we won. The magazine went back in. The editorial staff of *Ms.,* where I called frequently to report on events, was jubilant and the ACLU threw us a party with guest of honor Gloria Steinem her own self, who came all the way from New York and was nice to me. When she accused me of heroic behavior, I denied the charge, explaining that never had I feared I might lose my job. "You're like Rosa Parks," she said. Me and Rosa Parks!

Fortunately, nobody ever found out that in this same Women in Literature class, we looked at *Hustler, Playgirl, Playboy,* and *Penthouse,* too, along with *Ladies' Home Journal, Good Housekeeping,* and *Vogue.* We wanted to find out how women were presented in these magazines, how these women looked, and, omigod, is this a split beaver shot? Nobody ratted on us. Kids are cool.

We talk about all this, my college students and I, in the weeks following my return from New York. What would they think, I wonder, if they knew what I had been up to? Some would enjoy it, others not. Definitely, the college would not. Besides, knowing about my sex life would not make them good teachers, which is what we're about here.

ON MY E-MAIL is a note from Robert: *"I anticipate with pleasure spending your birthday with you. Come stay with me."*

I have been miserable without Robert. I have tried very hard not to write to him; I have made myself put down the phone before it rings in New York. I have been so unhappy that I don't stop to remember scouring his bathroom, hearing him call Sylvia my name—"sweetie." And now those two elegant sentences on my screen. Why does he write? Why does he invite me? Maybe he got lonely for a pal; I'm sure he knew that, without an implied promise of lovemaking, I wouldn't come. I shouldn't go, but I don't care; I get to be in love again; I get to imagine his hands and his mouth on me; I get to start all over.

My department chair agrees to take my seminar. My TAs agree to teach my prison class. When I explain my upcoming absence to my students at the prison—it is my birthday and I am going to celebrate in New York—they smile back at my foolish grin. At the end of class every single one of them pauses on his way out, shakes my hand, and says happy birthday, have a fine time, don't forget to come back. Steve is the last. Steve is very serious, very, still trying mightily, he has told me, to develop a sense of humor. He takes my hand and looks very, very seriously into my eyes and says, "You be careful. New York will chew you up and spit you out in little pieces." He is a prophet. Except it's not New York I need to fear.

TWELVE

Sex at the Morgan

I am notably solvent.

—SIDNEY

Robert's third wonderful sentence read, *"Happy Valentine's Day, sweetie, from the man who misses you."* How could I go? How much pain am I up for or maybe in need of? How eroded by my own lust is my common sense? How selective is my memory? It selected this: "Lie on your side, sweetie," Robert would say as we lay next to each other in his bed. He would trace me then, with the tip of his finger, the entire length of me, tip to toe, slowly, a most exquisite touching. How could I not go?

I land at JFK at four P.M., EDT, on March 7, my very birthday, in the year 2000. This time, being the New York girl I have become, I take a cab alone to Robert's apartment building and the elevator all the way up to his floor. The elevator door opens and there stands Robert, smiling, arms open wide. Inside his apartment, he wraps me up and kisses me, and while I am feeling that in his arms is absolutely where I belong, I sense that something is different, and I don't know what it is, but I don't like it.

We dine that evening at Café des Artistes. As an enthusiastic resident of what has come to be called the Gourmet Ghetto, the Berkeley birthplace of California Cuisine, I have not been impressed with the food in New York, except for the hot dogs and the knishes and the roasted nuts waiting for me on the street corners. But this restaurant is just about, no, it is, the classiest place I have ever been to; San Francisco's eateries, by comparison, seem *sooo* nouveau. Café des Artistes is famous for its murals, painted in the twenties, of naked nymphs cavorting daintily with one another, so it appears, in pastels and lots of chiffon. *Sooooo* romantic, so sweet, so pretty, just like me I am pretending as Robert guides me gently by the elbow into a booth—a booth! Privacy for lovers, that's us. And I don't know, but this place ought to be famous for its service: our waiter was lots more sophisticated than I and, at the same time, helpful and charming and not one whit condescending. In San Francisco, it seemed to me that too often the waitperson who came my way was less interested in waiting than in auditioning en route to my table for the part that would take him far and forever away from persons like me. On the other hand, somebody had told wait-persons they were supposed to be friendly—"Hi, I'm Ken, I'll be your . . ." And, this being America, they were equal, which meant they could get pissed at you if you didn't behave as a pa-tron should; many of them let you know that, were justice to prevail, they would be the ones seated at the table and you the one serving. To be fair, let me say that, in recent years, since waiting tables has become so lucrative, waitpersons exhibit a much higher degree of professionalism. Like in New York, in this *salle à manger magnifique* where I swear there was not one tourist, except me, and by now, of course, I had progressed way beyond ogling. "Sweetie," said Robert, "take a look at the menu."

"Don't look now," I tell him, "but when you can do it inconspicuously, look at the woman at the far end of the bar." She was a regular here, you could tell. Ever so thin, chic in black and gray jacket, skirt to match, hair dark, streaked with gray and pulled into an honest-to-god chignon away from her face, which someone, probably she, had made up subtly and utterly correctly, she sipped her martini (I can learn) from a glass smoky with cold. She would have two, smile at the bartender, who bowed (yes!) slightly, and walk steadily on high heels out of the bar. She was me as I would be in twenty, maybe fifteen, omigod, ten, years, dignified and just a little drunk. How old was I anyway? "Thank you, Robert, this has been a wonderful birthday."

On the walk home, I take his arm and he says, "I don't like that. Please don't take my arm. It makes me feel like a possession." If he had struck me with the back of his hand, it wouldn't have hurt any more. I stuff my hands in my pockets.

Back in the apartment, in Robert's great big bed with Central Park outside my window, I turn to kiss him and hear, "Oh, now, sweetie, really . . ." He goes on to explain: "Our passions simply do not match. You have no equivalent of Sylvia in your life, so you come to me needy." Can't argue with that or with the terrible, terrible dark weight that has taken possession of me. It began with a thud in my midsection with Robert's "Oh, now . . ." and spread quickly to every part of me. I am stunned. "Why did you invite me to come stay with you? Why did you tell me you loved me?" I lie rigid on the bed. Next to me, Robert says, "I admit, I may have sent you a few mixed messages. I value your friendship very much." "Mixed messages!" I rolled myself far away from him, as close to Central Park as I could get. What was I going to do?

Next day, after a sleepless night, I call Sidney from Robert's closet and make plans to meet. "I am going to the Morgan Library today," I say to Sidney. "I'll be there at two. Can you be there, too?" It's damn hot in this closet, though perhaps my brow is damp from frustration. Sidney hems and haws and says something about his apartment being painted and on and on. "Look," I say, "I'll be at the Morgan at two."

"How will I know you?" Sidney wants to know.

"I sent you a photograph."

"I lost it." He sounds like a little boy, appealing.

"I will be wearing a red knit hat. And I'm short."

"I feel silly," he says. "I have a Band-Aid on my nose. I was cleaning out the closet—you know, one of those Fibber McGee closets everyone has—and something fell on me, this was just yesterday and . . ." His voice is gravelly, his accent New York–sexy.

This Band-Aid of Sidney's is good, for I have managed to manufacture a pimple just below my eye, at the bottom of my left eye bag, something I grew in preparation for coming to New York to impress Robert. Over time it had reddened, swelled, popped, and was trying to heal except I fiddled with it, and now it is bleeding, it's a goddamn open wound. If I smile, it pulses. If I frown, it throbs.

"At two, then," I say. What the hell. This man is on my list. I am going to meet him. He is not going to escape. Fine with Robert. He is kind and puts his arms around me. "Look at me," he says from way high above me. "You are under no obligation to this man. You can leave anytime you want to." He pats my pimple, where it is oozing a bit, with his handkerchief. "You know where to get the crosstown bus." I nod. He kisses me. "Don't forget your key." I am all mixed up.

This is Sunday in New York. It is raining pell-mell and, beneath Robert's umbrella, which, by the end of the day, I will lose, I am off to one of the most wonderful libraries in the world. In fact, I won't see the library at all. I'll just see Sidney. Because he shows up. Right at two.

The Morgan Library is a serious building. It stands on the corner of East Thirty-sixth and Madison and occupies half a block in the heart of New York. It had been the home of Pierpont Morgan, a serious man, whose collection "was to rival the great libraries of Europe." It is a no-nonsense building: its stern façade and dark-paneled interior brook no frivolity, no levity, from those who enter. The Morgan Library on this particular Sunday in New York says, "Sit up straight, speak only when spoken to, and, this above all, Keep Your Hands to Yourself." My grandmother would have been right at home in the Morgan.

Sidney has directed me to meet him in the restaurant of the library. I go there. I am early. I loiter. I should be arrested and taken to a holding cell, except who would post bail? Robert? Maybe, maybe not. My mouth is dry. Again. I think about how little I know of this man, yet this is a public place, lots of people, he won't kill me here. I am so hot in this coat, which I absolutely do not plan to remove because the static electricity in this city will glue my sweater to me, my usual big, baggy sweater, which did so well for me when I met Walter. Why am I so intent on meeting this man? I could have stayed home with Robert, not so appealing to either of us at the moment. "Notably solvent," Sidney had described himself in his first letter. I never met a man who was that. I don't know anyone, man or woman, who is that. Is he rich? Could be. And then he just says it, not that he's "comfortable," which is what most of the men in their letters claim to be. I am just so curious.

I see him. I walk toward him, my red knit hat ablaze, like my pimple. Later, Sidney will refer not at all to my pimple but to "that funny red hat you were wearing." His Band-Aid is tiny, as discreet as a Band-Aid on the bridge of a nose can be. In our imperfections, we are a pair. I pretend to be confident. I extend my hand in introduction, with the other take off my hat, and my hair, electrified by New York City, sweeps up high above my face, making me look like a broom upside down. I capture most of it. Sidney smiles and says, "Shall we?" and, bending slightly from the waist, he sweeps an arm toward the café. I am in love. No, not really, but god, he is so New York. He is wearing a vest. His hair is dark, rough, shot with gray, lots of it sticking out from under his broad-brimmed hat, which he removes as I come toward him. He smiles shyly with what I will come to believe is the sexiest mouth on the North American continent. His glasses, probably bifocals, they must be, he is sixty-eight, have no line across the lenses as mine do, and behind them his eyes are dark and they are gray. I have never known anyone with gray eyes. And where are the lines in his face? Hard as I look, his skin is smooth as a baby's. He is notably attractive. But it is his clothes that fire me up.

All my life I have loved men's clothes. My father loved men's clothes, too, and spent a lot of money on his. My father looked like Scott Fitzgerald except tall. Athletic, like my mother, he moved with grace and style. He was not the picture of a small-town doctor, as his father—medium height, sweetly rumpled—had been. No, my dad in his Sulka ties, his dark navy pinstripes, wing tips polished and buffed, was the acme, the zenith, of men's fashion. Sartorially splendid he was. I loved looking at my dad. Everybody did.

When I first lived in San Francisco, forty years ago, he came to the American College of Surgeons meeting. I met him in the bar of the Clift Hotel after my day as a medical secretary (a career my father approved of) was over. Here, in this redwood-paneled, lushly carpeted room, doctors stood along the bar, elegant in their male finery, or sat at tables, now and then crossing one expensively adorned leg over the other. I wanted to rub my fingers along their lapels, run my hand up and down the smooth backs of their jackets and along their shoulders. I would never have dared, any more than I would have dared to touch my father. Now here, in the Morgan Library in New York City, was a man wearing utterly delicious clothes. Finally, I was going to get to feel the goods.

Sidney holds my chair, waiting for me to sit, and I become a tramp. I take off my coat. Slowly. And as I do, I stretch ever so slightly, feeling my sweater snuggle up to my breasts. Shameless hussy. I drop my coat on the floor. Not intentionally. "Let me get that for you," says Sidney, amused and unimpressed.

I look across the table at him, rather at his clothes: the rich blue, lightweight wool of his shirt, the dark green wool of his tie, the muted gold of his vest, and the brown and black checks of his jacket. No Brooks Brothers there, a conglomeration, you say. Still, in current lingo, it works. He looks good enough to eat.

Sidney orders coffee and I remember that, along with presenting himself as notably solvent, he had written that he did not drink. I order wine. When it comes, I raise my glass and say gaily, I'm almost sure, "To meetings."

Sidney leans toward me, leading with his right ear, a sure sign of hearing loss. He joins my toast with his coffee cup and says, "You have wonderful breasts." Shades of Walter. Gee, maybe I do.

"Sshhh," I say, looking around at the nearby tables, all of them filled; it is, after all, a rainy Sunday in New York. On the far side of the room is my grandmother, looking meaningfully at me while she shakes her finger at my mother, who nods a cool hello to my sister-in-law, who nods back from her seat right smack in the middle of all the women in my entire life who know better and are watching me behave badly.

"Move your chair closer," Sidney says.

I do.

He takes my hands and pulls them across the table toward

him. He begins to rub the spaces between my thumbs and fore-fingers and up along my wrists. I go dizzy from the sudden warmth. "I want you to know I think what you're doing is won-derful," he says. His voice is full of gravel, his accent Morning-side Heights with Columbia thrown in.

"What?" Again, my snappy repartee.

"The ad, meeting men." And then, suddenly, he says, "You have a kind face. You look kind."

"I am."

"Put your breasts on the table."

I do.

"Oh," he says, "you have big breasts, they're so soft." He is touching them!

This is outrageous. I heave my breasts back onto my side of the table and, having located my voice, say, "This is a public place, Sidney." I look neither to the right nor to the left, afraid of what I might see. I can hear, though, two people speaking what I am sure is Norwegian, very fast, and then some Scandi-navian giggling.

"This is New York, nobody pays attention," he says.

"This is New York with tourists," I say back. "Everybody pays attention."

He takes my hands again. "Tell me about growing up in Ohio."

So I do. I tell him the story about waiting tables at a resort in New Hampshire during my sophomore year of college, about the customer who looked at me and said, "So that's what the Midwest looks like."

Sidney laughs, grows serious, and says, "I don't see any judg-ment in your face; you are so warm, so accepting."

What the heck is going on? Am I that different from the women he must have known? Then I remember his description during our phone conversation of New York women with their sharp-cornered baggage and know that this elegant man has been knocked about more than once. I like him, solvent or not. "Tell me about your work," I say. "When will you retire?" The Norwegians at the next table have been replaced by the French. I relax; the French are used to outrageous behavior.

Sidney puts two hands around the coffee cup—a good thing, too, all that rubbing of my wrists, the inside especially, has got me sort of very warm; apparently the pimple is not putting him off. "I will retire in a year or two. I'll probably have to." He looks at me, knowing I retired years before, and says, "What do people do when they retire? I have no idea."

"They travel," I answer. "They see the world. You could do that."

"I am not fond of flying," he says.

"You're afraid of flying?"

"Not afraid, just anxious." And then, in tones so urgent, he says, "You've got to come to New York, you've got to live here. Move closer."

I do and so do my breasts and so do his hands and it feels very, very good. "Stop now," I beg. "Please, a little conversation." I am melting, I will soon be a pool of squish. Surely, the French are totally comfortable with this public passion, but maybe not. Is that Gallic tittering I hear? Do I care?

"Of course." He smooths his hands down over my breasts and returns to stroking the insides of my wrists. I am feeling faint. It is so hot in here and stuffy. Sidney says in a very normal, very matter-of-fact voice, "Tell me how things are going with the man you're staying with, this Robert."

I know that if I cry the tears will drip into my open pimple and it will hurt; worse, it could start bleeding again. "Well, there are a few problems," I say and continue to twist my napkin into a rope.

"Is the problem personal?" I am silent, afraid of crying. He persists: "Do you think the problem has to do with you or is it . . . mechanical?"

"Physiological," I answer, not sure of anything.

"So why are you crying?" he asks. "Here, give me your hands."

"Well, Sidney," I say, "there is a certain level of frustration I bring to this table."

"Me, too," he says. "Come, I'll show you a secret entrance, the Morgan family's entrance. And then I'm going to kiss you."

I follow dutifully as Sidney winds around the gift shop and out a rear door onto a small porch overlooking the street. It is early evening and the rain pounds the pavement. From behind me, Sidney puts his arms around me and cradles my breasts in his hands. "What do you think of New York?"

I look across the street at the huge apartment building whose many, many windows look down on us. "Look up there, Sidney . . ."

"I'd be willing to bet that not one person in that building is looking at us." He takes my hand and guides it to his fly. "Look what has happened," he says. "Feel what you've done to me."

I do that, too. I am a woman after all. I, just me, have inspired this truly impressive erection and I swell with pride.

"Touch it with your hand," he says. "Just a little, so I can remember what your hand feels like." I feel the rough texture of his jacket, the soft wool of his shirt, and beneath everything the part of him I have brought to life. It feels good just like everything else about this man. I remove my hand. All those windows across the street, all those people peering out from behind the blinds, the curtains, the shutters. My grandmother, having left the café, is in there somewhere.

"Tell me what you'll do," he urges. He struggles with his zipper. And you know what? I am so relieved, so goddamn happy to be wanted, I don't care if the whole city of New York hears what I'm about to do and say. I place my hand on his bare-naked penis, which throbs like what I read somewhere a red-hot prick is supposed to do.

"I will start at the tip," I say, "and suck just a bit, then move my mouth down you and twist you gently with my tongue."

"You will?" The whole East Side must hear his breathing.

I am not turned on by this erection, sizable though it is. But I am turned on by being able to turn him on. I say, "And you know what I will do then?"

"What?" he groans.

"I will open my throat and take all of you. I can do that."

"Really?"

"But now I must go." I remove my hand. I could get to be a real bitch if I kept at it. But Sidney will never let me. I will discover that he is too sweet, too loving, to make me into anything but my nicest self. Here, though, now, with Robert far away on the Upper West Side, Robert who said he loved me, then, no, he valued my friendship, then, "Perhaps we could just cuddle," finally not even that, here was this stranger named Sidney, who thought I was desirable, who couldn't keep his hands off me, who didn't mind at all looking at me and my pimple and my big, sweaty sweater. With Robert, it just had to be that the sight of me was more than he could bear. Sidney was bearing the sight of me just fine.

"See that awning?" says Sidney, pointing to a building on the next block. "That's where I live." He pulls me close.

"Come," I say. "I'll walk you home."

He puts his hand on the back of my neck and with the other holds the umbrella over us. "You're not going to sleep with me, are you?"

No, I'm not. And I'm not sure why. Robert, maybe, difficult

as he was making life for me. Maybe it was Sidney's eagerness, so immediate and urgent. "No," I say. "Not now."

Is it my imagination or does he seem ever so slightly relieved? "Oh, well," he says, "we'd probably drive each other crazy." He opens my coat, slides his hand around my waist, and pulls me close. "But if you lived in New York, oh, how I would pursue you." We stop in front of Sidney's building. "This is it."

I look into the cool, ivory interior of the lobby, just the right floral piece on the counter, just a single painting, large but not too large, on the wall. It looks like a place where a notably solvent person might live.

He stands still on the sidewalk and looks up at the vacant windows of his building. He says once again, "My apartment is being painted. Otherwise . . ."

Something is odd here. Impassioned as he has become over the long afternoon, surely he would not let a little paint interfere with what would normally come next. But something secret is going on inside this quite wonderful man. I am guessing that someone lives in his apartment with him. Whatever the reason, he is not going to ask me to come in, and even if he did, I wouldn't go. Too much too soon, too mysterious, maybe even too solvent. "Sidney," I say, "will you get me a cab?" As the cab draws to the curb, I turn to him, take his face in my hands, and kiss him on his beautiful mouth.

"Will you come to New York again?"

"Yes. And when I do, I am going to sleep with you."

"Next time."

"Yes."

Next time I do.

MY WOMANHOOD RESTORED, I return to Robert's apartment, where I watch him continue to fall out of love with me. It

will be one of the most painful experiences of my life. On this
visit, Robert is dyspeptic; his back and leg are not so painful, but
indigestion plagues him. Viagra especially makes him queasy,
and since his libido has taken a hike, no sense in popping the pill.
"The questions keep changing as one ages," he tells me. I don't
agree. I want to say to him but don't—I've got a whole week of
this friendship left—Robert, you are preoccupied with aging,
with answering the questions you claim change as one ages. But
there is only one question and it never changes: How will I live
with the life force? Will I adapt? Deny it? Repress it? Ignore it?
Oh, Robert, I want to say to him, I am the life force, and you
don't even know it. You are a fool to let me go.

New York is a wonderful place to cry. In the park, along the
river, behind the apartment building, all over town, I cry and no
one notices. I must thank Robert, whom I have been careful not
to let see me cry. New York is not a small gift. The tears come
with fatigue brought on by heartbreak. They will never stop.

But I have decided something. I have decided to do what I
have been good at my whole life—being a friend. I know how
to do that and, as I wrote in my journal, "All of my usefulnesses,
farmed out to groups, individuals, causes, have found a home in
Robert." So get on board, Jane. Don't fuck up a free place to
stay in New York.

Thank god for March Madness. Sports is my friendship
métier. I learned from my mother and from my dad. Near the
end of my father's life, he and I found a way to talk. We talked
about NCAA basketball and professional football. My sister
took over golf and tennis—she actually played them—so my
father lived a full conversational life in the years before his
death. Of course, my sister and I were not the chosen two; my
father much preferred my brothers, but they had preceded
my father in death, as had our mother, who was the queen of
sports on and off the field. My father's third wife participated

actively in buying and redecorating houses, a hobby that left my father confused and broke. So my sister and I won by default: we had been brought up well, that is, with a speaking knowledge and appreciation of all things sport and, most important at this stage of our father's life, we were alive.

My ex-husband had done me a tremendous favor, early in our relationship, by introducing me to the pleasure of male asses. He was a longtime and ardent football fan. In 1963 the San Francisco 49ers played in Kezar Stadium, a small stadium with a seating capacity of thirty thousand or so. Games were not sold out; one did not have to inherit the right to buy a license for ten thousand dollars in order to buy season tickets for even more; back then, the end zone was open and available right up to and after kickoff, and seats were cheap. Tom and I went often. Now, I knew the fundamentals: I knew about downs and running backs as opposed to quarterbacks and kickers. But I didn't know the fun stuff. The fun stuff was how the players, depending on the position they played, were built. Tom taught me. "Look at the players wearing numbers in the twenties," he said, handing me his binoculars. "They're running backs. Look at their butts." I did. "Now," he said, "look for the guys wearing numbers in the eighties. Those are wide receivers. Look at their backsides. What do you see?"

I saw buns of steel, like cannonballs, on the running backs, and long legs and flanks on the receivers, small-butted, relatively speaking. They were all beautiful. I had never, ever looked at a male body clothed or otherwise. Always, I turned away, from Jack, from Tom, respecting, I thought, their privacy. In truth, I was scared. I wanted to make love with the lights off, the curtains drawn; and if, by some chance, we made love during the day, with the sun shining in through the windows, I did so with my eyes shut. That way, they couldn't see me either, a good thing because my body was so ugly, not that I had ever looked at it. Once, when I was very young, I walked past the open door of my father's dressing room where he stood naked. He covered himself quickly; and it seemed to me he looked not only surprised but embarrassed, if not ashamed. So I had brought that modesty, that ignorance of the body, along with me, too. But gee! Here in Kezar, the man I would decide to marry was not only giving me permission to stare at men's bodies, clothed in uniforms that accented them, but had given me a pair of binoculars to do it with. My interest in football remains to this day.

I grew up with basketball. My mother played it—center on an all-star team, what else—and in rural Ohio, so close to Indiana, high school basketball was king. At Michigan, I went to all the football games, as many basketball games as possible, hockey, etc., etc. And now, here in New York, my hobby was paying off. Big time.

Occasionally, Robert and I went out to the movies, dinner, but mainly we watched March Madness. Michigan's team out of the running, Robert was a Duke fan. (The following year, alone, I would watch Duke win.) I knew enough of Duke's history and about the game in general to make me a worthy companion, so with me and a little scotch, which Robert began to drink around noon, this tournament would be great.

My main friendship talent is knowing when to shut up. Over the many years of my life, I learned, in the company of men, when to be silent (most of the time), when to comment ("He should take Battier out now"), and when to jump up and down (not often). Men believe women don't know anything about sports and don't appreciate sports, and have no business hanging around sports and sports-minded men during sporting events. This is as true in the twenty-first century as it was in the fifties, no matter how many female sportswriters have fought and won the locker-room battle. One would think that men and women would share comfortably their passion for sport, and from the outside it might look as if that were what was going on— girls and boys, men and women, sharing the couch, the stadium seats. "Do you think Williams will stay in college or jump to the NBA?" Now, that question could come from either gender, and will be speculated on by the other. However, when talk gets technical—man-to-man versus zone, change-up pitch, that kind of stuff—boys turn to boys and men to men. So, ladies, practice restraint. Be cool. And yet, I will remember forever when, in 1963, at Kezar Stadium, in the end zone (the best place to sit— you can watch the plays open up) with Tom, I was livid over the play-calling of San Francisco's quarterback, John Brodie. (Those were the days when coaches shut up, except for Paul Brown of the Cleveland Browns; when quarterbacks called their own plays.) "Why is he calling a pass on second down?" I stamped my feet and cursed mildly. I continued to critique Mr. Brodie, who apparently heard nothing I said, because the 49ers continued to lose. Finally, somewhere during the fourth quarter, a man in the row in front of us turned around and said to Tom, "Boy, I wish my wife knew that much about football." It was a compliment I will take to my grave.

However, here we are in New York and it's the year 2000, and I am trying my damnedest to be cool, not an easy task, for in between games, a little scotch adding fluency, Robert recounts his sexual history. There is Stacie, the professor—"God, I really loved her!" There is Judith, "flaky but adorable." There is Ruthie, who with her husband swapped with Robert and his first wife on a beach on the Riviera. And there is Sharon, his second wife, once his medical student, whom he clearly still loves: "We made love every morning and often at night." Some girls have all the luck.

I suggest he write his memoirs and I even offer a title—"Interstitial Women," the two fulcrums his first wife and his second wife, with all those women filling in the spaces for a time, like me, though I do not have a space here, not really. He cannot see how his tales hurt me, he doesn't care to know, though it is entirely possible he does know and is punching me out of his life. Aware of me or not, he is deliciously lost in the sexual past, in the fields of women who spread their legs from desire, upon command, at his request. And he comes erect and fucks them all. Ah, youth, ah, wilderness.

But I am a grown-up, and I have my pride. I don't have to sit on Robert's couch and listen to all this. I can . . . I can . . . I have no pride whatsoever. Whoever I was is gone; whatever strength of character, sense of humor, self-regard I had is a sodden mess staining the sheets jammed against the foot of Robert's bed. "Robert, can I come visit you again?" I beg.

"We'll have to see."

"In June?"

"I don't even know if I'll be here in June."

"Will you let me know? Do you want me to come if you're here?"

His anger flares: "You're writing a script for me! You want me to say things I don't want to say! I have to write! I can't write if you're here!"

I go mute, though not inside where I am screaming.

At the end of the week I pack up what's left of my life force and go home. On the plane my stomach aches from holding back sobs. Tears stream down my cheeks. What will they think, the other passengers? They will think I have been to a funeral. They will think I am crying over the death of a loved one. They will be right.

Back home my college students wait. My students in San

Quentin wait. And, in my chorale, Johann Sebastian Bach and his B Minor Mass wait. Somewhere over Iowa, I dry my eyes and listen to the pilot tell us that the weather in California is good and that we will be landing three hours ahead of now.

At home, I e-mail Robert: *"In the interest of regaining my equilibrium, I will not phone or write you. Please do not call or write me."*

Time and distance, the great healers. And words.

THIRTEEN

Going Backward

My house burned down
But anyway, it was after
The flower petals had already fallen.

—CHIBANA HOKUSHI (ca. 1665–1718)

Were my father alive he would be as puzzled about my current life as he claimed to be about the rest of my life once I reached high school age and then adulthood. He never understood, so he told me, the articles I wrote and got published about teaching. He never understood why I took his grandson to live twenty-five hundred miles from home. He never understood the hardship, financial and otherwise, that accompanied single parenthood. He never asked because he didn't want to know or didn't know how to ask—which it was I never knew. As for my mother, if she were speaking to me, and, of course, she would have been after her first glimpse of her grandson, she would shake her head and murmur something about sadness and how there was enough of it in the world without her daughter adding to it. It would take the freedom from parenting, from full-time teaching, from shame, from fear of failing, for me to, as they say, get a life. What would my parents say about the ad I placed in the *New York Review*? Take a guess. You get one.

"BIGGEST TURNOUT I've ever seen," said Reuben Short, the funeral director. "Came from all over, didn't they."

My mother died in April 1965. Here I was at the funeral home, which stood next door to my grandparents' house and across the street from my childhood home, and where, down in the basement, Mr. Short's son kept furry animals of all kinds in cages and on tethers of one sort or another. "I don't know," said Mrs. Short, "Jimmy just seems to like live things."

The visiting line reached out the door and down the sidewalk. The whole town and then some had come to pay their respects to the family of the woman they had admired for so long. I stood unsteadily in the receiving line, shaking hands with people who had watched me grow up, people whose children my father had brought into the world, whose gallbladders he had resected, whose hernias he had repaired, tonsils removed, spines fused, limbs set. And yes, they came from the towns, the farms, everywhere my father had ever been. Here came Rhonda, the hairdresser in town. "Did you see how I did her hair?" she wanted to know. "I think it looks real nice." I nodded and said nothing for fear that if I did I would scream. My mother lay not far from us in an open casket. More than anything in the world, my mother dreaded being stared at. And there she was for all the world to see. On the shoulder of her suit jacket I had pinned a bunch of the violets whose hiding place she had shown us every spring and which had done the right thing by blooming early this year. My grandmother was not pleased: "Surely, we can do better than that," she said. No, I thought, we can't.

Down the line my brothers, tall and stoic, their faces the

color of chalk, smiled at the visitors. My sister looked the way she felt, exhausted and terribly sad, and stood next to Aunt Cara, who was holding her up on one side, me on the other. "Oh god," said my sister, "here come the Fergusons; they've come all the way from Fort Wayne." Her mouth was contorted, tears threatened to spill onto her cheeks, and I felt my own lips tremble. My aunt, a funeral veteran, tightened her hold on our arms and said, "Don't you dare cry."

My best friend in high school was there all the way from Cleveland. She reached for my hand, held it tightly in hers, and said, "Jessica Mitford was right." I smiled. At least, one other person recognized the absolute banality of this occasion. At least, Harriet knew none of this was right. When, later, I expressed my disgust to my uncle, he said, "In small towns, funerals have got to be open casket. A closed casket causes too much talk that never goes away." Harriet would have turned up her nose at this explanation, but I sort of understood; I just didn't like my mother being the center of a tradition that honored no one but gossips.

I turned to my father, put my hand through his arm, and said, "That's not Mom in there. That has nothing to do with her." My father said nothing. He knew better.

SETTING UP HOUSEKEEPING in your mother's house is not a good way to begin a marriage. But doing that was my last chance to win my father. All I had to do was become my mother. A window of opportunity, you might say, not to be ignored. At that point in my thirty-two-year-old life Oedipus was still only a character in a Greek play. Of course, I knew of the Oedipus complex and applied it to other people all the time: Sarah and her lifelong battles with her mother; Dick and his struggles with his father. Me? I was smug. I believed myself to have had a trouble-free childhood in a trouble-free family in a trouble-free town. Currier and Ives, Norman Rockwell: that was my life.

Even in graduate school, way past the age of smugness, or so one would have thought, I looked on my fellow students with a superior eye. How was it, I wondered, that these people studying for advanced degrees in literature, in touch with the wisdom of the ages, were so screwed up? I felt sorry for them; obviously, they had not had the advantages bestowed on them by parents who loved them in towns that sheltered them.

No, the reason I gave myself for my return to that sheltering town (and to that family and that childhood) was that my father was alone, he needed someone to look after him. Add to that, my youngest brother, who was moving back to live in our childhood house and begin his teaching career in the local, trouble-free high school; he would need taking care of, too. Men did not do well on their own; they would probably not iron their sheets and would drink milk straight from the carton. Then, too, my husband's parents lived in Cleveland. They had not been able to attend the wedding, had never seen their grandson, and wished daily for us to move closer. At least, Cleveland and my town of Archbold were in the same state. Finally, Tom wasn't doing much at Berkeley, had decided to change his field from math to psychology, and why not start in the Midwest? So I quit my perfect job, supervising English teachers for the credential program at Cal, withdrew all my money from my teachers' retirement fund, and off we went. I would do it right this time. What a mess.

My father, as you know, was a mighty handsome man. He was also, in today's parlance, emotionally unavailable and, more than likely, alcoholic. I know my father loved us, but it would take me most of my life to understand that he did not know how to show that he did. In a rare display of intimacy, he said to me while I was doing my Mom II number, "After all these years in practice, I still can't get used to a woman sitting on the other side of my desk and crying. It just embarrasses the heck out of me."

During my growing-up years, once I got to Ann Arbor and got sophisticated, I decided I really did not love my father. His conservative Republican values, his attention to appearance, his drinking, his golf, his wife my mother, were far cries from what I was coming to believe was important. And he was always, always busy. In my twenties, I asked my mother, "Did Dad spend time with me when I was a baby?" "Oh, my, yes," she answered. "He was so proud of you; he wheeled you up and down the sidewalk in your buggy; he thought you were the most wonderful baby on earth." Too bad I had no memory of that fine event.

The best times with my father were when I was a child, no older than nine, and got to go with him to make house calls. Each night, after dinner, my dad and I would climb into his Buick, the latest model in an endless series of Buicks, and drive off into the country, where his housebound patients lived on their farms. Sometimes, when the patient inside was in peril, I was ordered to stay in the car, but at most of his stops I was allowed to climb out of the car and go with him into the farmhouse. There he examined the patient and then turned to me. "Ten Seconal, please." I would zip open his medicine case, take out the glass tube containing the red capsules, and count ten of them into a white envelope. "Thank you," my father would say, and write the instructions on the front of the envelope. I was his partner then. I was on his team; I was the only one on his team.

I'm not sure when or why I got sent down to the minor leagues. I suspect that, when I became a girl—and I did so at an embarrassingly early age—I made him uncomfortable. I suspect that he did not know what to do with girls, especially a girl who didn't seem able to play a decent game of tennis or golf or even the piano. "Play for us," he commanded too many times. "What should I play?" "Just play something you can play all the way through without making a mistake." I would sit dutifully at the piano and play one of Bach's Two-Part Inventions for the very short time it took before I made a mistake. Then I was excused to the tune of my father's huge sigh. I was a disappointment to him, no doubt about it. And once my brothers were born, any attention left over from his long days at the hospital and the office went to them. They didn't get very much either.

So the pleasure in my father's company came unexpected and unbidden. One night I rode with him in his Buick convertible, top down, summertime. We were driving home from our cottage at the lake, where we spent every summer, where my father had spent every summer as a boy, some forty miles from our town; no one else—not my sister or my brothers or my mother—was along for the ride. I sat in the front seat, the seat belonging to my mother, and looked up at the stars. On the radio Sammy Kaye or Tommy Dorsey or Glenn Miller (who had died in the war but his spirit lived on) played "Stella by Starlight" or "Stardust" or "As Time Goes By" or maybe all in succession or at once; no matter, the strings and the saxophones soared into the summer night that, despite the stars above, was so dark that nobody, not even I, could see that my breasts were too big and my legs were too short and that pimples, some closer than others to popping, decorated my chin and forehead. At fourteen, I was utterly unconscious of what might cause the pleasant warmth in my upper chest, lower tummy, and inner thighs. All I knew was that this was what happiness felt like. That's a nice kind of sex, when it just comes at you and you let it.

Not all the sex between me and my father was so pleasant. One summer day, I crewed for my father in his Comet. He of course was the skipper, and our destination was the cottage of friends of his across the lake, where he would have a drink or two and then another. "Well," he would say, raising his scotch and soda on high, "it must be five o'clock somewhere." I was afraid to sail with him. "There can only be one skipper," he said time and again. "Crew members have to take orders, not ask questions, and be quick about it." I was terrified I would fail to pull the sheet in quickly enough, afraid I wouldn't shift to the other side quickly enough, afraid I would tangle myself in the jib, afraid I would be in the wrong place when my father, the skipper, decided to come about, afraid he would be disgusted by my ineptness, my awkwardness, my ignorance. No wonder he preferred to sail with my brother.

My mother told me more than once how lucky she was that my father had married her. She also stood up to him. To my father, the whole world was his operating room and he expected those of us in it to behave like his nurses, quick, efficient, alert to his every command. Every so often, my mother exploded. "Ed, I am not your nurse!" Then he would calm down and start over.

On the day of our sail, we sailed as close to the friends' shore as possible. My dad turned the boat into the wind, I loosed the sheets right on time, pulled up the centerboard, and we climbed out to walk the rest of the way in the water. At the water's edge, the friends, martinis held aloft in one hand, the other shading their eyes from the sun, stood watching. "Well, Ed!" they called as we came up the dock. "We wondered who you had with you! We thought maybe you had gotten yourself a girlfriend!" Laughs all around except from my dad and me. My bathing suit was horrid, all stretched out from my fat breasts and belly and a summer of daily wear. My hair was a tangled mess from swimming and being ignored. And why hadn't my dad told me before we set sail that we would end up at the Morrises' cottage? I would have worn the old shirt my uncle had given me (my father had no old shirts) to cover myself when I wasn't swimming. I had no shirt, no cover-up, no camouflage, and these dreadful people on shore were accusing my dad and me of being a couple. I was embarrassed for him. My father saw nothing funny either, but it had nothing to do with his new girlfriend. He was simply embarrassed. As for me, secretly, way down deep beneath the humiliation, I was happy. Anything was possible; maybe, I could turn out a girl after all.

Once in a while, I saw the man, the doctor his patients saw. Another summer, on vacation from my secretarial job in San Francisco, a vacation I should have taken in Mexico or Tahoe or Mt. Shasta or anywhere but with my family—I was twenty-five years old, for god's sake—I stood on the porch of our cottage watching the moths beat their wings uselessly against the screen and listening to the waves, whose sound would soothe us all into a sleep usually available only to the very young. My youngest brother was in his teens and, according to my mother, spent far too much time in his bedroom. The middle room was the worst room in the cottage: small, hot, the penalty for being the youngest of four. It was directly above the living room. On this night, my mother had had enough. "He's up there again! Ed, do something!" My brother was masturbating; at fifteen he did it a lot; he oughtn't to have done it at all, my mother believed. I spoke out: "Would you rather have him impregnate some girl down at the City Drug?" My mother rushed out of the room and returned with the broom. "I'm going to put a stop to this!" She held the broom by its bristles and slammed the tip of the broom handle against the ceiling again and again. "Ed," she screamed, "do something." My father very gently took the broom from her and led her out onto the porch. He didn't say anything, he rarely did, but the way he drew my mother away from her own humiliation made me understand why she believed herself the luckiest person in the world. Eventually, my mother reconciled herself to my brother's style of premarital lovemaking, though, on those now rare occasions we made the beds together, she would murmur, when we got to my brother's room, "At least he could put the Vaseline away." A few years later, she got downright jolly: "I found Chaucer in the bathroom; that's a step up."

Now, though, in 1965, the queen was dead, long live the queen, and here we came: my new husband, my new baby, and me, who couldn't cook or iron or play tennis or golf and who no longer played the piano. I did, however, continue to make mistakes.

The town thought I was a saint.

It was the laundry that did it. Every Monday morning, I washed the sheets. I hung them up to dry on the clothesline in the backyard; and when they were not dry but damp, just the right damp, I took them down and folded them into the laundry basket. They smelled of the fields and the sky and the sun and the richness of the loam from which my little town grew. In my life across a part of the world, some of it in the finest hotels, no smell, no fragrance of the elegant women and men who reside there, no sheets on the beds of the most exquisite hotels, can match the perfume of those sheets on my mother's clothesline in my town in Ohio. I took them down from the line and carried them across the street to my grandmother's basement. The whole town watched.

In the beginning, I ironed those sheets on my mother's mangle down in the basement, where she had been so happy smoking Luckys, drinking Coke, and listening to the Tigers on the radio. But her mangle was small; it required greater patience, greater coordination, than I had, along with a lot more time, which I didn't have. Across the street, in the basement of my grandmother's house, stood my grandmother's mangle.

My grandmother's mangle (my grandmother had been dead for many years) sat like a pipe organ against the cool, damp wall of her basement. It was hotel-sized. It operated on gas. It took a match to get it going. *Vwooom!* went the flames. It scared the hell out of me. But I grew to love sitting high on the bench, smoothing the sheet over the roller, slapping the lever down to bring the hot metal plate onto the sheet, pushing my knee against the control that set the roller in motion, its speed dependent on the pressure of my knee, threading the sheet, my fingers on either end, keeping it tight, slapping the lever up when things got too hot. It curled my hair, all that steam and the pride that went with it. I was a conductor, a maker of music, a smoother of sheets that would line the beds of the men who needed me.

Behind me in the fruit cellar were jars of pickled peaches and watermelon pickles and apple butter and strawberry jam, canned and stewed and sugared up and bubbled by my grandmother until her death and then by her maid, Ann. For almost fifty years, Ann lived in the house, the caretaker of everyone who came by, the baker of the best sugar cookies with a raisin in the center any child ever got for being good. I was an uninspired cook, so once in a while, laundry done, I would help myself to one of the jars, whose contents would complement the dinner I cooked that night for my men. Oh lord, I was trying so hard.

Then back across the street I trudged, laundry basket piled high with perfectly ironed and folded sheets and pillowcases, plus all the handkerchiefs my father might need. Mrs. Plettner peered from behind her lace curtains in the house on the corner, just as she had thirty years ago when I was five. Mrs. Leichty, in her house next to my grandmother's, peeked, too. As they watched and, I'm sure, smiled, I grew wings, a halo appeared just above the crown of my head, and soon it was all over town:

That Janey, Doc's girl, why, she's a saint. Next door, inside the Short Funeral Home, down in a basement totally unlike my grandmother's, Jimmy kept on with his live things.

My son grew strong and loud. He dragged all the pots and pans out of the cupboards and banged on them. When I put him in his playpen, he yelled. I took him out. He yelled some more until I put him in his little red wagon and pulled him around and around the dining-room table until I got dizzy. He yelled when I stopped. I pulled again, faster and faster around the corners, hoping that he would fall out onto the carpet and never want to ride in that goddamn wagon again. The reason babies and small children are so adorable, so cute, so beautiful, is that, if they weren't, not many would make it to kindergarten; accidents would befall them. My son, of course, was beautiful; his grandfather thought so, too.

My father would come home around six or even later. I would be at the stove, my son on the floor, slamming lids and kettles around and yelling. My father thought this was funny. He loved it. He adored this baby. He laughed aloud when it was all I could do to keep from screaming. He pulled that goddamn wagon around the dining-room table and never once did he think, If this beautiful little boy fell out and just stunned himself on the carpet for a little while, maybe we could get some sleep. We were happy, the three of us. Even the arrival of my brother from his teaching day at the high school didn't interfere. We were one big happy family.

But whoops, there was my husband. Oh, dear. My father got my husband a job. Floyd and Dale built roads. They were friends of my dad's. They gave my husband a job building roads. My husband was good-sized, muscular, manly, you might say, with a body by Phidias. Back in Berkeley, he had gotten interested in Buddhism and had begun to meditate. In Berkeley, in the sixties, meditating was the thing to do; everyone did it more or less successfully. In Archbold, Ohio, in 1965, meditation was unheard of, and when my husband began to practice it during lunch break, when he stood on his head, for god's sake, the rest of the road builders had had it. This was Doc's son-in-law, so they wouldn't take overt action, but they wouldn't have anything more to do with this alien from California than was absolutely necessary. They froze him out. My husband must have been terribly lonely, though how would I know? We never made love, we were too tired; we never made love, we'd forgotten how. Shame on me, too bad for us; I just never paid the slightest bit of attention.

But I didn't. I was busy, busy, busy. Being a saint was exhausting. I just sort of forgot my husband, and the dreadful life he surely was leading. He moved out of our room (my parents' bedroom in the early days of their marriage) and began to build a sort of shelter in a bedroom in the back of the house. He put dark blue cloth over the windows, he made it dark, so dark no one ever went in it, certainly not me, and after dinner, which he ate mostly in silence, he went to his shelter. We spoke less and less. We never went anywhere together, not to dinner or a movie or a party. None of this bothered me at all. I was on speed during the day and tranquilizers at night. Next day I did it all over again. This routine worked to my advantage: for the first, and last, time in my life I dropped to a size 8. Finally, I was thin. I wish someone had noticed.

That summer, I moved, with my son, to the lake just as my mother had when her children were young. My father came up on his day off and on weekends. My husband came, too, though not so frequently, not so charmingly, not so handsomely, as his father-in-law. When he did come, he sat on the end of the dock and looked out over the water. It was easy not to notice the man I had married.

In August, my father betrayed me. Late one night, I heard his car pull up to the cottage, then a stumbling of feet, and then, "Jane! Wake up!" I climbed out of bed, shushing him not to wake the baby, and stood in my nightgown at the top of the stairs. At the bottom he stood not altogether steadily, his face lit with happiness. "I've met the woman I'm going to marry," he said, and rushed on, "She won't hear of it until after a year, but then . . ."

"Congratulations, now go to bed."

"Her name's Mary," he called after me.

My heart turned to stone. I brought all my small-town, old-fashioned prejudices to bear on this dreadful circumstance: it was too soon, do we know this woman's family, does she have money of her own, how old is she, is she beautiful, more beautiful than me, than me, than me, oh you have tossed me aside again, how could you after all I've done for you? My father was fifty-nine years old.

It was a summer of lead.

I would try once more in my life to be my father's chosen one. I would pimp for him. After my divorce, for of course my marriage was in trouble from the first, when I was living in California with my son, after the death of my father's second wife, Mary, a woman who turned out to be a wonderful human being, my father journeyed to California to see his grandson and his daughter. His visit coincided with the comeback appearance in San Francisco of Tempest Storm, stripper par excellence.

My father had always been fascinated by naked women, by beautiful naked women. From the twenties, when he vacationed in Chicago—"the girls danced naked right up there on the bar," he told me—through all the issues of *Playboy,* which he kept in plain sight in the bathroom he shared with my mother, my father the doctor had this hobby: naked women. Once, my brother came right at him: "How can you be interested in those foldouts when you see women without clothes all day long?"

Our father answered, "That's different." Well, that was more explanation than he usually gave us for anything, for everything, that puzzled us. Usually, he would say, in answer to our questions, "Go look it up." This we could not look up.

In his second widowhood, I sent him porno books. I went down into the Tenderloin in San Francisco to porno shops and picked out these awful books: *Head Nurse, Student Teacher, Upstairs Maid.* These I would wrap in Santa Claus paper and send back to Ohio for his Christmas present. Finally, during one of his phone calls, calls he made at seven A.M. Ohio time, four A.M. California time, he asked for "more plot." So I had to look a little harder. I don't know what it was—the women's movement, impinging adulthood, incipient common sense—but I stopped. What the hell was I doing providing anyone, and my father, of all people, with hard-core, badly written (I peeked at a couple) porn? Well, gosh, I was just trying to be a good daughter, trying to please my father in the only way I knew how. I pretended to myself that all this was funny, but it wasn't. I don't even like to put it in here. I am embarrassed even now. My god, would I stop at nothing?

So anyway, off my father and I went on a date to San Francisco—my son being underage, like seven, and forced to stay with a sitter—to see Tempest come back. These were some of the good days in North Beach, the time of "Topless," the time of "Male Strippers" as well as "College Girls Onstage!" And "Lewd Sex Acts!" up and down Broadway. Okay, they probably weren't good days, but everybody looked like they were having a lot of fun, including the topless girls, who jiggled into the faces of men who left their desks in the Financial District for a business lunch in North Beach. I suppose girls were exploited, but they didn't seem to mind. I suppose girls pandered to men's basest desires and men succumbed to them; they didn't seem to mind either. The scandal was that the performers weren't paid enough, and gradually that changed, so that Carol Doda, the reigning Queen of Topless, made a ton of money.

In The Pussycat on Broadway, the main street of the section of San Francisco once called the Barbary Coast, my dad and I sat together, swizzling our scotch and sodas, and waited for Tempest to appear. The music swelled, the loudspeaker did, too, and "Here she is: the one, the only—Tempest Storm!" Cymbals. Tempest Storm was beautiful. She had gorgeous long legs swathed, like most of the rest of her, in pale peach chiffon the color of her hair. She glided across the stage, exposing nothing and at the same time everything. "Gosh," I whispered to my dad, "she doesn't look a day over thirty-five." My father, the doctor/porno-fan/naked-women expert, leaned over and said, "She's fifty-four."

Across the street was The Condor, home of Carol Doda, famous for her forty-two-inch bosom. Carol Doda was not fifty-four, not thirty-five; she was in her prime, which, unless you prefer them really young—and my dad didn't—was now. We stood in the back of the room and watched her descend from the heavens to the top of a grand piano: first her jeweled feet, her slim, trim legs, swathed in nothing at all, her twenty-three-inch waist, twinkling away in a jeweled corset, and then—cymbals—her breasts. Way outsize, way out of proportion, way way silicone. My father was mesmerized. Gee, if I had played my cards right . . . We were escorted to a table. In the front row. To get to it, we had to pass right in front of Ms. Doda, now sliding her little tongue across her bee-stung lips and her little hands up and down the microphone. The stage lights bright, the rest of the room dark, my father was momentarily blinded and stood before Ms. Doda, like a bat caught in the light. Ms. Doda smiled down at him, leaned down from the stage, forty-two inches struggling to stay within the confines of her corset. Whoops! There they came. Cymbals. She took the glasses off

my father's face, held them up to the light, and said, "No wonder you can't see!" And with that, she rubbed them, my father's
trifocals, back and forth, up and down her breasts. Returning
them to their rightful place, she said, "You have a fine evening."
My father was in seventh heaven. He was amused. He smiled.
He laughed. He had a fine evening. So did I. I had finally been
of use. What a date!

But all that came long after I abdicated my throne as the
martyr of Archbold. Perhaps it would be more accurate to say I
was deposed. By a pretender named Mary, whom, to give myself
a little credit where little is deserved, I grew to admire and respect and love right up until her death from pancreatic cancer in
the eighth year of her happy marriage to my father.

And so, not long after my father announced his plans for
marriage to this then-stranger named Mary, I climbed down
from my grandmother's mangle and—for the last time—left the
security of my little town and followed my husband to Minneapolis, where he had been awarded a fellowship in psychology. Whither thou goest. In Minneapolis, I would give up my
wings and the halo that went with them. I would don the cloak
of infidelity, of duplicity, and I would launder it in booze. In my
father's house I had discovered that, if I had a drink around five,
the amphetamine I had taken that morning would be reacti-
vated. If I needed serenity, whoever said alcohol and pills don't
mix never tried scotch and Valium. If I had trouble sleeping,
there was always the Seconal, which years before my mother
had shown me how to prick with a pin if I wanted fast action.
From my father's medicine cabinet I had filched an ample supply of everything it might take to ignore the frozen north, my
unfortunate husband, and my own screwy self. My secret phar-
macy would see me through the winter no matter how cold it
turned out to be.

It turned out to be pretty cold, freezing, in fact. In Min-

neapolis, out of anger, I suppose—we never talked about it—
my husband withheld sex on purpose, unlike in my father's
house, where he was too exhausted to offer it at all. If he had
had money, he could have withheld that and we might have had
a healthy sex life, though I doubt it. Still, a healthy sex life might
have kept us from behaving badly. At the university, where his
fellowship lay in wait, he pretended to go but didn't. He had affairs. He spent my teaching salary on therapy. He couldn't stand
being near me, an altogether reasonable response to my behavior and to his.

"We all have school," I told my son, who right then and
there began a long career of hating it. "Mommy goes to school,
Daddy goes to school, and so do you." He scrunched up his
face. "Mommy and Daddy like school, and so will you." Ah, dis-
trust in one so young. In fact, I was the only one of the three of
us who liked school, and I loved my school in Minneapolis. It
became a haven. It reminded me every day that there was something I knew how to do, something that no one could take from
me, something that demanded my entire and complete and in-
tense concentration every hour of every day. Along the way, I
could be certain of laughing, for this school seemed to be
chock-full of funny kids. There were times when I was the one
who had to leave the room and regain control by pressing my
hot forehead against the cool tile of the hallway. Even the principal was funny: "I want you all to remember," he ended his
opening-day speech, "that if you have any problems, my door is
always closed." I laughed. I liked him, so I couldn't quite figure
out why he put me in a converted storeroom along with thirty-
five kids, some of whom, for lack of desks and space to put
them, sat on the windowsills and the radiator that ran the length
of them. I had been told that, if the principal *really* didn't like
you, he would assign you five classrooms, one for each period
and each on different floors, so that you might find yourself

climbing and declimbing four flights of stairs, plus descending to the half-basement, whose windows were half-covered with snow during the winter and tall grass the rest of the time. So I shut up until I got mad and knocked on his door—closed, as promised—and demanded another classroom. "There are people," he said from behind his desk, hands clasped behind his head, "standing in line for your job." I said, "I'm calling the health department." Next day new room.

At home, I was not so aggressive. I stopped cooking. Every evening at five o'clock, just like my father, I made myself a scotch and soda, stirring it with my finger, the natural swizzle stick my mother had schooled me on. From the couch, beneath a cloud of Marlboro smoke, I listened to my husband in the kitchen lay out the pizza and tacos he had brought home for dinner. And so, at the same time my son was developing a lifelong antagonism toward school, he was also developing a lifelong taste for junk food. His blue room far behind him in Ohio, my husband hid out in the bathroom. As for me, smoking and drinking were enough, with a Valium thrown in every once in a while.

I had sex with Henry. Remember *Our Miss Brooks* on TV? She was the English teacher mad for Mr. Boynton, the biology teacher. They never did anything, of course; the biology teacher was too shy. Henry taught biology at my school and he was not shy. Every day Henry and I and Gunnar, the geometry teacher, had lunch together in the teachers' cafeteria. Gunnar—whose opinion I respected after he described a particular proof so elegant, he said, that when he presented it to his students (Gunnar didn't teach kids, only students), he had to stand next to the window of his classroom in order to cool off—urged me to sit in on one of Henry's lectures. So one day, during my prep period, I went up to the small auditorium, whose seats were slanted, like at the Colosseum, down to the stage below, where Henry, shunning film strips, overhead projectors, transparencies, all the paraphernalia available to lesser teachers, spun romantic tales of pistil and stamen and bees in words that fairly vibrated with promises of pleasure and fulfillment. Not above vibrating myself, I felt a tingle in my nether regions and wondered about the kids, tenth-graders, who appeared mesmerized by the music of Henry's voice and the lure of his stories. Not long after, despite the wise counsel of the librarian, who, from way across the cafeteria could see what was going on, Henry and I made plans to Be Together.

On a Sunday afternoon, I excused myself from home and family for a special department meeting. Off I went to our prearranged destination, where Henry promised he would meet me and drive me to his home. Henry was married, just like me, so I understood at once when he told me to duck down beneath the dashboard until he got the car into the garage. His wife and kids were at the hockey game, but there were always the neighbors to consider in this very, very respectable neighborhood, Henry told me. It was a bit cramped down there, but not for long, and besides, I was laughing at Henry, who was not laughing in case anybody might be watching.

We had done some kissing in Henry's Mercedes before this assignation, one time parked on a hill. Henry's hand had tugged my skirt up to somewhere near my ear, and I was fumbling with his zipper, when there came a knock on the window. It was a policeman, for god's sake. I straightened myself up, and Henry opened the window to hear the policeman remonstrate with him for parking on a hill. "Could roll right down. Better be on your way." We continued to whet our appetites here and there after school and before I collected my son from church and Bible school, then the only affordable day care in the greater metropolitan area. With the cops on one side of us and the Lutherans on the other, we were squeezed right into Henry's sauna. What else could we do? Where else could we go?

It took hours and hours, it seemed, before I began to sweat in that sauna. I had never been in a sauna, had only read about them and how the Swedish people ran from them into the snow and whipped themselves with saplings. What fun could that be? And now here I was—naked with Henry. Thank god, I finally began to drip. It was a requirement that I sweat, just as it had been a requirement for me to hide out on the floor of the Mercedes. So far, I had completed both, though not as quickly or as quietly as the teacher might have wished. "I thought you were never going to sweat," said Henry, trying to hide his disappointment. I thought briefly of running into the snow to look for birch branches.

Henry led me on a tour of his house, both of us in towels, both of us careful not to drip on the carpet. The whole house was blond. Henry told me that every piece of furniture had its original in the Museum of Modern Art in New York. It was all blond, Danish modern. It was a very Lutheran house, very northern, Nordic, like Henry's blond wife in the picture on the piano, like Henry's son, the junior wrestling champion of Minnesota, and Henry's daughter, queen of the eighth-grade winter carnival. The pistils and stamens of Henry's school life were nowhere in evidence any more than my fiery lambastings of the Puritan hypocrisy with which I regaled my students. Maybe a sauna at school, at least in the teachers' cafeteria, would solve a lot of problems before they turn into adultery.

In his study Henry had already laid out a blanket on the floor right in front of the very large television screen. I wondered briefly if I were in a lab of Henry's making, if this Sunday afternoon was meant as an experiment, if I would be pinned to the blanket, observed, made note of, and written up for a journal. I lay down and pretty soon we were kissing and Henry was naked, too, and then there was this strange thing that Henry did. "Put your head up there," he said, pushing me so that my head pointed toward the television. I did as requested, Henry laid himself beside me, and, as we rubbed and kissed, Henry raised his head occasionally and watched TV. I had never had an affair before, so I reminded myself that one couldn't expect everything to be normal and that if I wandered from my uxorial duties, as surely I had, I had better be ready for whatever happened and not complain. I was lucky not to be in jail or struck down by a hockey stick.

In answer to my question, Henry said, "I'm watching the game. You have to be out of here before third period begins. My wife and kids will be home soon after, maybe even sooner if the game isn't a close one. That's why I'm watching. Come on, roll over here."

We never did have sex, not the kind where the man inserts his penis into the woman's vagina. Henry believed that, as long as he did not penetrate, he was not being unfaithful to his marriage vows. It would take Bill Clinton, the true education president, the man who educated the entire country about sexual practices the Puritans never wrote down, to make me realize that Henry's peculiarity was not his alone. As one day our president would proclaim on national television, Henry could say to himself, "I never had sex with that woman." To that end, Henry and I rolled around on the floor of his study, his eye on the TV screen, until third period of the game. I got dressed, so did Henry, I got down on the floor of the car, he drove, and I went back to the apartment I shared with my husband and son.

I was sad. I so much wanted to be held and, if not loved, then liked a lot, cared for. The next morning I woke and thought, I used to be happy. I decided to be happy once again. I decided to pack up my son and my books, leave my husband in the care of his psychotherapist, and return to California, where I had work I loved, friends I loved, and maybe someone someday to love me.

On June 12, my parents' wedding anniversary, five months after my affair with Henry, two days after the end of school, at nine o'clock in the morning, I put my son in the backseat of the VW Squareback, a six-pack of Coke in the front, a map on the dashboard, uppers and downers in my purse, and off we went. I turned up the volume on Jimi Hendrix's *"Are You Experienced."* Sort of.

It was the end. It was the beginning.

FOURTEEN

The Education
of Andy's Mom

*Whether or not I shall be the hero of my own life or whether that
station will be held by someone else, only these pages shall show.*

—DAVID, in Charles Dickens's
David Copperfield

I reckon I got to light out for the territory ahead of the rest.

—HUCK FINN, in Mark Twain's
The Adventures of Huckleberry Finn

I n the week my husband and I had agreed would end in my
leave-taking, Andy going with me, I watched from our bedroom window as, day by day, Tom took the Volkswagen apart.
When he wasn't doing that, he and I were having sex. In the living room, standing or sitting, hard up against the kitchen sink, in
the shower, on the bed, on carpet, tile, on hardwood and soft,
wham bang, all the sex he had ever refused me came at me now
and I couldn't get enough. This was truly great fucking. It was
pure, unencumbered by love, spurred on by anger, made urgent

by imminent loss. Tom told me about his affairs, I told him about mine, and we became for each other all the partners we had ever had or wanted to have. A helluva week. It would be almost thirty years before I had another one.

Andy, confused and upset by packing boxes and suitcases and the dismantled family car, not to mention his parents conjoined all over the apartment behind hastily slammed doors, ran up and down the hall, banging on doors, ran outside and in, banging his trike into the walls of the apartment and over the auto parts that littered the sidewalk out back. By Friday, the seats were lying on the sidewalk, alongside the tires and some things that looked as if they had once belonged to the motor. "I just want everything to work," said Tom, and, sure enough, by Sunday morning, everything seemed to be back in place, and off we went, Tom running alongside the car calling to Andy, "Bye, son, have a good vacation. See you in the fall." Huh? What had he told Andy during the little talk the two of them had had?

Like the car, only far more fragile, Andy's life was dismantled and I didn't do a proper job of putting it back together. I took him away from the father he loved to a land he could never have imagined, to a life that depended for any stability on his mother, who, high on amphetamines throughout most of the trip, couldn't have been entirely reliable. At a motel somewhere in Oklahoma, we forgot he couldn't swim, and Andy, in the deep end of the pool, sank. Whoops, I pulled him out by the hair, hey hey, what happened there? On the road again, Andy asked, "What's that smell?" I replied by composing a song, "Manure." It was a call and response. Andy would sing out, "Hey, what's that smell?" and I would sing back, "Manure, manure, O lord, I smell that manure." Much ruckus from the backseat: laughter, hiccups, kicking the front seat of the driver, small body falling to floor, gasps for serious air, and then, "Hey, Mom, what's that smell?"

We sang a song for every state: "I was born in Michigan," "Oooooooklahoma!," "I was born/in a trunk/in the Princess Theatre/in Pocatello, Idaho," until we got to Nevada, where, stymied at last, we bumped up "California, Here We Come" and doubled it with "San Francisco, Open Your Golden Gate." We would sing and laugh and tool on down the highway free and happy with the adventure of life.

Just across the state line into California I wept at the beauty of Lake Tahoe spread out before us and in relief that we had made it this far. I stopped the car, got Andy out of the backseat, pressed his face close to a mountain stream, and announced that he no longer had asthma. This turned out not to be true. I promised him a backyard. This turned out to be true, though he had no interest in backyards, never having had one. I got him one anyway, in the town of Orinda on the east side of the Berkeley hills. Orinda was and is an upscale settlement of mostly white people, mostly Republican, many of them nice. It is one of the most beautiful towns you'll ever see: houses, a few monstrous and ugly, others small and charming, tucked in among the live oak and madrone, built up and down the sides of hills, some teetering on, even sliding down, those hillsides when the winter rains loosen the earth beneath them. Neither Republican nor upscale, I found a small house on a hillside for rent. In 1970, property taxes were lower in Orinda than in Berkeley, so many professors lived on the same hill we did and commuted ten minutes over the top to the university on the other side; it was called Red Hill, from the days of Senator McCarthy, when professors were accused of being pinko Commies, reasons for the Red Scare. I was proud to live on this hill. I loved our little house. The backyard was surrounded by huge pine trees, and their scent kept the inside of our house cool and fresh. It was the best of outdoor living.

While the out-of-doors is democratic—it invites everyone—

income streams are not; they are divisive, and mine was at the bottom. As a lower-class person, I turned to music, which, like the out-of-doors, lets everyone in; and one day, when we were in the middle of the Orinda grocery, I made up this song, its burlesque beat requiring my hips to swivel ever so slightly as I sang it out to Andy while we wandered up and down the aisles of Safeway:

Verse:
Orinda woman (bump)
Dressed in your tennis white (grind)
You play around the livelong day
And then go home at night.

Chorus:
Orinda woman (va-va-va-voom)
Orinda woman (Repeat and fade to whisper)

At night, we bundled ourselves together in my bed and slept. Mostly. Sleeping next to this little boy was like sleeping with a pony. His arms and legs pummeled the darkness, and I woke more than once when a small but powerful heel slammed into my stomach. And then there was the notion somewhere deep in my lonely head that five-year-old boys oughtn't to be sleeping with their mothers, comforting though they might be to each other. I sensed that Sophocles and Freud would have agreed with me, so Andy slept in his bed and I slept in mine until I was asleep, when Andy crept in and snuggled beneath my blankets. I woke when an elbow slammed into my thyroid, and dutifully carried him back to his own bed. I returned to my bed, fell asleep, until . . . This was not working. Let's try money. "I'll give you one dollar for every night you stay in your own bed, time not to exceed one month." "Okay." Twenty-nine dollars later, he was his own boy and I resumed a full night's sleep.

In the midst of all this frivolity, when we weren't marching in San Francisco against the war in Vietnam along with three hundred thousand other like-minded folks, we went to school. Just like in Minneapolis, Andy and school hated each other from the first day of kindergarten. "How was school?" I asked. "I went," he said. "Well, tomorrow . . ." I began enthusiastically, and stopped at the look of astonishment on his face. "I already did that," he said, refusing to believe that school wasn't over, wasn't a one-time thing, a sometime thing, but instead a thing that would take up the best part of his days, that would interfere with everything he wanted to do, a thing his mother loved and paid the bills (sort of) with, a mother he was mad at. In his mind, his dad's words rang: "See you in the fall, son." Well, it was fall, vacation was over; his mom was supposed to take him back to where his dad was. Instead, look at what she did: she took him to school. What had she done with his dad?

School did not make up for being half an orphan, but it did provide the one immutable rule of our family: no matter what, we went. In the winter, another one of those cold and rainy ones, I came home from school to find Andy on the doorstep with a note pinned to his jacket: "Do not send this child back to school until he is well." I looked at my little boy. His eyes were running, his nose was running. I felt his forehead; it was hot. I burst into tears. So did he. And I was angry: how dare Miss McDougal tell me I was a bad mother, a mother who would send a sick child to school! But I was, I was, and what was I going to do about it?

I called in sick the next day and took care of my son. It was a joy to do so, a joy of the kind known only to working mothers. Next day, though, I had to go to school, and Andy was definitely not well; the chance was very high that that teacher would send him home again with a note that said, "Not yet." Back in Minneapolis the nursery school provided extended care until six P.M. The people were kind, the Lutherans ran it, so what could go wrong? Nothing, until one day Andy said, "Does it hurt to hang on the cross?" Bible stories with full-page illustrations; damn those Lutherans. "Yes," I said, "it did, but people don't do that anymore." No, but they still scare children half to death. Here, though, in the advanced civilization of 1970 California, I could find no extended care, not in the school, not in a church, not in a private home. So, in times of headache and runny nose and hot little forehead, I sent him off to the neighbors, to their charming houses, each one different from the other, scattered up the hill, across the road, and down the hill. They were wonderful, our neighbors, but they weren't Andy's mom. I was, and I hated myself for not taking care of him the way my mother had cared for me.

Not everything was hard. Sometimes, I slept through the whole thing. On our hill, the kids built stone forts, got poison oak, and learned the ways of the wilds. At night the cat, Bessie, lurking in the darkness outside, snared wood rats. Wood rats were big and ugly, almost as big as Bessie, but she managed to leap up and through Andy's bedroom window, rat in mouth, and, in the dark hours of the night, run it to ground. In the living room the dog, Tear (short for Tear Up and Terrible), chewed silently on my driver's license, rousing himself only to shit on the carpet, saving his energy for the daylight hours when he chased cars and bicycles and, occasionally, just to keep up his strength, bit small children. Elsewhere in the house, a hamster, dumped without warning from its plastic town house, cowered, awaiting sudden death or a return to life imprisonment. In my sleep, I heard scampering, scuttling, thumping, and what surely were death rattles. Where? Andy's bedroom? I slept on, the deepest sleep of all, the sleep of the ignorant. In the morning, the wood rat would be gone, except for an organ or two that Bessie had gotten too finicky to finish. Tear stood proudly in the middle of the living-room carpet next to his doings; the hamster waited in the closet for me to step on it. As Andy reached fourth-grade science, he grew knowledgeable about the various parts of rodents. "Look here, Mom"—he pointed to a slimy glob on the floor next to his bed—"this is the liver." He learned to read scat: "Look, Mom, Tear ate something with writing on it."

Sometime during fifth grade, I began to tune out. I know, I know, parent involvement and all that, christalmighty I was too tired and I was too fat. And I was too tired to get myself not fat, too scared really. In my expanding body, I didn't have to worry about sex and not having any, which was why I had gotten that way, aided and abetted by the end of my lifetime supply, or so I thought, of amphetamines; what a comedown of a week that was. Appetite inhibitors no longer mine, I ate. So it was, his mother comatose or close to it, that Andy learned about sex, not from his science book but, the way most kids do, from his friends. One day after school, I was lying down on the couch, where I lay every day after school. Suddenly, faster than a speeding bullet, Andy streaked across the room and landed *ker-thump* on top of me and began pumping his nine-year-old behind up and down. He said, "Is this how you do it?" Well, what would you do? I laughed and answered, "Pretty much, that's how you do it." He wanted to know, "Why do people do it?" and I said, "Because it feels good. When you do it with the right person." Puzzled but willing to rest and brimming with information new and old, he continued, "I know how many times you and Dad did it. Once." Triumphant, he climbed down from my belly and ran off to tell Michael next door how to do it, too, and that Michael's parents had done it four times.

Like me, he grew up without a no-nonsense talk from either parent about sex, about the naturalness of desire, about taking care of the other person, about unexpected consequences. How was I to do it? I who was avoiding even thinking about sex. So I didn't. One day, when Andy was twelve, I said, "I suppose you know all about sex, don't you?" In those words I heard my mother, who had said exactly the same thing to me. Thoughts of being a parent who was improved by time collapsed when I heard Andy say, just as I had, "Oh, sure."

I was a better teacher than I was a parent. For Andy, school got worse; for me, it got better and better. It was the seventies, and School was Happening. These were the times when schools had money for books, when teachers were trusted to decide what to teach, when kids thought poetry was Far Out, when accountability was real and true and happened between teachers and kids, when every so often everybody got stoned. In my Russian lit class we read *Crime and Punishment* and discussed Sonia's options (none). In my British lit class we agreed that no one, not even Andrea Dworkin, could have withstood the hunkiness of Mr. Darcy ("Elizabeth and him are totally equal, you can tell!"). In my Athletics in Literature (known as Jock Lit), we discussed the symbolism in *The Natural;* actually, I discussed the symbolism, the boys wanted to know Roy's ERA, which in no way stood for the Equal Rights Amendment. In my Women in Literature class, we read *Playboy, Hustler, Penthouse,* and discussed this photograph, that foldout. "Hey, Mrs. Juska," said Lori, holding *Hustler* aloft for all to see, "is this a split beaver shot?" Oh, that again.

I thrived. Gloria Steinem and Betty Friedan were liberating me, telling me that sisterhood is powerful, empowering me with self-esteem up the wazoo, along with righteous anger at the patriarchy my father had been king of. All around me women were burning their bras, doing gynecological inspections with mirrors on one another's kitchen tables, taking the pill, having sex with more than one man before, during, or instead of marriage. They were having legal abortions and their mothers were shutting up. History was asserting itself and the pull of its tide was strong. I rode the waves. I masturbated in the bathtub without guilt, just with loneliness.

In my new feminist persona, I stopped cooking again, but not, as I had back in Minneapolis, out of anger; this time it was out of some misguided sense of entitlement, to what I had no idea. Around five o'clock each evening, I did what Andy came to call the Swanson Shuffle. (We were a musical family.) Still dressed in my school clothes, which were actually my at-home clothes, too, I would lumber toward the kitchen, scuffing the floor as I went with my Dr. Scholl's clogs, my ever-burgeoning body hidden in one of my XXL muumuus. In cold weather I added knee socks and an L.L. Bean chamois shirt. "What'll it be, Andy?" I would call from the kitchen. "You want fried chicken, veal parmigiana, Salisbury steak? What'll it be?" He chose, I placed two dinners in the oven, fixed one more scotch and soda, and, when the timer rang, served them, irresistible in their aluminum trays, on the TV tables in the living room, where we watched cartoons. So, well, yes, we had a family dinner every night just like all good families are supposed to, just kind of different. Andy and I were a good family because he and I were in it, we were just kind of different. After one of our yell-outs, Andy stood next to me, shifting from one foot to the other, and said, "Do you think we should get a divorce?" Never, never, ever; I hugged him into quiet and wiped the tears from his cheeks. Our family was small but intact, nuclear to the core and indissoluble, though we would be tested, boy, would we.

For Andy, middle school, more demanding of his time and energy, became a nightmare. A learning disability? I wondered. Did he know how to read? "Andy," I said, casual as could be, "read this story to me, will you?" He took *Time* magazine from me and read fluently several pages. "I got confused a little," I said. "What did the story say about . . . ?" He told me. A word to our test-happy legislators: it's not hard to tell if a kid can read, can decode, can comprehend. All you have to do is listen. My son could read as well as I. Still, nine weeks into every quarter the failure notices came home, the announcements that my child was in danger of failing, was in fact failing, notices familiar to me as a teacher, notices I sent out to parents, most of whom reacted as I did, by yelling, berating, begging, blackmailing, promising expensive gifts, threatening to rescind telephone privileges, allowances, food, clothing, shelter, and junk food. To no avail: he refused to do homework, slapped together tooth-picks to look like stalagmites when an earth science project came due, scribbled onto a piece of paper a summary of *The Red Pony*, which he never read. In Orinda, in those days, children did not fail, so his teachers passed him, and he steeled himself for high school. What torment it must have been to follow our one rule: No matter what, we go to school. With what despair he must have looked ahead to four years of high school.

With that history behind us, I oughtn't to have been sur-prised, much less upset, when midway in his freshman year of high school, he came home with his head shaved. His beautiful golden-brown hair was gone, nasty little bristles in its place; also gone was his appetite for anything Swanson's. He took the collar off the dog, put it around his neck, and announced his new identity: a vegetarian skinhead. I went next door and got drunk.

And so began the long haul that would end when he was seventeen, in the fall of what would have been his senior year had I not disenrolled him from the high school, where he ele-vated passive-aggressiveness to an art form. His schedule—mind you, I had been by this time a high school teacher for twenty years and so not naïve in this regard—put him in a government class that he never attended and into two periods of I.W.E.—Inside Work Experience—provided for those kids who couldn't tolerate five periods of sitting down in classrooms and listening to teachers talk. Andy's I.W.E. periods took place in the cafeteria, where he was expected to help the cooks and where he refused to carry vats because they contained chicken parts. The rest of his school day consisted of two periods of O.W.E. (Outside Work Experience), where he was expected to help the janitors clean up the school grounds and during which he hung out at the creek smoking something. This was not going to get him graduated.

No longer required to attend school, Andy became a Bartleby for his time: He preferred not to. No household chores, no job, no allowance, no social security number, no driver's license. He preferred to ride his skateboard the six miles up and over the hills and down into Berkeley, where he performed every so often with his band, Hammerhead, songs he had composed down in our basement, my favorite titled "Fuck Yo Mama." At Mabuhay Gardens, a punk palace in San Francisco, he threw himself off the stage into the pit; in Berkeley he hid out on the roof of a college dorm, and experimented with drugs, alcohol, sex, and dodging the cops. A Sentimental Education for the eighties: Whatever would Flaubert say?

I was helpless, powerless to do anything but go to school, and worry about my son's future, my past failures, and his present whereabouts. I was not stupid; I knew my son was fighting me by way of the thing he knew I loved: school. What the hell could I do about it? At last, out of desperation, I did something. I called his father, who lived far away in Atlanta and had seen Andy rarely since we had separated, once or twice and not at all since his adolescence. During the early years of our life together, Andy's and mine, I gave serious thought to changing my name from Juska, which belonged to my former husband and had nothing to do with me. I talked about this possibility with Andy. "What would my name be?" he wanted to know. "It would still be Juska," I said. "Can I go out and play?" Several days later, he stormed into the living room, where I lay collapsed on the couch yet again. "If you change your name," he sobbed, "I won't belong to anybody." And he cried. And I cried. And my last name is still Juska, and Andy and I belonged to each other until it was time not to.

"Tom," I said into the telephone, "I have come to the end of my rope. Andy is . . ." and I listed all the things Andy preferred not to do, to be, to think. "It's time you took over."

Such stammering, such ahems, such ahaws.

Weeks passed. Nothing changed. One night, in Andy's hearing, I called Tom: "I have bought Andy a ticket to Atlanta. Will you meet his plane?" How I was going to get this big boy into the car, let alone onto a plane, I had no idea. In the silence emanating from the other end of the phone, I said again, "Will you be at the airport?"

The next morning Andy was gone, run away. His note said, "Don't worry, Mom, I'll make it."

So began my descent into hell. It was November, a November of day after day, night after night, of driving rain, of close-to-freezing temperatures, of no sun, no hope, nothing but fear for my son's safety. My son, my beautiful, funny, smart boy, was living on the streets of Berkeley. He was homeless. He was broke. He was a denizen of Telegraph Avenue along with scores of homeless people, many of them psychotic, some of them dangerously so. It was 1982, and oh, how it rained. These were dangerous times, the summers of love behind us, and Berkeley nights were dangerous places. Where would he sleep? How would he keep warm?

Every so often, the phone would ring and I would hear, "Talk to me, Mom. Just talk to me."

"Where are you? I'll come and get you."

"I can do this, just talk to me."

"Oh, please, let me come get you, please."

"I'm going to make it, I can do this."

"Are you warm?"

"Better. I found a water bottle in a trash bin and I hold it over the sewer and the steam, the steam, and I put it under my T-shirt, and . . ."

"Where are you? I'll bring you some warm clothes."

He hung up.

Alone, at home, I consumed ever larger quantities of scotch and fell into bed, where I dreamed the police had come to my house to tell me terrible stories of my son, and when I refused to come to the door, they slammed heavy chains around the house and beat the walls until I woke screaming.

He came home Christmas morning for one hour. He was thin. He was cold. He was exhausted. Merry Christmas. What does one give one's child when one's child is homeless, penniless, cold and tired and hungry? Money? "I don't need money." Warm socks? "I've got socks." Where are they? "I sleep in the stadium. I got socks there." The stadium? "Cops don't find me there." Breakfast, eggs, cheese, are you still a vegetarian? "Yeah, I could eat." And then, "I'm going." Oh, please, please don't go, I will cook, I will find money, I will . . . "I've gotta go. I'll be okay." And he went. Omigod, and Merry Christmas.

Andy never came home again, not really. He got himself warm, dry, and educated. He got himself off the streets, got a job, an apartment, and one day, seeing an ad in a magazine for firefighting, got himself a future. Off he went to the high Sierras, where he talked his way into the junior college nestled into a lovely valley and where one of his teachers—a forester who walked the John Muir Trail each summer—taught him about the woods. He supported himself by washing dishes, clearing trails, mopping up pizza joints, and he paid his student fees at the college with Pell Grants. He never, ever asked me for money.

I was thankful he was safe. I was confused over what he was doing up there, nine thousand feet above sea level. One Thanksgiving, on my visit to the mountains and my son, his best friend, Al, and I sat together and watched video after video, Al having told me from the outset "I don't have many words." Movies creaked by, one after the other, and finally I asked, "What do you think Andy's doing up here?" Al of few words answered, "I think he's looking for how to be a man." Indeed, he was. He was looking for how to be self-reliant, strong, and independent, like the man he remembered as his father.

And so we separated, god what a wrench. How else could it have been, though, but violent and painful for both of us when, for most of our lives together, the two of us, mother and son, liked and loved each other and laughed and sang together? How else could he make himself into his own person except to find a world utterly different from the world of school and his mother? My son is the hero of his own life.

Now comes the happy ending.

In the mountains Andy learned the forest from the men who worked in the woods: the choke setters, skidders, fallers, and bullbucks. He got himself into the University of California at Berkeley, where he learned the forest in another way and earned a B.S. in forestry. When he talks about trees, he becomes downright spiritual. He is happily employed by an admired firm. He is funny, smart, and still very thin. He is kind. He is good. My wonderful new daughter-in-law, Karen, says about her husband, "Andy lives his integrity." He totes the most ethical chainsaw in the West.

My son would be perfect if he read Trollope. But he doesn't and shows no interest in repairing this flaw. Oh, well, can't have everything.

FIFTEEN

The Man Who Got Away, or What Price Trollope?

*As a longtime fan of Trollope, you are no doubt acquainted
with the Berg Collection.*

—MATT

It was Matt who knew about Trollope. Matt zoomed all the
way from northern Wisconsin, where he lived, to the top
of the list of men I was determined to meet. Of all the letters
that overwhelmed my mailbox, his was the only one that spoke
knowingly of Trollope. Of course, many of the letters from men
who answered the ad confessed to not knowing anything about
him—"though excited to learn from good teacher." Some wondered if I had misspelled *trollop,* others thought it was a cute play
on my willingness to become one if I wasn't one already, "which
soon I hope to meet if Venus rises in my house like I am when I
read your ad." Furthermore, I was not acquainted with the Berg
Collection; I had never heard of it.

I wrote Matt at once, enclosing my address, my phone number, and my eagerness to know more, and did he have an e-mail
address? No, he wrote back in longhand, he was a Luddite, did

not own a computer, wrote sometimes on his old Underwood, did not own a television set, and went to the movies all the time when he wasn't filming them himself. He was a photographer way up there and often sold his work, went to New York frequently, sometimes to Los Angeles, and surely would stop by. But he never did. "Come to Brentwood this weekend," he wrote, Brentwood being a lovely section of L.A. where smart people lived and worked. Oh, goodness, I couldn't, I had to spend the weekend in the dreary offices of the Educational Testing Service, reading those dreadful essays written by persons in other lands hopeful of passing this test and coming to America or at least rising in the ranks in their own land. I hated the work but needed the money, now, in partial retirement, more than ever. And over the years ETS, the outfit that gave us the SAT, the GRE, the MCAT, the GMAT, and the AP, not to mention the TOEFL, the TWE, and the CHSPE (pronounced "chispee"), had been good to me and the other teachers who spent their weekends reading dreadful writing for money. So, attractive as Matt's letters were, as well as the photograph of himself that he sent, I refused his invitation. Surely, another time would come along. Indeed, other times did come along, but Matt did not come with them.

Occasionally, a phone call from him did. His voice was sexy: medium-low, varied in pitch, controlled like an actor's, and practiced in vocal seduction. He had been married for a long time but wasn't anymore, his daughters were grown and wonderful, how did I feel about Roethke's poetry (I liked it very much), how many men did I plan to sleep with (eight, including him), how many had I already—"In my whole life?" "Yes"—(four), and did I know how unusual I was (so what).

His letters came, too, written in the fine hand of one who took pleasure in words written not printed, by fountain pen not keyboard, on thick vellum not computer monitors. His hand was strong; I liked him more with each passing letter. They were letters that told me about New York: where to go—the Rendell Gallery, the Morgan Library; where to eat—small restaurants with good food that cost very little; where to stay—a shabbily charming and affordable hotel in Midtown; what to see—the Sargents at the Metropolitan, the Stoppard at the Circle in the Square, and, of course, Trollope at the Berg. Eventually, I did them all. But it was the Berg that headed my list because that's where Trollope lived now.

In January, on my first visit to New York, leaving Robert, who was placating the pain in his back by lying down on it, I donned his down jacket, put on his mittens and my hat, and went to the New York Public Library.

THE NEW YORK PUBLIC LIBRARY IS guarded by those stone lions you've seen in the movies, one on either side of the many stone steps leading up and into the library itself. The sight of those lions was, for me, like a lot of New York, a heart-stopper, as were the street sign that said WALL STREET, the Statue of Liberty, which rose out of the water when I wasn't even looking, Times Square, the Empire State Building, and all those places I had seen in the movies and read about for years and years of my life. Suddenly, they were live and in color, and they looked just right, just the way they looked on the movie screen and on the pages of the books I had dreamed over. In New York I stopped traffic—omigod, there's Bloomingdale's/Radio City Music Hall/St. Patrick's Cathedral/Battery Park—when I stood stock-still in the middle of the street or the middle of the sidewalk and people and cars would slow, even stop, sometimes almost bump me, often yell at me, and here came New York's finest on horseback, right down Madison Avenue, six of them, watch out everyone, I'm stopping to gape to ogle to adore the sights and sounds of New York City. Whoops, pardon me, excuse me, isn't this wonderful? Look! There goes a hansom cab! And that must be the Ritz!

Eventually, what I came to love most were the places I had never seen in the movies or read about in books, places like the New York Society Library, the Red Ball Bar & Grill, the Coliseum Bookstore, the Morgan Library. And the Berg.

One does not, however, just go to the Berg Collection. One has to earn the right. My hiking boots and my ready smile had gotten me anywhere and everywhere I wanted to go: London, San Francisco, Florence. Surely, the New York Public Library would welcome me. The gift shop did, and I'm wearing, as I write this, the $17.95 NYPL baseball cap (red) they were kind enough to offer in exchange for my Visa card. I could be wearing my Metropolitan Opera baseball cap (black), which I got for only $60, the contribution requested of a nonresident, small-time, fixed-income supporter. I no longer—yet another boon from New York—sign my full name on Visa purchase slips, just my initials and last name. I found that a shorter signature allowed time for more gifts, the large majority for me. New York City, like no other city I've ever visited, extracts one's money with a smile, makes one happy to turn over money one didn't know one had. The shops in San Francisco are intriguing, but there is always the pull of the out-of-doors: the hills and the sky and the water; in Florence the art tugs one away from the shops; in London it is the theater. New York is pure: it's money. Since returning from New York, I have managed to continue my accumulation of things unnecessary to a basic good life. But in January, still innocent of New York's seductions, I trotted up to the fourth floor, the Berg Collection; it was free.

It was locked. I could see through the iron grate and the glass behind to a small room, with four tables long enough for three chairs on either side, wide enough to hold papers and books. The walls, with the exception of the back wall, were book-lined, most of the books behind glass. On the back wall were oil portraits of the two Drs. Berg, I would eventually learn, though not without replacing my pride, my self-respect, my integrity, with lying and cheating.

People were in there. They sat at the tables, books and papers spread out before them, heads bent, pencils scribbling furiously, and how was that possible in the dim light? They would make themselves blind, my grandmother whispered. And there was a man who sat at a desk by himself who just had to be the librarian! I rattled the doorknob, rapped on the grate, waved at the librarian, who turned from his desk in time to catch my ready smile and mouth back to me, "No." I spread my arms wide, palms up, and raised my shoulders toward my ears. I mouthed back, "How?" He pointed to a sign, a very small sign, on the lower right-hand corner of the door: ENTRANCE BY PERMISSION ONLY. I mouthed, "Where?" He pointed to my right. I reshouldered my backpack and trudged down the hall.

In a large room that looked just like a room in a library with a desk in the middle that looked just like a circulation desk behind which stood live people, who, just like librarians, would answer . . . "How do I get into the Berg Collection?" I asked the man behind the desk. "You can't," he said. "You can't simply go," he said, enjoying my incredulity. Now, as the sophisticated traveler I fool myself into thinking I am, I had seen this before, in the British Library, the new one. One has to get credentialed to get into where the actual books are, into the reading rooms. One has to be certified a reader, by whom I was never able to determine. However, this was America! This was the country of Benjamin Franklin and Thomas Paine and the Common Man! Anybody who can read *can* read!

"You have to have a bibliographical entry; you're allowed four." The man behind the desk gestured toward the walls, whose books, I noticed, were all bound the same, a solid sea of green bindings, gold letters on their spines. "Whom"—I hadn't heard that pronoun in a while—"is it you wish to research?" He glowered. Didn't anybody in New York smile?

"Trollope," I said.

"Which one?" he said. A nasty little sneer curled a corner of his upper lip.

"Anthony."

"Of course," he said, as in, This woman would know only the famous one.

"Up there," he pointed. "Those volumes on the top shelf."

"Thank you." At least he talked to me. Oh, dear, the top shelf was way, way taller than I am, and I saw no ladder, no cherry picker, no long arm of the library, by which I might extract the proper volume from its aerie. Aha, there was a chair, and if I stood on it and reached . . . Once more, I eased my backpack onto the floor and, in the interest of good manners, took off my boots. As I climbed onto the chair, praying that my socks were sweaty enough to hold me fast to the slippery seat, I could hear behind me rufflings and subdued snorting, then the heavy step of the Man behind the Desk. "Here," he said. "Allow me." He stretched a bit, reached up, and pulled a green volume down. "This is the one you'll need. Be careful you don't fall."

Was I grateful? You bet I was, for now, getting into the Berg Collection had become more than just seeing Trollope; it was my own cause célèbre, my raison d'être, my finish line. I looked at this volume of biographical entries. I had no idea what to write down. I just wanted to see a manuscript. I wanted to see what it looked like, if it showed the speed at which Trollope wrote, which, given his output, must have been very fast. I wanted to see if Matt's comments about his first draft being pretty much his last showed. I wanted to be in the presence of writing I had so much for so long admired. But I had to have four bibliographical notes, so I copied four items and marched to the circulation desk, where I thrust them triumphantly beneath the nose of the librarian. "No," he said. By now I was no longer smiling, but the librarian began to smile, a glacial move for him, and said, "It is not I who can grant entrance. You must go across the hall. Knock first. Good luck to you." Was that a smirk or a sneer? Or could it be he really meant it? You just can't tell about New Yorkers.

Four annotations pinned to my mitten, pack once more strapped to my back—I was feeling more and more like a Sherpa without the Sherpas' lifelong conditioning—I trudged across the hall and knocked on the door. "Come in," said a Voice from behind the door. I opened the door and resumed smiling. "You can't come in here with that," said the Voice. "With what?" I asked. "Your backpack. All belongings must be checked or lockered on the first floor of the library." The Voice got up and left the room.

It had gotten very hot in this library. That's the thing about places with seasons like New York. Winter is very cold, so inside is hot. Why they don't make it just warm I don't know, but they don't; inside feels good at first, but before long you're mopping your brow. Which was what I was doing, that and worrying I would smell up the wool turtleneck tunic, which was practically all I had to wear on this wintry visit, and which was now soggy beneath Robert's down jacket. So I hurried down the stairs to the first floor to get lockered. (A note: the New York Public Library does have elevators; however, they went the opposite way of me—up when I was going down and vice versa. Besides, I considered all this climbing sort of like the Stations of the Cross, like I had to suffer along the way in order to be worthy of the Holy Grail soon to be mine.)

Where do you put things once you've lockered? I was cooler,

but, pocketless, I was devoid of anything useful, such as paper and pencil, photo ID—what if I died in there? And the locker key: where was I supposed to put that? I felt denuded, easy prey to thievery, to chicanery, to loss of identity, and to depravity as yet unimagined. I put the key in my boot, my hiking boot, which they let me keep, along with the four annotations by now crumpled and kind of pasty in my hand.

Back up the stairs to the fourth floor, lighter and freer without most of my worldly possessions, confident that I had at last followed all the rules, I entered a new room, this one nearer the Berg but still far away, where the Voice, the one that had commanded me to get myself lockered, now sat behind a long, long table. And now there were two, another one at the other end of the long, long table. I was about to be interviewed.

I hadn't seen herringbone like that since Fraternity Rush in 1954. Rep ties, either. But these two, these medium-young men, were right out of a John Cheever story about two fellows who hadn't quite made it at Yale so decided to come out in library school. Gay men are the same as straight men; there are lots of different kinds, just as there are lots of different kinds of women, some of whom are even girls. But among all the variations, there are, in particular, two kinds of gay men: one kind likes women, the other does not. Behind the table sat a man of the latter sort, no question about it. To his left, three chairs down, sat a second man whose tolerance I could not immediately discern.

"I'm back," I announced as if everyone would care.

With his chin, the man who did not like women pointed to a chair onto which I was to sit. He was to be my inquisitor. "Why is it"—he looked at a space somewhere beyond my head—"you wish to visit the Berg?"

Well, here goes. Feigned insouciance was all I had and, hopeful that my Shirley Temple dimples would finally disarm him, I said, "I am a longtime fan of Trollope, Anthony"—I was going to get it right—"and understand the Berg Collection might possibly have a manuscript and I would really, really like to go there because . . ."

Ties number 1 and number 2 looked at each other and smiled, almost. They shook their heads at each other as if to say, Can you believe this woman?

"I've come all the way from California," I said, three thousand miles having counted for something at the Metropolitan Opera, which gave me a seat to a sold-out *Der Rosenkavalier;* and the Metropolitan Museum, which provided me an escort who took me into the Sargent wing when it was closed. Herringbone number 1 spoke: "I'm afraid the argument you present is simply not adequate." They smiled at each other openly now with utter disregard for what New York might think of such bald-faced jollity. They shook their heads in concert. No.

Goddamnit. "Gee," I said, "I guess I should have lied."

Number 2, showing his colors at last, said, "Too late for that, isn't it?" They performed an open-mouth smile, awash in hilarity, united in misogyny.

You sonsabitches. I said, "Let me add to what I have told you." My dimples were no more. I leaned forward and began to lie. "I teach at the University of California at Berkeley, a course in writing. My interest in Trollope has to do with emendation, that is, to what extent did he make use of revision, what might a manuscript show that might impress, or not, the efficacy of revision upon my students at the university in terms of their own work. As writers. As scholars." By the end of my eloquent falsehood, I was very close to, you might say in the face of, number 1. It was clear that I would not be moved. Number 1 looked down the table at number 2. They bowed their heads in silence, raised them, looked unblinkingly and profoundly into the eyes of the other, and nodded. Yes. Number 1 pushed across the table an application form. At the bottom, I was directed to write two university contacts who would verify my need to know. After borrowing a pencil, I filled in the form and wrote the names of friends who just had to be at the university, they used to be, surely they still were and would be sitting by the phone to take the call from this two-headed Cerberus. Number 2 handed me a card that read "Good for one day, 21 Jan. oo, unless revoked." I signed my name on the line at the bottom of the page, swearing that every item I had entered on the application was true. I tottered off to the Berg.

By now, my bibliographical notations were no longer pasty, they were pulp; however, I showed the little wad to the man inside the Berg, who let me in after I flashed my permit. This was not the same man I had seen earlier; in fact, it gradually dawned on me that I had not seen a woman in this library at all anywhere over the four hours of my visit. This man was very, very tall and big all over. This man, you just knew, could fit only one job in the entire city of New York and this was it. He looked like Lenny in *Of Mice and Men,* except this Lenny, Lenny de Berg, I think of him, didn't talk at all. He pointed to my bibliography, then to the card catalog. I deduced that I was to match the mess in my hands to call numbers in the catalog and give him the numbers and on and on, jesus h. christ, sweat was streaming down my back. I said to him, "Look. All I really want to see is an original manuscript. Couldn't you just see if you have one and . . . ?" He pointed at the card catalog, and said, "You get four." "But I've already got four, here they . . ." I was talking to his back. Sigh. I found a listing in the card catalog that looked as if it might be a manuscript, wrote the numbers down on a sheet of paper I borrowed from Lenny with a pencil I picked up off the floor, and handed the paper over. He disappeared. I sat down and put my forehead on the cool surface of the table. The time was drawing nigh. The Holy Grail would be mine or it wouldn't be. My entire life would have been wasted or not. My worth as a human being, diminished as it already was by lying and cheating right down the hall, would be restored or not. I would leave the Berg Collection triumphant or . . .

Here came Lenny. He was carrying something book-size and red. He placed it on the table in front of me and disappeared once again. Whatever he had found was in this red leather case with a gold clasp. I lifted the clasp gently and opened the lid of the box to find red silk covering whatever lay beneath. I parted the layers of silk—like stage curtains, they were—and there it was: the original manuscript of *Miss MacKenzie.* It was the most beautiful thing I will ever see. I began to cry. My snuffling—of course, it was loud, I had no Kleenex, no handkerchief, no pockets—interrupted the concentration of the scholars bent over the other tables and I was made to shush. Wiping my nose on my sweater, which would now have to go to the cleaners for sure, I read *Miss MacKenzie,* marveling at the legibility of Trollope's hand, the fineness of it, and the fact that there were almost no emendations, perhaps one or two crossed-out words on a page. Page after page, perhaps eight hundred pages in all, this is what makes a book, this is where genius goes, what he does, what a privilege to be in his presence, to touch, to see, to read him as he writes. I wished I had a class to share this with, or Dr. V, because here on this very page, in Trollope's own hand, was Miss MacKenzie her own self sighing into the mirror over her advancing age, then moving forward to kiss her very own reflection. It would not do, would not do at all, for tears to stain these pages, so I wiped my eyes on my sleeve, yucky by now, and bowed my head over the words as I turned page after page upon page. There are churches of all kinds; this was mine.

After a long time, Lenny reappeared. Flush with wonder, I looked up at him, smiled (what the hell, it might work this time), and said, "I would give anything for a photocopy of just one page of Mr. Trollope's manuscript." He pointed to a sign on his desk: PHOTOCOPIES FIFTY CENTS. "I'll be right back," I said. "My money's down on the first floor in my locker and it won't take but a minute and . . ."

Lenny spoke. "Which page?"

"Huh?"

"Which page you want copied?"

"Oh, any page, any page at all."

"Which one?"

I turned to any page at all and pointed. "This one."

He took the manuscript and disappeared. Back he came, in his hand a page copied from the manuscript. He held it out to me.

"Oh, thank you, thank you, I'll just go down and get my . . ."

"Here," he said, and placed the copy in my hand. "It's a present."

Some things in New York are free. I cried all the way to the bus.

BACK HOME IN Berkeley, I photocopied Lenny de Berg's gift, page 247 of *Miss MacKenzie,* and sent it off to Matt along with my gratitude. Our phone calls became more intimate, more frequent, and more drunken. They came sometimes from me, more often from him, sometimes in the early evening, more often in the late hours of the night. Sometimes Matt was stoned, sometimes he wasn't. But if he wasn't and I wasn't, we would be before we ended our conversation, which ranged from the questionable dramaturgy of Ionesco to where we liked our orgasms to come from. I fueled myself with wine, Matt with what I came to call his M & M's, martinis and marijuana. Neither of us passed out, at least not while we were on the phone, not while Matt contested the desirability of having sex with another person, such as a woman, asserting over and over that his daily jerk-off was just fine with him, that women in northern Wisconsin were too fat to bother with and usually too dumb. "I'm not fat [very]," I said, "and I'm not dumb. Come here and have sex with me or I will come there and have sex with you." This seemed a reasonable next step given the growing frequency and deepening intimacy of our phone calls. I liked him a lot. "Meet me in New York," I urged. "We would have such fun." Yes, he agreed, we would. But we never did. Always, he was somewhere else. Always he was shooting in Vancouver or seeing an agent in Chicago or visiting his daughters in Missouri. And never closer to me. "Matt," I asked, round about one midnight, "when did you last have sex with a woman?" "About twelve years ago," he answered. I could hear him sucking on his joint, sipping his martini. "I met this woman in the hotel bar in New York. When she left, she dropped her keys in my lap and I used them." "How was it?" "Good," he said, "very good, actually." Jeeze, another Cheever story. "Let's meet in a hotel bar in New York," I offered, "and I'll drop my keys wherever you say." Matt was getting like the Berg Collection, not open to just anyone, just for the asking. But he was still on my list, near the top, and I had no intention of giving up. God, he was fun. He knew so much poetry, so much theater, he was funny, he was sexy. "But Jane," he would protest, "you're so old!" Matt was sixty-two and here I was, all of sixty-six, very soon to be sixty-seven, and he was a man I liked and wanted to have sex with. It didn't matter to me if I was older; actually, it didn't matter to him except as an amusing way to avoid the actuality of me.

I would put a stop to this. On a lovely day in June, I flew to Madison, in Wisconsin, where I would live if I didn't live in Berkeley. Like Berkeley, Madison is full of Democrats and a couple of Republicans who are also smart. My longtime friends live in Madison and so I went to visit. "I'm coming to Madison," I told Matt. "I will come visit you." That was a short conversation.

From Madison, I called Matt. "I will rent a car and be up this weekend. Is there a place to stay you would recommend?" I wanted him to say "Stay with me"; it was just logical, for crissake.

"Why are you coming?" he asked.

"To meet you!" I was astonished at the coolness of his voice, though it was morning, too early for an M & M.

"Guess I can't stop you. There are motels outside of town."

"You are not welcoming."

"We have no business to conduct, no conversation that can't be carried on over the phone."

"Do you have all your arms and legs?" I asked. "Is there something you haven't told me? Are you living with a woman or a man or a dog or in a place you want to keep secret from me?"

He went into a tear. "Goddamnit, I don't see why the hell you can't be satisfied with just talking." His voice shed every dulcet tone it ever had. "You're going to spoil the whole fucking thing with your pushiness." He was out-and-out yelling. "You've got to have your way. Just leave it alone. Just leave me alone!"

"I'm coming anyway."

Click.

I don't have a lot of money, you can tell by now; but I have a lot of determination. I get stubborn, especially when I get curious. And I was angry. People don't swear at me, not since 1962, teaching high school, first period, when George Swinton told me to go to hell and I kicked him out of class, something a teacher could do then with impunity more or less. Here was Matt, this three-quarters wonderful man going off on nothing. Well, we would set things straight. He would see me for the unthreatening, accepting, wonderful woman I could make myself into. "We don't have to sleep together, you know," I told him over the phone. "We can have coffee or a martini and I can just turn around and leave if we decide that's best." How could he resist me? But he had. No longer. So, in my Madison guest room I packed my bag, checked my map, and set the alarm for seven, which would get me to where Matt lived by noon. Five short hours, by god, the sun was coming up, the trail was getting warm. Head 'em up; move 'em out.

The alarm rang at seven and so did my head. What had happened during the night? Thick goop had invaded my sinuses and fired cannon volleys into my frontal lobes, the ones necessary for driving. I struggled for the clock, turned off the alarm, and pushed myself out of bed. I would be fine, no matter what the symptoms, what dire prognostications they spoke. In the shower, I practiced my greeting to Matt: "Hi, how are you," I wanted to say. Nothing came out. I was laryngitical. I was voiceless. I was psychosomatic. My throat burned.

On the phone, Matt was sympathetic and clearly relieved. "Another time," he said. "Take care of yourself." I went back to bed all alone and happy to be so.

I gave up. I flew back to Berkeley and missed Matt. He had become a friend, a sort of soul mate, an intellectual companion, a funny, real person the Midwest had coughed up and looked after, a person I recognized from my time, from my part of the country, without the lousy parts that had bedeviled me in my childhood. He had become a person with whom I felt safe.

A few weeks later, at nine P.M., the phone rang. It was Matt. "Are you healed?" The tinkling of ice from his end signaled the coming of fun. I was healed and so we played, we laughed, we argued about Arthur Miller and Edward Albee and about Eric Rohmer and Peter Bogdanovich and about sex in the shower and on the floor, and then he said, "What do you think would happen if we met?" and I said, "I don't know, I'm kind of nervous now, you sort of frightened me . . ." He went into a tear. "Goddamnit, don't be one of those women who back away from the slightest remark that isn't exactly what they want to hear." And I said, "I'm not one of those women, I'm this woman, and I am more cautious of you than I was . . ." And he said, "What is your fucking problem, lady, that we can't have a reasonable conversation, goddamnit, listen to me, don't you dare hang up on me, don't you dare." So I did.

He got away. Not all my determination, not all the charm I could muster, not my willingness to travel great distances or to meet his plane, his train, his automobile, could convince him of—what? What do you suppose he needed convincing of? What caused him to go into a rage, to become so violent in his words, so explosively angry that I held the phone away from my ear and shuddered at the change in him? It was not me, at least not just me. But I never got a chance to find out. Even now, sometimes when it's nine P.M. in California and eleven in Wisconsin, I look at the phone and hope it will ring. It doesn't. Probably better that way. He gave me Trollope at the Berg, though, and for that I will always be grateful.

SIXTEEN

Kyrie Eleison

Many music lovers are apt to get Bach mixed up with God.

—JAN SWAFFORD, in *The Vintage Guide to Classical Music*

M att's phone calls made being away from New York more bearable; our conversations about theater and poetry and sex made New York seem closer, put it right on the other end of the phone, all the way from far-off Wisconsin. However, a phone call, no matter its length or intensity, is not New York. And, I have found, being away from the city for too long puts me in a dismal state of mind; it is as if back home in California, I run on fumes and eventually must go back to New York to re-fuel. None of this is comprehensible to Andy.

Andy has supported my teaching in the prison and my vol-unteer efforts as an abortion escort. Still, he worries a bit: "Why do *you* have to do it?" He agrees with me that it is important for a woman about to get an abortion to make her way to the doc-tor's office unmolested by jeers and obscene placards. He agrees that everyone, in prison and out, needs an education. But, while he would like to worry less about me and while I have worried a lifetime about him, we are passionate in our support for each other.

So I did not worry that he would turn away from me, divorce me, when I told him about the ad. I told him about what it said. I told him that I got sixty-three responses and that I was going to New York to meet some of these men. I even told him about the fiasco with Danny Boy that had happened only a few weeks before, which I expected would reassure him I had not lost all of my reason. He was mildly amused, silently worried, and in the end, he said, "Go get 'em, Mom. It's your turn."

But, naturally, he was and is puzzled by me and the things I have done. Why does it have to be *his* mother who goes off and does nutty things? "I'll just never understand you," my father confessed once to me. I wonder at what point he gave up trying. My son doesn't need to understand me, and he knows that. He needs to be available for In Case of Emergency; he needs to let me put his name on that line. He needs to be the one to whom I leave all my worldly goods, even though they aren't many and may not, by the time I die, be any at all. And he is all those necessary things without question or complaint. So when I e-mail him that I'm off to New York again, will return end of May, he writes back, "Have fun." And shortly after, "Again? Weren't you just there?"

Well, yes, I was, but this time I am going to sleep with Sidney, though I don't mention this to my son, his need to know extending just so far. Now, I could wait to sleep with Sidney, I suppose, but once again New York has worked its magic. The final presentation, in early May, of the Encores! series at City Center is *Wonderful Town*. In his youth, Sidney sang and danced in *Wonderful Town*. And now, in this revival, Ruth and Eileen will once again sing and dance their way out of Ohio and into the heart of New York City. Just like me. We make plans to go. We will have a date.

Still, there are three events happening in May that I must attend to before I fly off to New York. They are endings for projects I began the previous January: the final ceremony for my student teachers, all of them waving job offers as they parade down the aisle; my final class at the prison, where Frederick will hold us spellbound with his rendition of "Eensy Beensy Spider"; and my chorale. I am passionate about them all.

When I was young, I had no use for Bach. I could never get his Two-Part Inventions right enough for my father or for my piano teacher; although, against my will and better judgment, she entered me in a juried recital in Toledo, the big city fifty miles away, where I blew up in front of the jury before I even got to the middle of the first invention. I left the room much dejected but nothing like my piano teacher, who, in the hallway outside the performance room, sat sprawled in a chair, eyes glassy, mouth agape. Guess I showed her. Bach and Haydn and those Czerny pieces, all that music in those Schirmer editions, were tasks I undertook because girls did that; girls learned to play the piano the same as they learned the piano a hundred years earlier and for the same purpose: to make themselves more suitable companions to men who were suitable right off because they were men. I didn't know about this then, of course; all I knew was that I was supposed to practice and didn't, and that my thirty minutes at my teacher's spinet demonstrated, week after week, a succession of errors almost more in number and kind than either of us could bear. Every so often my teacher would take over; she would play the Bach I was supposed to know by now. She showed me how it should sound; she showed me how badly I was failing. I dropped out at fifteen after nine years of trying not very hard at something I wasn't especially interested in. She retired not long after.

But something must have crept into my unconscious, something must have taken, because late one cold winter night, when

I was sixteen, as I sat in the corner bedroom of my house staring into the darkness, at the frost on the windowpane, snow on
the ground below, listening to the crackle and hum of the radio
next to my bed, suddenly, the air cleared and out of my little
radio came the sweep of the strings of the Philadelphia Orches-
tra playing Rachmaninoff's First Symphony. My first orgasm, I
just didn't know the word; I had never heard a whole symphony
before. My dad's taste ran to Benny Goodman—gauche, I
would stupidly have said if I had known the word. Across the
street, in my grandmother's house, my great-uncle collected red
vinyl records. They were beautiful—if you held them up to the
light, you could see through them—and every so often I would
creep over there when I knew my grandmother was off quilting
or out back wringing the neck of a chicken for Sunday, and I
would sneak Rossini's overture to *The Thieving Magpie* onto his
big Stromberg-Carlson hi-fi record player, lie down on the floor,
and wait till near the end of the overture, when the rhythm
changes; it is so sexy how he does it, brave even, definitely jazzy.
But no one in my family—not even my great-uncle, who seemed
to collect but never listen to his records—no one I knew in my
little town or on the farms outside it listened to music. Church
was where the music was and Bach had not found his way into
the churches of Archbold; hymns like "He Walks with Me and
He Talks with Me," a soppily sexual love song to Jesus, had, and
so had "The Old Rugged Cross," which exhorts us all to cling
to it. Bach? Never heard of him.

Of course, I played in my high school band. Everybody who
wasn't the strictest Mennonite played in the band and sang in
the chorus and, if you were a boy, played on the basketball,
football, and baseball teams, too. This was a town where the
boys on the football team huddled at the sidelines at the end of
the first half, changed into their band uniforms, picked up their

cornets and trombones and drums, and performed the halftime show. There just weren't enough of us to go around. I played flute, which wasn't loud enough for the outdoors; there, I was supposed to play the piccolo, but I quit when we got to "Stars and Stripes Forever," where the piccolo solo always brings down the house. We'd get to that part, and the whole band plus the director would pause, look at me, and play softer so that the tricky obbligato of the piccolo could soar the way John P. Sousa had meant it to. I never did it, I hardly ever even practiced to do it. Once, I started out, but before we got to the middle, I blew up. The director was tougher than my piano teacher, maybe because he had a lot more kids to support, but he made it clear that I had disappointed a lot of people and not just Sousa. The boys on the football team were especially irritated.

In college, I joined the university chorus for about five minutes. The music was hard and the director made us rehearse till all hours, and even suggested that there were those of us who would benefit from practicing at home. See ya. At the other end of the musical spectrum, I spurned Frank Sinatra and Jo Stafford and Peggy Lee. I mean, "I'd like to get you on a slow boat to China." Really.

I was close to sixty when I let Bach into my life. Over the years, I had been warmed by Mendelssohn and charmed by Schubert. But Bach, especially Bach for voices, left me cold: his vocal music in particular seemed starchy and unnecessarily complicated and long. I didn't have time. But my neighbor in Orinda did. Every Monday she drove off into the night for rehearsal with her choral group. One September Laura said, "Why don't you come along; I think you'd enjoy it." "Are there auditions?" I asked. "Yes," said Laura, "but you don't have to worry, everybody gets in."

What could happen but that I would blow up and humiliate

myself again. But then my analyst, Dr. V, the object of my affection at the time, was a fan of Bach. I suspected he was, he never actually said he was, but then he never actually said anything that might reveal a personhood; however, I had read enough about psychoanalysis to know that analysts, especially older analysts, were Bach fans. So I began to pay attention to the Goldberg Variations and the Brandenburg Concertos, and I liked them more with every listen. This was a sign. Surely, my growing appreciation for Bach's music meant that I was becoming the woman for him—my analyst. If I talked thrillingly about this music, not long from now he would realize that we were meant for each other. Alas, while my love for Bach—and my analyst—continued to grow, my analyst's adoration of me never surfaced. Bach, on the other hand, returned my passion tenfold.

Laura at my side, in the rehearsal room I filled out a card listing all my musical experience. Filling out one entire side of a three-by-five-inch card, I put down everything I could think of, including my participation in the University of Michigan mixed chorus. The form didn't ask how long, just what.

The last time I had sung a note was in 1970, driving across the country in flight from my marriage. After that, I sang the outlandish songs I made up for Andy. Before 1970, my last note had been sung in 1955. It was now 1997, twenty-two years later, and I was ready to sing again.

The director sat at the piano and played a list of notes that went all over the scale. I was supposed to sing them. "Can't I sing the Doxology?" I asked. "I do a mean Doxology." The Doxology, as you may know, is composed of about seven notes, all of them in mid-range. He nodded, puzzled into acquiescence. I sang away. At the end, he said, "You don't have much range, your tone is jarring, you don't sight-read at all. Let me see your card." He looked at the card. "You went to the University of Michigan?" I nodded. "When?" "Graduated in 1955," I answered. "You must have sung under Maynard Klein." I nodded. So that was his name. The director beamed up at me from his piano stool: "So did I. You're in." Some things hold true: It's not what you know, it's who.

According to people who know, one of whom is now me, Bach's B Minor Mass is the greatest mass ever composed; lots of us would go on to say it is the crowning achievement of all Western music. And I'm going to sing it. In May of the year 2000.

The words of a mass are easy. They're usually in Latin, which is pretty easy to pronounce since nobody really knows how it's supposed to sound. In the B Minor Mass (and lots of other masses and requiems) you just go "kyrie" a lot, as in "kir-ee-ay," "kyrie." There's always a "gloria," often "in excelsis," which anybody can pronounce once the director tells you if it's *exchelsis* or *exselsis,* which he will. He will not put it to a vote, I can tell you that, choruses and probably orchestras, too, being the least democratic organizations this side of the Kissinger family. Musicians put up with this dictatorship because we and they and the conductors and the directors all agree that we are in the service of the same master, in this case Bach. Anyway, the *gloria* is where you get to sing loud and fast and where, even if you get lost in the fugue, you can figure, since it's a *gloria,* it will end on a major chord, so if all else fails, don't blow up, don't quit, just wait for the last chord and belt out your note. Feels good. Near the end is the *hosanna.* Boy, is this fun! You sing only those three words—"hosanna in excelsis"—the whole way through, so you can concentrate on all the sixteenth notes that practically obliterate the page and that you're supposed to sing along with the other singers in your section, and not ever without them. I lip-synched right up to and through the performance. Not all the time, but man, Bach expects a lot, not to mention the director, who never quite forgave me for not being up to Maynard Klein.

The B Minor Mass is a transcendent experience for both atheist and believer, and I was grateful to Bach and the director for letting me in, novice that I was. Most of the singers had been singing regularly all their lives, just as I suppose they had been having sex regularly all their lives and I hadn't. As new to singing Bach as I was at having sex, I wasn't sure at first what to do in this chorale or how to do it, like who was running the show, who should be on top, and was it okay to *pretend* to be singing when I got tired and lost and things just got beyond me? So the Alto II's, my section, were nice to me; they sang loudly into my ear, pointed to the part in the score where everybody but me was, and encouraged me to try again, just like the men in my new life. In Philip Roth's *The Dying Animal,* David Kepesh in his later years plays Bach on his piano. He uses the music and his knowledge of music to seduce a young woman. He uses music to seduce himself; he masturbates to Beethoven, Mozart, Haydn (Bach does not make this list), Schumann, and Schubert, which has got to be kind of hard if you think about it: playing music like that requires both hands. About sex, he says, "only when you fuck is everything that you dislike in life and every-thing by which you are defeated in life purely, if momentarily, revenged. . . . Only then are you most cleanly alive and most cleanly yourself." I would argue that in singing the B Minor Mass "everything you dislike in life . . . is revenged." When, in the Sanctus, the basses descend the scale in octaves singing "Sanctus Dominus" as they go, now, that is sexual music. I sub-mit that participating in art and in sex allows us to transcend the certainty of our own death and the destruction of all that is beautiful and good. Art compensates for life.

By the spring of 2000 I had a lot to transcend. On May 3 we

offered up ourselves and Bach's music to an audience. The next day I left for New York.

When I was not practicing my Alto II part for the B Minor Mass—and yes, I practiced a lot—I was preparing my students in prison for their final exam. I was inviting people to come for the last night of class, when the men would tell their stories. I did not, I could not, anticipate anything so dramatic as Frederick leading us in "Eensy Beensy Spider," so I did not expect this night to equal our best final night ever, three years earlier, when Randy had told his story. On that night, from his seat in our Circle of Kings plus One, Randy transformed us all with the music of his voice and the power of his words as he told the story of his life. Like the B Minor Mass, Randy Wethers and his story were another transcendent experience.

RANDY WAS THEN forty-six years old. He had spent thirty-two of those years in prison. He was of medium height with the body of a man who has worked out: strong, muscled, compact. Randy was scheduled for release on the Saturday following our last class, though early that week the prison accused him and his cellie of trying to start a new religion and tossed the cellie into the Hole. Randy was the last to tell his story. He did not need notes; his memory served him—and us—well. "They tell you to tell the story of what you know best. So I will tell the story of my life." Randy was a basso profundo, and his voice rolled over us like the River Jordan.

"When I was two, I saw my mother stab my father forty-two times. I went to live with my father's mother, my grandmother. All the rooms in her house except three were locked. In the room where she sometimes sent me, there were clothes piled all over the floor, and a picture of Jesus on the wall that glowed in the dark and his eyes followed you wherever you went. My grandmother told me over and over my mother was a murderess and that one day she would come and get me. When I was seven, she did. She took me away on the Trailways bus, and I don't know why people complain about sitting in the back of the bus; the seat was big and wide and the view out back was better than the view in the front." Randy's voice was calm, soothing, the voice of a man in control of himself, his life, and his audience.

"My mother took me to New York City, where she entertained her visitors in the bed next to mine. Sometimes, she gave me a dollar. The subway was fifteen cents, and I had a whole dollar. I discovered Coney Island. I loved Coney Island. I listened and learned and looked, so when my dollar ran out I knew how to get more.

"As I grew older, no one knew what to do with me, I was so wild. So they put me in Creedmore State Hospital. By the time I was eighteen, I had been in and out of every jail, every court, every juvenile facility in New York City and beyond. I hated my mother. It took me a long time to appreciate what she done for me. She had fed me, clothed me, she never did drugs, and the visitors she entertained were always on the other side of the curtain. She taught me this: 'Always remember, to every reality there is a shadow. Just because you see a woman standing at a bus stop don't mean she's waiting for a bus. Eyes closed don't mean sleep. Good-bye don't mean gone.'"

He looked around the circle at each and every one of us and said, "Pray for me on Saturday." Every one of us, believers and not, bowed our heads.

Word has it that Randy was released but that he is not gone. He returns to San Quentin regularly to visit his son, an inmate.

———

NEW YORK WILL HAVE to be very good to me to compete with that. But whaddya know, on my arrival, the marquee over Carnegie Hall announces the performance of Bach's Mass in B Minor by the New York Choral Society. Of course, I go. So *that's* how it's supposed to sound. It is magnificent.

Creedmoor State Hospital, where Randy spent his adolescence, is in Queens. I sometimes think I should pay my respects, but Queens and Creedmoor seem very far away and, at the same time, not far enough.

SEVENTEEN

Hard Candy

But then, perhaps you live in Tupelo and have a wasting disease.

—JOHN

M ay is the most wonderful month New York offers. Go there. The weather is fine, the people are happy to breathe the last of winter, the cops are on horseback, ducks swim in Central Park, all is right with the world, and the world in all its rightness is New York City. It is possible to feed oneself for very little money from the sidewalk stands in New York: a hot dog for $1.50; a bag of warm nuts, $1.00. In San Francisco, a hot dog from a sidewalk vendor costs $3.75. Of course, in San Francisco one can choose from an array of Aidells gourmet sausages: apple chicken, basil tomato, cilantro spicy. The bun is big and crisp but not too, the stuff one can put on it endless: onions, ketchup, mustard, chiles, sauerkraut, tomatoes, relish, pickles, cheese. A San Francisco hot dog is a dining experience. I like New York hot dogs: a wiener slapped into a steamed bun, maybe some mustard, maybe some sauerkraut, often nothing. It feeds the stomach. And sometimes, the vendor who sells it to you feeds the soul.

In January, on my first visit to New York, on Broadway and Sixty-eighth I had my first knish. The vendor was a small, old, older than I, bent-over woman. She smiled up at me. "One hot dog, please," I said. She paused, looking at my red nose and watering eyes. "I think you want knish," she said.

"I never had a knish," I said. I stamped my feet in the bitter cold.

"I thought so. I make this one for you." She took the sort-of patty made from, she tells me, potato, deep-fried, and split it at one end. "You like onions?" she asked. I nodded. She tucked some fried onions inside. "You like mustard?" I nodded. "You like applesauce?" Yes, but with mustard? Oh, okay. "This Jewish food, good Jewish food," she said, and handed me my first knish. It was delicious, utterly delicious. "I thought so," she said. "You look like you could use good Jewish food." She put out her hand for the $1.50. I handed her $5.00. "That's fine," I said, "thank you for my first and very wonderful knish." The woman beamed, well, of course she beamed, and I beamed back. Lots of people in New York beam at me, well, almost beam, as beaming as New Yorkers ever get, which is hardly at all. It is, I suspect, because I beam first and I tip big. Cabdrivers line up for me. Doormen race to hold doors for me. Porters vie with each other to carry my bags. I am happy in this city.

But, my god, I was just here in March! One month at home and back I come again. Three reasons: 1. Sidney has got the tickets to *Wonderful Town;* 2. I have yet to meet John, the New England John whose letters and phone calls intrigued me, that is, his language on paper and over the telephone is extraordinary: formal, sort of, syntactically varied—a varied syntax sends shivers up and down my spine—interested in me, always a seductive tactic against which I am hopeless; and 3. there is Graham, whose letters have gotten even more interesting since his first in December, whose luncheon invitations in January and

March I accepted with increasing pleasure. Of course, I view Graham, years younger than I, as a sort of adjunct to all this, not notably significant, just someone to amuse me, to make me jittery and dry-mouthed, that sort of amusement. I haven't had hot flashes in fifteen years; those lunches saw their return because from across the table Graham looked at me funny, like he didn't want me just to talk to; it was a sort of priapic look, if you know what I mean, and I couldn't believe it either. However, that sort of thing does pique one's interest.

This visit, finally, I have done something smart. I have accepted my niece's invitation to stay with her in her Midtown apartment. Caroline is who I would have been if I had gotten to choose era, personality, looks, intelligence. She is thirty-three. She likes me. She is self-supporting, funny, independent, well educated, well traveled, well read, and well dressed. She thinks these adventures of mine are a hoot, well, I'm not sure of that, but she finds them interesting. On my two previous visits to her city we have met for a drink or brunch; one evening, we go to Arthur's, our favorite bar in the Village, old, real, too scuzzy for most of Caroline's friends. Over a beer, Caroline says, "Men lie, you know."

"They do? More than women?" I ask. I am enrapt and completely trusting in Caroline's insights, the insularity of my history having limited the scope of my own insights. Earlier in the evening, I told Caroline of Sidney's admiring words, his instant appreciation of me. So now I am listening especially carefully.

"Yes, I think they do. Well, they don't think they lie. When they say it, they believe it."

I nod, seems true enough.

"But somewhere down the line they forget they said it. Or they admit they said it but have changed their minds." She looks more intently at me. "You might be wary of Sidney's flattery." Suddenly, I feel very young and very foolish. But then, she might be wrong; after all, in January she met Robert and pronounced him a very nice man.

For as long as she has lived in New York, Caroline has said, "If you ever need a place to stay . . ." Now I do. And it will work out: I will be in New England for part of the time, she will be in Asia part of the time, so I won't bother her, won't invade her space or her privacy, won't disgrace myself in her eyes. Of course I won't.

BUT I HAVE MILES to go before I sleep. I am bound to meet John. In his letters and phone calls, he has made three things clear: 1. he has no funds to travel; 2. he has a long-standing relationship with a woman with whom he does not live save on the weekends, so I am not to phone then; and 3. he would enjoy meeting me. Why am I driving a rental car from the airport to this little no-account town somewhere in New England? Why didn't I stay in New York?

His letters, for one. In November: "A visit when mutually agreeable conditions prevail is very much to be hoped for." Don't you love the passive voice when it's used right? Then, in December: "If you were here, I would feed you well, take you sightseeing, and encourage you to have multiple orgasms." I call the airlines. In January: "If you come all the way from California, it is incumbent on me to accept in advance, without protest or rancor, that you may or may not fancy me." This is one elegant writer. "May," I write back. "I will be there in May."

Until then, John, who abjures television, automatic transmissions, and the computer, does answer his telephone. It is John I call in time of need, as when, this very month, Sidney got weird. "Is it normal," I ask John, teary-voiced, "not to want to kiss?" I am confused, not for the first time; I don't know, maybe lots of people don't like kissing, but I don't think so. The only thing I can think of from all my book learning is that prostitutes don't allow kissing; does that mean Sidney wants me to be a prostitute? I don't know; he simply will not tell me, he won't talk to me about this, he drives me nuts! On the other hand, he seems very much to like me and to appreciate the pleasure I give him. He tells me I am smart and sexy, and then, "There are so many endearing things about you," he says. In the conference room of his office, we have made love, I think, though with no kissing I can't be sure, and I tell him I am off to New England tomorrow to meet John. "I will miss you," Sidney says. I tell him, "I will leave my earrings and combs all over your office so you will find pieces of me when I am gone." He smiles and says, "I already have a piece of you." He has, too. I smooth his trousers, scratch at a spot on his tie, rub my fingers over the shoulder of his jacket, touch his nubby vest, the silk of his shirt, and listen while he tells me about the horrors that would arise from a Bush presidency (every one of which comes to pass). In the elevator, coming down from the twenty-fifth floor, I take his face in my hands and say, "Hold still." I kiss him on his beautiful mouth and say, "I have wanted to do that ever since I first saw you." He is as immobile as he is delicious. He pulls me close and growls into my ear, "You are adorable."

So what's so compelling about John? John has said, in response to my telephone blubbering over Sidney's nonkissing, "You know, Jane, you don't have to be sensual all of the time. Go to the Whitney." It seemed to me the best advice anyone had ever given me; my head cleared and my shoulders relaxed. Next day, I went to the Whitney. There every piece of sculpture was phallic or vaginal or both. I had never seen so many sensual constructions in my life: what wasn't erect was cavernous; what didn't stick out sucked in. That night I called John. He laughed and said, "I guess the first thing I'll have to do when I meet you is kiss you." Okay. "Watch for me by moonlight;/I'll come to thee by moonlight, though hell should bar the way!" I didn't actually say Noyes's words out loud. What I said was, "Noon, Tuesday."

There's something else irresistible about John. In a late-night phone conversation—he seems to have ample funds for phone conversations—he jokes about stealing books from the library. I am aghast, of course, and then curious: "What books would you steal if you actually did, which you actually wouldn't." And John says this surprising thing: "There's a small volume by Margaret Fuller I have always longed for."

I'd go thousands of miles (and did) to meet someone who knew and appreciated Margaret Fuller, the feminist writer and journalist, a female intellectual respected even in the 1830s and 1840s, even in Concord, Massachusetts, and by no less than the men of Ralph Waldo Emerson's circle, a woman whose powerful mind and the need to make her own living drove her from this country to Italy during its time of war. For a long time she has been a hero to me, and here is a man named John who, out of the blue, says that he, too, is an admirer. People like this must not go unattended; they are rare and getting rarer. Not only is John conversant with Margaret Fuller the woman and the writer; he went to grade school at Margaret Fuller Elementary way far away in northern Minnesota in a time when her ideas and achievements were a model for the young. I have been hungry for people like John for so long, people who would talk to me about what I hold near and dear. On the phone, John asks me what about Margaret Fuller draws me to her. I answer, "She seems to have borne great suffering with dignity and grace." John says, "I suspect we won't have difficulty finding things to talk about."

Margaret Fuller was not beautiful in the way George Eliot (an admirer of Fuller's, incidentally) was not beautiful—their faces are sometimes described as "equine"—and she was very brave. As editor of *The Dial,* a sort-of house organ of the transcendentalist philosophers, she was reluctant to publish Thoreau because she thought he was a bum and his writing sappy. She thought the Brook Farm experiment in communal living was silly. She thought women ought to learn to think for themselves. As a woman she loved the eternally married Ralph Waldo Emerson, the man; as an intellectual, she was his equal, and he came to regard her as such; however, finding insufficient encouragement on the romantic front, she turned the energy of her disappointment to writing for little to no money at all. She traveled to Italy for Horace Greeley and his newspaper and sent back her observations and analyses of the Italians' fight for independence from the papacy. She fell in love with an impoverished and much younger Italian nobleman, a freedom fighter; he fell in love with her; she gave birth to his son; soon after, they married (there's some debate about this) and—here's the killer—on their way to live in America, the ship foundered on the rocks within seeing distance of the New England shore. All aboard were drowned.

Margaret Fuller did the right, the brave things—according to her lights—in a time that celebrated physical beauty in women and paid them hardly any money for their talents. I must be truthful here and tell you I find her essays unreadable: they are filled with classical allusions (the wont of transcendental writers), so full as to crowd out the sense of what she wishes to tell us and, finally, exhausting to the modern reader, though as modern readers we may blush from our ignorance of the Greeks and Romans, once second nature to the educated person. In her journals she is less learned, and it is from her journals and the facts of her life that I came to admire her completely. "With the intellect I always have—always shall overcome, but that is not the half of the work. The life, the life, O my God! shall the life never be sweet?" Her yearning is mine. And, from a letter to a man who fled her ardor, "Perhaps it is that I was not enough a child at the right time, and now am too childish, but will you not have patience with that?" She writes for me.

INSPIRING AS John's conversation about my hero was, his photograph gave one pause. "I had to look all over the place to find this," John wrote. I guess so, I thought; if I looked like that, I would avoid the camera, too. In the photograph, John stands in his kitchen, peering furtively over one shoulder, which appears to be somewhat higher than the other. His dark hair, the few strands that remain, falls greasily back over his head, revealing a brow that does not suggest a high intelligence or invite my confidence, let alone lust. He looks like someone in the witness protection program. Or Richard III. The fact that I will travel all these miles to an unknown place to get kissed, maybe, by the guy in this photograph should convince you of my dedication to Margaret Fuller and my eagerness to find someone who knows her.

So here I go again, in my rental car, visited by familiar symptoms: dry mouth, shortness of breath, blurred vision; what am I doing behind the wheel of a car? I ought to have been used to this; after all, John was not the first, he was more like the fourth or fifth. But I have not gotten over the fear that on first sight, the man, whoever he is, will find me old, fat, just plain wrong in ways he will never explain. I have never gotten over the picture in my mind of a man lowering his gaze, fumbling for an apology—"I'm sorry you came all this way, but . . ." So far, though Robert shook it up a good bit, my luck has held. Nonetheless, the law of averages is not on my side. Neither is time, which it is just a matter of. Let me go back to New York, where it is safe.

Except I can't, for in this most beautiful of months in the

finest of all cities, Robert found me; he phoned my niece, she told him where I was. Was I happy? I don't know, a little, maybe more. He tells me that he and Sylvia had a fierce and final fight, and that he is free at last. For what? Robert is a very good kisser, but in the six weeks since our last meeting, he writes me, he has gone impotent, yet another system down for the count. Viagra still makes him nauseated; even Sylvia, with whom he confessed to being in love way back in March, had not been able to restore function, he tells me. Worse, for me at any rate, he has no desire. And yet—Would I like to do the *Times* crossword puzzle with him at his apartment? Yes. Would I like to have breakfast in our favorite restaurant? Yes. Would I like to go to the ballet at Lincoln Center? Uh-huh. I am so weak. At his invitation, I traipse up to his apartment. From the chair on the other side of the room from where he sits with the Sunday puzzle, I ask him very shyly, "Does impotence preclude your giving pleasure?" He is offended: "I have always considered sex to be a mutual affair." As usual with Robert, I feel confused. I want more than anything in the world for him to take me to bed. He has no intention of doing that; he has not lied about why. I feel ashamed and embarrassed and needy. I feel like a beggar. Which I would become in a minute if I thought he would be generous. But I know he won't. I am glad to have a reason to leave him behind. He makes me cry.

SPRING IN New England has been unusually rainy, so everything is beautifully green. Behind the fences are cows and horses and, particularly refreshing after New York, space—lots of meadow and empty fields just sitting there. I open the window and breathe deeply. John has given me directions to a small shopping center in the small village outside of which he lives in the woods in a house whose location, he says, is too complicated for me to find on my own. Ted Kaczynski had a house in the woods. John promises he will meet me in the parking lot. That's safe. Back when I was running for exercise, whenever nasty dogs ran out to greet me, I screamed, bringing the owners to attention. I perfected this scream. It's better than mace, which you have to remind yourself to tuck into your shorts. My scream is built in; so far, it has been infallible. This is what I tell myself as I leave the livestock behind for this village right off a picture postcard. Listen, I say to myself, anybody who lives in this lovely, lovely place can't be a murderer or even a plain, ordinary degenerate. I am ready. Bring him on.

A car pulls up next to mine. A man looking nothing like his photograph gets out, comes 'round to my door, and says, "Jane?" I get out, and he is tall and he is great-looking, and he is smiling truly, and then he puts his arms around me and kisses me. Right in public. "Follow me home," he says. You betcha.

John's house sits on the edge of a stream that runs through a meadow. It is a little house, a very old house, 1832, with an upstairs and a downstairs and a basement. It is a very nice house, nothing fancy unless you count as fancy (and I do) books lining every wall. John writes. He writes very slowly on that manual typewriter of his, so slowly that he has had nothing ready for publication in five years, though he works daily.

He sits in a chair across from me in his living room and crosses one graceful leg over the other. Wait till you see him with his trousers off. His legs ought to be stuffed (not yet) and put in a museum for everybody to enjoy. "I hope you passed on your legs to your daughter," I will say, upstairs in his bedroom. "I did and she appreciates them," he will say.

Honest to god, I am stunned. I try not to look at him below the belt, my favorite part of men, just below the belt buckle, that pelvic plain, flat and broad. Above the belt tells how much and how long the man has eaten and drunk the wrong stuff;

below, where I carry a lot of my extra pounds, in most men remains enviably firm and flat. John is lean above and below. I put a finger to the corner of my mouth to check for spittle.

John says, handing me a glass of wine, "I haven't had a drink in thirty years, though I know you appreciate good wine." God, he's a mind reader, too. "I play tennis," he says in answer to my gaze fixed on his nonexistent gut. He smiles at me fidgeting in the chair, whose edge I sit on so my feet can reach the floor. How can I be expected to be graceful or sophisticated or cool when sitting in almost every chair in the world necessitates a certain amount of scooting so that my feet won't stick straight out like Lily Tomlin's creation, that devilish kid Edith Ann, sitting in the huge rocking chair? "And that's the truth," Edith Ann sputters. I feel like her. John is still smiling. "You seem so buoyant," he says.

Buoyant. I could never have thought of that word in my whole life. But isn't it nice to be called "buoyant." "I am," I manage, once again struck by my own linguistic inventiveness.

John continues, "I would have expected this odyssey of yours to have worn you down a bit. In my experience, women want affection, after the act, for a time beyond. Aren't you letting yourself in for a lot of pain?" He is honest to god interested in what I think. "Tell me, what have you learned about us, about men?" He is irresistible. I find my voice.

"I haven't drawn any conclusions about men," I tell him, "and yes, I have made myself vulnerable, and yes, I have suffered some." I choose *some* over *a lot,* the latter being closer to the truth. "But a great deal of pleasure has come my way, not just physical but intellectual, absolutely unexpected but as wonderful as any of the flesh, maybe more." He does not look at all doubtful. He looks as if he is liking me, as if he finds me interesting. Even I am beginning to find me interesting. I continue, "I have decided to appreciate men for who they are, not trouble myself with who they aren't." John looks skeptical. I explain, "I have decided to appreciate men for what they can do, not fuss about what they can't." John ought to know, given my late-night phone calls, how hard-won this new philosophy of mine is. But he is incredulous: "You're running for goddamn sainthood!" I've got him on the edge of his seat.

"No," I say, "I'm being practical. Too much energy, too much time, gets lost in frustration." How I wish I were telling the truth. I am, in a way; I really have decided all this as it applies to Sidney; he doesn't kiss, why make it a big deal; he's wonderful, he likes me, he tells me wonderful things, calls me "darling" in that sexy New York accent, so what if he doesn't kiss. But Robert? I don't know if I can be in the same room with him without wanting him to undress me and take me to bed. I don't know if I can watch him move his long fingers, blunt at the end, over his beard, slowly and deliberately, the way they moved along my body, without wanting him to the exclusion of everything and everyone else. Robert wants me to be his friend, just his friend. I don't know if I can.

John smiles at me. "It's good to have a conversation with someone who doesn't turn everything into an argument." I like this man. "How do you feel about cemeteries?" he asks.

"They're great to visit, but I wouldn't want to live there."

John's smile is indulgent. "I thought we would visit one or two this afternoon, come home so I can feed you, and then, if you like, explore the upstairs."

"Okay."

WE STAND UNDER gray skies before grave markers, our shoes damp from the wet grass, and make up stories about the people whose names are engraved on the stones: "Hepzibah Fulsome Bullard, b. 1612, d. 1644." Hepzibah, we decide, died in child-

birth; sure enough, nearby are three very small stones, like little
lozenges lying on their backs: "Clara," "Thomas," then "Anna."
Oh my, she had lost all three, two in an epidemic and the last at
birth. Or so we imagine. John is a historian. He knows that the
epidemic might have been influenza or diphtheria. Our stories
about birth and death become very real.

"Elizabeth Holmes, Wife of Albion," reads a stone. "Truth-
full Holmes, Consort of Albion," reads the stone nearby. "Re-
liance Holmes, Relict of Albion," reads a third. And finally,
"Albion Holmes, b. 1613, d. 1689." We decide the women had
died in childbirth and Albion had gone right along to the next
one. We stand together, our heads bent toward the stone, imagining aloud the lives of each successive wife, the number of
children in her charge increasing until she, too, died giving birth
to yet another whose care would be provided by Albion's next
wife. "Those were hard days," I say.

"Those were simpler days," says John.

"No days were simple."

"I prefer them to today."

"Tell me one thing about today that is an improvement."

"Medicine," John says. "Great strides there." His tone is abrupt.

BACK HOME he feeds me curry, which he has made himself,
and sauvignon blanc. Then he kisses me a long time and I follow
him upstairs, which is like his downstairs: plain and comfortable
and books all around. This will be the first of three lovely nights.

I have never had sex with someone who sucked on hard can-
dies as he labored in my vineyards. John explains. He gave up
tobacco only three days earlier; only three to go, the doctor said,
until the physical addiction would abate. He doesn't believe it
will ever abate. "I predict I will be sucking on candy until I die
or until my teeth fall out, whichever comes first."

"Uh-huh," I say and continue my efforts toward orgasm. Finally, I fake one and John doesn't, and we lie side by side. "You're remarkable," he says. "You're at least ten years younger than your age."

"If you say so." I am pleased, of course, but at that moment I am more concerned with my orgasm, or, rather, its absence: my failure. All that plunging he did; surely, I should have come. What is wrong with me? Good lord, after meeting all these men and sleeping with quite a few, I am as troubled about vaginal orgasms as I was at the very beginning, six months earlier. Performance anxiety, as you probably already know and I should have long before this, is not restricted to the male sex. In our fertile years, according to evolution, sex results in pregnancy and the continuation of the species, pleasure not figuring into this equation. In our postmenopausal years, according to *Cosmopolitan,* sex leads to orgasm, which is supposed to result in pleasure, which we are supposed to get a lot of and not feel guilty about. So if I don't have an orgasm, what does that mean? I had no pleasure? Come now, I had a lot of pleasure. John is nice. He is fun. He is warm and feels good on the outside and on the inside. So who do I think I needed to fool when I pretended? Me, I guess, stupid after all this time. Here is a man who will listen to me. He is a man with a mountain of experience who likes me, who thinks I am smart, who even admires me—"I admire you for what you are doing," he said in the first moments of our meeting. I lean over and kiss him, and, appreciating him for what he can do, say, "Tell me a story."

"Emily Dickinson's brother, Austin, carried on a long and torrid affair with a very married Mabel Loomis Todd, usually at noon, in front of the fireplace in Emily's house."

I am happy.

———

The next day we walk around little villages whose inhabitants of the cemetery outnumber the living, whose libraries are monuments to stone masonry, where the latest of five generations dips ice cream out of freezers in the grocery store that dates back two hundred years, where the children go to school in the same building as their parents and grandparents before them, where the floors, old wood oiled ebony, sag from children's feet and rise again beneath the desks bolted to the floor and, back to back, to each other.

"The James brothers," says John. Oh, good, he will tell me a story about Frank and Jesse. "Henry and William," says John, "you remember them." I laugh and explain my disjointedness. He smiles down at me and tells me a story about Frank James and Cole Younger. "They decided, after their retirement from lawlessness, they ought not ever to be seen in a bank together. No matter their lack of criminal intent, one or both of them, they agreed, would get shot." This is a wonderful man. When he smiles, which is often, the creases in his cheeks deepen. Sometimes, I reach up and run my fingers along them. He does not seem to mind.

That night, I hurt. The pain had begun seconds before I yelled, though it was not unbearable, and at first I considered not saying anything, hoping John would drive past whatever obstacle my body was presenting. The name of my disease—the wasting disease John had mentioned in his very first letter—is creeping martyrdom. My mother had it and tried to pass it on to me. I hate myself when I see signs and symptoms, silent suffering heading the list. Not this time. I yelled. "Oh! I think you hit something in me!"

John paused. "I'm sorry, I think I hit your cervix. I'll be

more careful." And he was, slower and gentler, but I was drying up; pain is not a lubricant.

"Maybe we can rest a bit; otherwise, you're going to get stuck in me."

"Would you mind if I did?"

"No," and this time I didn't lie. I liked him in me. I liked his liking to be in me. I liked his full attention. I liked that he didn't talk during sex. I liked that he talked after.

"When did you lose your viriginity?" he wants to know. I tell him about blooming late, about the sadness of Jack. "Why did you marry your husband?" he wants to know. "I was pregnant," I tell him. "Those were hard days," he says. And then, "I have some K-Y jelly right here should the need arise. In the twenties, this kind of lubricant was called Johnson's Joy Juice."

Someone once told me I was a fool for learning. What a nice classroom John has provided and what a terrific teacher he is. Then, I tell him a story. I take hold of his penis, which is now outside me, and hold it gently in my hand. "I once had a lover."

John laughs. "Oh, really, you had a lover," as if that's how I spent my entire life. I give his penis a little tug. "I'll behave," he says.

"This man had a bend in his penis, right at the tip," I say. I hold up my index finger and bend the top joint. "Like that." John's penis is straightening out. I will have to pick up the pace of my story. "I thought it was cute. But he was embarrassed, wouldn't talk about it, didn't want to acknowledge it."

"Which way did it bend?" John wants to know.

"Down, just a little bit," I say, not sure of the accuracy of my memory of those years before, on the rug, in front of the television, in Minnesota.

"Actually, if it bends up, it's good. It's more likely to hit the G spot."

"If you say so," I answer, and I let go of his penis so it can find where it is the happiest. But this G-spot thing is still driving me nuts. The G spot is supposed to give me a vaginal orgasm. The vagina is where I'm supposed to have an orgasm, right? The other kind, the clitoral orgasm, is what it's okay to have when no man is around to give me the right kind. And John is into giving me the right kind.

"Take me on the outside," I whisper. He strokes me very nicely. "Don't stop," I say, "I'll come with you there." But I am whispering so softly, so shyly, that he doesn't hear me, and he does stop and straddles me, putting his penis where he believes it will do us both the most good. And it does. I stop this stupid worrying about how and where and if I should come. The fact is, I like everything about sex—the kissing, the touching, the whispering, the entering, the filling of me, his collapse on me. If what this man and I do in bed doesn't culminate in vaginal orgasm, then so be it. The pleasure of what the two of us are about up here in his bedroom is mutual. That much is clear. The closeness of a man I like, and right now that's John who likes being close to me, is sometimes overwhelming; sometimes I am just plain grateful. So I give up on my G spot; it's been dormant too long or I was born without one, who knows. If it happens, fine; if not, there's so much more.

ON OUR LAST EVENING, John takes me to dinner in the village and tells me a story; only this time it is not out of the past, it is not about historical figures. It is about now and it is about him. Sharon is the name of John's consort who lives in a town not far away. "I decided, when I answered your ad, that if you and I met and if we got along, I would give up other women, I would remain faithful to Sheila."

"And did we get along?"

"We did indeed."

I am confused. "What if we hadn't?"

"I would have continued seeing other women."

I don't get this. Nothing in these three days has prepared me for what seems to me to be an assault on all that is logical. It is so illogical that there is no arguing against it. "So, then," I say, "I am a milestone." John is pleased with my response. I am not. I do not like being a milestone—for him, for Jonah, for Robert. "Gee," I continue, "I should get a marker, a historical marker. Where would I put it, here?" I tap my lower tummy.

John laughs, he thinks I am funny. "I think of a milestone as an honor." And then he sees my tears. "You surprise me. We hardly know each other. It's only three days—"

Of course. "It's not you," I say. And it isn't. It's that for just about every man I have met on this journey I am a swan song, a test case, a last hurrah, the tail end—"You came in on the tail end," said Robert. I would have liked someone to want to keep me. Would I have stayed? I don't know. But the truth is that no one wants me as a consort. I am a bend in the road. I am the dusty pile of stones along the road marking the site of an accident. I am an unmarked grave in the cemetery. I am feeling sorry for myself. What the hell did I expect from men my age or older? Well, I expected this, but, more and more, I wanted to be wanted and for more than three days and, if I must tell the truth, by Robert. Falling out of love is a lot harder than falling in.

Outside the restaurant, I tell John this. John puts his arm around me and, for the first time, has no story at all.

THAT NIGHT I touch the scar on John's belly. "What's that from?"

He lowers himself gently onto me and says, "I used to have a bit more colon than I do now." He raises himself off me and begins anew, and I notice that the skin on his face is loose, it falls forward, it is freeing itself from the bone, just the way the skin on my upper arms and inner thighs is loose. Our bodies are dying. Soon we will be no flesh at all, just bones. I reach up for him, to pull him to me, to hold him against the dying of us both. But I am not skillful enough and John falls, *whap,* onto me. I feel a slight ping but no real pain, nothing to cry out about.

It seems now that the candy rolls around his mouth in time to his rhythmic forays into my inner recesses. On a particularly deep drive—my cervix having moved to a more comfortable location—John cracks the lemon drop apart. When he comes inside me, the pieces make little sounds, like the pebbles that rolled around in the fishbowl I insisted on having when I was little.

IN THE MORNING, John is dressed early. "I don't mean to rush you," he says, "but I have an appointment."

"What could be more important than me?" I ask. I am bold with bitterness.

"A CAT scan," he says. "The doctor wants to find out if my liver has cancer."

"Have you had symptoms?"

"Yes."

"Will you let me know?"

"No."

BACK HOME in Berkeley, the doctor assured me that my rib— the right third rib at the mid-clavicular line—wasn't broken, just bruised, and would take some weeks to heal. Ribs are like that, he said, and shrugged, just the way John's doctor had shrugged when he told John, "Cancer of the colon is a random event." John had never figured out if this was supposed to make him feel better. It didn't. As for me, I hurt only when I turned over in bed, wore a bra, or took a breath.

EIGHTEEN

A Merry Old Soul

I realize that there is a somewhat substantial age gap between us
(not quite Harold and Maude, but in the neighborhood).

—GRAHAM, January 2000

Graham is a gift I am happy I did not refuse. He is a joy, a
delight, a treasure. He is exactly who I needed on my return from New England. He would be careful of my rib.

Five months before, back in Berkeley, in an effort to stanch
the flow of blood from my cuticles and my heart, I lay on Dr.
V's couch, where I gnashed my teeth over Danny the Priest,
Jonah the Thief, Robert the Liar, Sidney the Peculiar, and now
Graham the Younger. In March, after my second go-round in
New York, I was still gnashing, and might be gnashing still had
Dr. V not retired. A guy can take just so much. I had, by this
time, met Graham in the flesh. And it was his flesh that un-
nerved me.

So I told Dr. V the following, though not in so many words:

Amid the Sturm und Drang of Robert, the contumely I
heaped upon us both, the tsunami of emotions that left me
gasping for breath, I accepted the invitation to lunch that Gra-

ham had offered in an earlier e-mail. In the beginning were the words and Graham had a way with them: *"I realize that there is a somewhat substantial age gap between us (not quite Harold and Maude, but in the neighborhood), but I'm unconcerned about age when it comes to the people I care about."* This, in his first letter, arrived in my mailbox in early January. I was in love—ahem—with Robert by then and immune to entreaties, even to the last one, as Graham's turned out to be, the final packet, number 7. So I decided not to answer. As you will recall, my cup was running over.

During the days that followed I kept remembering the end of his letter: *"I hope to hear from you soon. It could be a lot of fun."* Nothing wrong with that. His letter had also included *"You should know that sex is extremely important to me, and my proficiency is quite good."* Well, I would ignore that. We could just write, maybe even meet someday, though probably not, and in the meantime, his letters would entertain and amuse me. They would lighten the load of lustful e-mail with Robert under which I staggered. And so I wrote back.

Now there grew on my desktop an e-mail file that in length would rival Robert's. To Graham, I confessed my love for Sargent's portraits; he confessed the same. I queried him about Chekhov; he answered with a provocation: *"His characters suffer from the talking disease, fatuously spieling away their lives, Chekhov's point but oh so tedious to make."* I disagreed but only with half. We agreed entirely, though, that Graham was having fun writing to me and I to him. *"On menus where numbers herald each dish—think Chinese, Bangladeshi, Uruguayan—#1 is not very interesting. In fact, it takes until #5 or higher (sometimes even #15) for the menu to brighten. Why is this?"* And he knew all this stuff: *"I would love to take you to the tomb of Scott and Zelda in Rockville, Md. It's the most appropriately ironic place in America and thus perfect for the Fitzgeralds."* And he had done such interesting things: *"After Yale, I spent my wanderjahr in India where I was born. I took only Proust with me."* I know, he sounds elitist, which, this being America, is okay for somebody to be but which Graham is not really. No elitist is going to write to a sixty-six-year-old woman who advertises for sex. He's discerning, let's say, though would a discerning young man write to a . . . ? He's curious. And brave. What in the world went through his mind when he read my ad?

"I'm coming to New York in March," I wrote. *"Wonderful!"* he wrote back. *"Let me buy you lunch. We could even turn the whole week into Jane's Birthday Week with a host of festivities and fireworks."* And *"I think we're virtually guaranteed not to run out of conversation."* Just in case, he included a list of conversational possibilities: odd integers, viz., *"What were you like when you were seven?"* and *"Which of the 9 muses do you like most? Least?"* Irresistible. Besides, it was only lunch, and the hospitality on the Upper West Side was wearing thin.

And so, on the appointed day, Graham's instructions clutched in my hot little hand—Robert would have pinned them to my mitten had I had one—I took the number 9 subway downtown, walked onto a very crowded street, stood on the street corner, my face turned up to the street sign that read WALL STREET—oh golly, I've read about this—closed my mouth, went into a skyscraper, and stood at the foot of the escalator. I was one hour early, ample time to faint and recover before Graham showed up. If he did. Surely he wouldn't. Please, Graham, don't show up, if you don't show up, I'll go right up to your office, no I won't, I'll go to the water, the ocean, out there and jump in, likewise if you do.

I rued the day I ever sent that damn photograph to him, you know, the one where you can't see one frigging line in my face. I looked about thirty-three, just his age, the age he looked—and was—in the photograph of himself that he scanned into his computer and e-mailed to me. In it he is on a mountainside in Spain: a sunburst of red hair, nonchalant in blue shirt open at the neck, which, even then, I could see, was lengthily attractive. And here, on my screen, came a second photo, this one of Graham's legs naked below his khaki shorts. *"I send you a picture of my legs,"* he wrote, *"of which I am justly proud."* I guess so. A guy who mailed himself with confidence like that was going to show up. Graham would show up and he would take one look and I would see "Mistake" written all over his face, flashing like the signs in Times Square, SHE'S OLD! SHE'S OLD! I prayed to god to give me a heart attack. No luck this time either. Here he came, he was smiling. For how long?

I have no recollection of getting to the restaurant or of the restaurant itself except that on the wall were multiple television screens with the doings of the market scrolling indifferently along; while, from their tables in the restaurant, multiple faces glued themselves to the screens. Good, they would not be glued on us.

Fortunately, no crimes were committed. If they had been, I would have been utterly useless as a witness to anything but my own discomfort and, I was certain, Graham's. My jacket kept pulling open and I felt Graham's eyes on the forty-five-dollar T-shirt underneath, which I had bought because it was loose and would hide my breasts but obviously didn't. (You realize, of course, that what used to be L for large is now XL, and what was S for small is now XS. Oh, women of the world, we are getting shafted again.) I kept pulling the jacket shut and Graham kept looking. He looked all over me and paused now and again at my hands. Those are liver spots, I wanted to say, and when he looked at my mouth, Teeth yellow with age. But I didn't. I didn't need to. Without any help from me, Graham was taking me in. He was digesting me. So far, he had kept me down. I ordered a hamburger and a glass of white wine. Classy. Graham ordered a spinach salad and tea. This wasn't going to work, it just wasn't. I twisted and turned in my stomach, knotted my napkin, wished it were long enough to put around my neck, then we could strangle me, at least it would give us something to do. From his knapsack Graham took a bottle of champagne, handed it across the table to me, and said, "Happy birthday, Jane. May you have many more, all of them as auspicious as this one. What did you read on the plane?"

"Thank you, Bartleby," I whispered. "Bartleby, you know, the Melville . . ."

"Do you agree it is the most perfect story ever written?"

I did, and we fell upon each other, starved for talk. We feasted on a banquet made sumptuous by us, replenished by us, free for our asking, and portable so that we could take it with us wherever we went. We never got full. We got happy.

Outside the restaurant, Graham said, "I want to show you something." I followed dutifully, and as we walked, Graham swung his arm wide and said, "Look at all these people! There are far too many people."

"And they all live here or in California where I live," I said.

"This is not good. Something must be done."

I suggested that, since the Upper Midwest continues to empty itself of its native-borns, we go to whatever lengths are necessary to make that part of the country attractive, thereby inducing immigrants to east and west coasts to return home.

"Fine and dandy," said Graham, "but there's still the problem of the weather."

"We dome baseball, basketball, football, why not North Dakota?"

He was thinking. "The problem continues to worsen in our North American continent. I have another suggestion." He jammed his fists into his pockets. "We could get rid of the Canadians."

We were now in front of the Customs House. Inside, the great room is a circle, its circumference lined all around with perhaps one hundred wooden desks. They are the desks of the customs agents, one of them Melville, who sat keeping the books on goods from abroad. "Which one do you think was Melville's?" I asked Graham.

"Can we be certain that he sat at the same desk? Were desks assigned? Is it possible he moved from one desk to the other?"

"If he sat in the same desk every day, which one would it be?"

"That one," he said, and pointed to a desk very far from where we stood. The huge, round, marble room, domed and echoing our every movement, was empty of people save for the two of us and the hundreds of ghosts who had spent their days bent over these very desks. I felt the way I had when Lenny de Berg placed Trollope's *Miss MacKenzie* in front of me; I bowed my head in reverence, not the last time I would feel like that with Graham.

On the way out we passed a reception desk, where a few overly casual Native Americans sat ready to answer questions about how this monument to literary history, this triumph of architecture, had become a center for Native American studies. I didn't say to the Native Americans behind the desk what I was thinking: Sit up straight, button your shirts, mind your loud voices, show some respect, if not for a white society that failed you, then for yourselves and the job you have agreed to do. Silently, I reprimanded myself for thinking like my grandmother, who persisted in showing up at all the wrong moments.

Long ago I had made an observation which appertained as we walked toward the water, into which, only an hour ago, I had been thinking of jumping: very smart people lead with their foreheads. Graham is very smart; ergo, when he walks, his forehead precedes the rest of him, so it is not immediately apparent that he is tall, probably six feet, and slim as a reed. Ideas come to him so fast and furiously, he swallows them and chokes slightly as they tumble from him: "What books do you ex . . . pect will stay with you forever? Not the ones you'd take, say, to an island, the ones that are a p . . . art of you." He is utterly charming.

His question was not hard to answer. *"The Canterbury Tales."* Then, before I could say "and *Lear,*" Graham was running, galloping, occasionally leaping and twirling in midair, across the plaza as he recited with joyous and, need I add, youthful vigor from the "General Prologue." "Whan that Aprill with his shoures soote/The droghte of March hath perced to the roote" all the way through to "And at a knyght than wol I first bigynne." His Middle English was impeccable. He was a delight. He made me smile. He made me laugh out loud.

Graham was writing a novel. He worked at a job he detested but that paid him a lot of money so that in two years or so he could quit and just write. "You need a patron," I said. "If I had enough money, I would be your patron."

"Today, people with money don't support artists and writers; they give their money to universities and get a building named after them."

Graham makes pronouncements like this all the time, and, mostly, they're true. I think about them, sometimes argue a bit, but by and large, well, like this: "Do you think there are any absolutes?" I ask.

"Yes," he answers. "Cruelty is wrong. I am a fan of Kant—with a *K,* not a *C.*"

I argue a bit. "Surely, you know the categorical imperative is a philosophical sieve."

"What Kant wants is for us to be nicer to each other. The world would be a better place. I'm all for people being nicer to each other." He looks down at me. "Aren't you?"

"Mm-hm." His eyes are almond-shaped, flecked with green.

Or this: "An appreciation of irony is necessary to survival."

Now, I agree absolutely but wish to prolong our conversation: "Oh, Graham, irony is old hat; it went out with the sixties."

He is so serious. "It is never out of date. Irony lives and breathes. Irony saves lives."

"There are those who claim that California is irony deficient," I say.

"And the Midwest?"

"The Midwest is irony."

"Talk Midwest to me," he says. He has seen *Fargo* nine times.

"Okay." I summon the purity of the midwestern vowel, a sound untinged with remnants of British speech or fancied up by California for nationwide distribution via satellite, a sound I had spent years ridding myself of, embarrassed because it marked me a hayseed. It all came back to me here in this most sophisticated of cities in the company of this most sophisticated man and I say, "O," and then, "O yah," and I am back on the farm. Graham laughs delightedly.

I will speak midwestern for Graham again and he will make more pronouncements. But all this will happen over time— there will be four lunches—these conversations that tickle my brain. He is like a puppy determined to play, teasing me out of my dusty corner, tossing me high into the air. I am infused, enlivened, happy.

On that cold and blustery March day, our very first meeting in the flesh, I have a more immediate question: "Here is something that has puzzled me since arriving in New York. People seem to look at me, and I don't think I'm making this up." Sidney has said, "Of course, they would be aware of you. New Yorkers are always alert to the possibility of being mugged or mishandled by strangers." Robert has answered, "Are you certain?" Not long after, Dr. V will answer with, "People recognize the libido when they see it."

Graham says, "Appearance, how one dresses, is the only way New Yorkers can announce our status. We don't have cars or houses, so it is dress that tells others where we live on the ladder of class. I am," he adds, "a cynic."

"You are not old enough to be a cynic."

"All right, then, I am a disappointed romantic. Besides, all my friends tell me I have an old soul."

Back on Wall Street, at Graham's escalator, I hold out my hand and—well, how does one thank someone for a perfectly lovely time?—I lean forward and kiss him lightly on the cheek. It is clear from his grin that Graham has all his own teeth. "Write to me," I say. "I will," he answers.

Over the short time we had been together, Graham had gotten older, and I had gotten younger. By the time he returned to his skyscraper we were just about the same age.

"ARE YOU LISTENING, Dr. V?" I ask, slip-sliding away on his genuine leather couch like Freud's. Dr. V has mastered several kinds of silence: one in which he is totting up my bill, another in which he is restraining himself from throttling me, and this one in which he is intent upon what I am saying. I go on. "Graham is an absolutely wonderful . . ." I cannot say "man." I cannot say "boy." I burst out finally ". . . person. But he is thirty-three years younger than I am, he's thirty-three, for god's sake, this is ridiculous. And not only that"—here comes the confession—"I think he might want to sleep with me." This cannot be, of course, but I have learned here on this venerable couch to say that which comes to mind.

Dr. V speaks: "Do you like Graham?"

"Yes."

"Does he like you?"

"Yes."

"Then I fail to see the problem."

"Did you hear me? He might want to sleep with me."

"As I said . . ."

"Okay, okay."

THAT WAS THEN. This is now. That was March, this is May.

I have designated myself to bring food for a picnic. Graham will bring dessert. Or, well, screw this, shall we just get to the hotel? Shall we just get to the part where Graham makes love to me?

Out in the harbor, the white sails of boats skim along the surface of the blue water. The grass has never been this green. Today we are having a picnic, a French picnic, *déjeuner sur l'herbe*. To that end, Graham is wearing a beret, a black turtleneck, and Basque sheepherders' socks. I try not to look at the middle part of him, and fasten my eyes on his socks. "Ah, yes," he says, "I see you're interested in my socks. They're quite long." He pulls up his pant legs to show me just how long they are and how far up they go. The photograph of his legs in Spain didn't begin to do them justice. As he pours wine into my glass, water into his, he says, "You're fun to write to." I mutter something about the pleasure being mutual and he says, "How is your visit going?" On every meeting, Graham will ask me this question and every time the tears will crowd into my eyes, a simple matter of over-flowing when a person is nice to me and the fact that my visits to New York include hope, despair, exhilaration, and frustration, along with a soupçon of trauma relieved by ecstasy. I snif-fle. I can barely look at him. Graham has been to Majorca on business and is a lovely color. He just gets better-looking all the time, and I look like hell, no makeup, why bother to hide any-thing from this young man. I start to blubber. Graham hands me his handkerchief. "My grandfather always carries three, but I find one quite sufficient." His grandfather! My god, I'm probably older than his grandfather! I don't care.

When Graham is not dissecting me with his eyes, when he looks off into the distance and talks about Nabokov and butterflies, I look at him, at his long, oval, currently light-brown face, his very red hair swirling around his head like a halo, his very straight nose, his perfectly molded lips, his long and slender neck, and wonder what goes on in his mind when he thinks about me. What kind of mental and emotional and aesthetic gyrations has he put himself through that would allow him to want to spend time with me? How has he managed to free himself from the fact that I am old and look it and that he is young and looks it, that he is beautiful and I'm not? How on earth has he brought himself around to the notion that he wants to sleep with me? Because he does. Every so often, I peek at him and catch him looking at me in a different way. His face gets lustful. It looks a little bit like those paintings where there is a satyr lurking behind a temple. I am totally embarrassed when I see it and terribly afraid and utterly excited.

His kindness undoes me. I weep into Graham's handkerchief my woeful tale of maybe being a prostitute because Sidney won't kiss me and how Robert said he bought Viagra but where is it, and about John who might be dead. At the end of my tale, I blow my nose—oh god, I can't hand this dirty handkerchief back to him—and he takes the handkerchief from me and says, "I have to see someone at least twice before I believe in their existence. You definitely exist." He brings from somewhere two madeleines. *"Un petit gâteau, madame."*

On the walk back to his office, he tucks my arm in his and says, "I'm free weekends, after work, for lunch."

What do I do now?

Fate intervenes. Caroline calls to announce her early return from Malaysia on the following day. She has the flu. She is miserable. We agree she will be fine with orange juice and a lot of sleep. She puts up no fight at all when I suggest moving to a hotel. That's the plan. That night I don't get exactly drunk, just woozy enough on wine to call Graham for a bit of conversation. I ask, "Do you think Fred Astaire ever had sex?" Graham answers, "Occasionally. But he never enjoyed it." And he asks me, "Have you ever slapped anyone in the face?" No, I have to say, "though once I pushed a plate of potato salad into a boy's face." "That's even better," he says. And then I invite him to the hotel. I can't believe I did that, but hell, nobody's touching me; I might as well be back in California instead of here, where promises are made and broken hourly. Besides, how can I refuse what might well turn out to be an extraordinary interlude with a man whose ass, so far clothed yet nonetheless terrific, promises delights of the highest order. Graham had written in the very beginning, *"This could be a lot of fun."* So far he had been right. What if I didn't do it? What if I missed it? What if I got to be ninety and all I could think of was what a fool I had been in my youth? At the end of our phone conversation, I say, "Graham, my body is every inch my age. I am sixty-six years old all over."

"I find you interesting on many different levels. I'll see you tomorrow between six-thirty and seven."

I check into my hotel three hours early, plenty of time to pop a twenty-ounce can of Sapporo to freshen my breath. Graham does not drink, nor did he ever do drugs. "I have no inhibitions," he explained, "so nothing to release." If I try really hard—so far nothing seems to have discouraged him: not my tears, not my wine-swilling, not the lines in my face, spots on my hands, yellow on my teeth, bifocals on my eyes—maybe this Japanese beer breath will scare him off. If not, never fear. I remain in possession of my secret and most powerful deterrent: my body.

At 6:45 there is a knock at the door. I open it and Graham

hands me a parental frown and the room key, which I have left in the outside lock.

In my hotel room there is a bed and a chair and a footstool and over there a desk. I take my place in the chair and knock back a few ounces of Sapporo. Graham pulls the footstool close and sits down facing me, watches me squirm, and says, "What are you afraid of?" His face has that look on it. And I say, "I'm afraid you won't like me. Maybe if we just . . ." I lean forward to just sort of kiss him maybe on the cheek. He leans forward, turning his head so that my lips miss his cheek and land squarely on his mouth. He kisses me back, raises me from the chair, ever so quickly lays me down on the bed, and before I know it my clothes fall off. "You are sexy," he says.

How did he get naked so fast? On his knees, he straddles me and I gasp. "Oh, my goodness!" He is prodigiously affixed. "I know," he says, "my hands are small. The old saw about hands being the telltale of a man's intimate parts doesn't apply, does it." My cervix is in for it this time. "Come here." I reach for him. He does not fall on me. He does not hurt me ever. Somewhere in the first lovely hour I cry out, "Oh, Graham, this is joyous." It is as if he listened carefully to my woes and has set about to cure every one of them right here in bed. And then, when it's time, like the gentleman he is, he takes me home. He holds the door open and, at just the right moment, nudges me gently inside. "May I come with you?" he whispers. "Please," I say, and presently he does.

We are silent for quite some time, a long time for us. Finally, I say, "I know one is not supposed to be grateful, but . . ."

"You're welcome." He perches on an elbow and looks down at me. "The greatest pleasure for me in making love is giving the other person pleasure."

I am in bed with a fucking genius. It could be that the only real problem is that this man is too good to be true. If you need proof, listen to this: the light was on the whole time.

We lie in bed and talk and talk and talk. I tell him about my regard for Margaret Fuller. "Tell me about her." "It's too long," I protest. "Tell me," he insists. He lies back onto the pillow, cradles his head in his hands, and listens. In return, he tells me about George Eliot's manuscript at the Morgan. "You must go." "Tell me about the book you're writing," I say. He does and then, "Tell me about yours." He turns on his side toward me and smoothes my hair away from my forehead. "You can't imagine how long it has been since I have had a real conversation." And then he whispers into my ear, "Shall we take another turn around the park?"

Afterward, Graham says, "I think your book just got a lot more interesting."

"I'm not a good enough writer for this." I feel him smile.

"You are cogitative. Tell me what you are thinking."

"I haven't a thought in my head. It's wonderful."

"Didn't you know? That's why intellectuals have sex."

"I'm not an intellectual."

He laughs. "Oh, yes, you are."

It is late. Graham says, "Hemingway says the earth moved only three times for him."

"I lost count."

NEXT MORNING, I returned to Caroline, a goofy smile on my face, wondering if Graham had gotten to work on time. Caroline was feeling better. Even flu-ridden she was beautiful. She stood at the kitchen sink running hot water over her Steuben wineglasses. Her hair was pulled back in a ponytail, her face, free of makeup, shone in all its natural prettiness. She wore a pink and white slip dress and looked like the little girl I had loved all her life. "Were you with Robert last night?" After meeting Robert over brunch, she had pronounced him "a nice man, good-looking." She could have gone on and said "age appropriate," which he is, and "safe," which is what Robert looks like. He can even talk safe. He can make himself seem gentle and kind. He fooled me, too.

Without thinking, something I had gotten very good at, I answered, "I was with Graham."

Caroline's smile became a grimace; her face paled. "Please, Jane, don't tell me you slept with Graham."

I didn't have to. Caroline's disgust was visible. She said sarcastically, "So how was it?"

I could have said that it was a one-time thing, that Graham had been drunk, that I had forced him. Hell, I could have lied and said, "Yes, I was with Robert." What in me, aside from a serious lack of imagination, made me tell the truth? I said, "He is a most generous . . ." Oh shit, now I had done it.

Caroline began to pace up and down the kitchen, wringing the dish towel in her hands as she went. I could feel my throat constrict; I could feel the towel around my neck. "So," she demanded, "where do you think this is going?" As if it were going anywhere; I could read Caroline's mind, and in it I was a fool and no longer her aunt.

"Well," I said, "I don't think he's going to take me home to meet his parents." This did not help. Nobody was laughing.

Caroline's back was to me as she emptied the dishwasher. Suddenly, she whirled on me and said, "And what do you think your son—your thirty-two-year-old son—is going to say about this?"

"Nothing. Not if I brought him up right."

"Oh, I think he will have plenty to say!" Her voice rose, I wanted to clap my hands over my ears, jesus, I was getting mixed up here, who's old and who's not and who did wrong and who didn't, and I was supposed to feel ashamed and I didn't. Caroline threw the dish towel over the back of the chair and banged on into the living room, kicking the kitchen door as she went. Ouch.

She was not finished. "So," she called from the living room, "is Graham going to call?" I read her mind again: What's wrong with this Graham person, he won't call, he's got to be as disgusted as I am if he's got any sense at all. Is this guy a pervert, a weirdo? "Jane," she continued, "he's so young!" She stood at the kitchen door.

"Actually, he's very old."

Caroline's outrage had reached the corners of her mouth, pulling them down toward her chin. As her mouth went down her voice went up. "Is he smart enough? Aren't you smarter than he is?" The windowpanes rattled.

"No, Graham is much smarter than I am. Than anyone I have ever met." I answered her question, "If he doesn't call me, I'll call him." Caroline slammed the door to her bedroom.

Now I had done it. Evil distortions of my brain had made me think that Caroline—and everybody else, rational or not—could share the delight, the wonder, the fun, of Graham. Months ago, when I had told Caroline's mother, my sister, whom I adored and admired, that I was writing to this young, this very young, man, she had said, "I'm sending you money for a psychiatrist. Or him. He's the one who really needs help." I do this, you know. I assume that because I like something or someone, so will everybody else. It's so naïve. When I taught all those high school kids, I thought, of course, they would love *The Merchant of Venice;* I did, so would they. I am such a slow learner. Still, I have had a long, long time to catch up with sensible people, so I ought to know that it is not just common sense that tells a person when to shut up, when to keep quiet, it is courtesy, as in

Thinking of Others. Not everyone wants to know about you, Jane; in fact, a lot of people don't. I had fucked up this time. Seventy-five dollars to change my plane reservation to an earlier time. Better do it.

Instead, I went to the movies. I saw Ethan Hawke's *Hamlet*. It was the best *Hamlet* I had ever seen. I smiled all the way through it. As I walked back to my ex-niece's apartment the thought jumped into my brain: It's not Graham Caroline finds disgusting. It's me. Of course. I must be even uglier than I thought. I considered going back to the hotel, but my Visa bill must surely have hit *bankrupt* by now, so what was a little crow. I could just shut up. I would try.

Caroline was quieter but not terribly friendly. I missed her calling me Aunt Jane. No more Aunt, my fault, my fault. She plopped down on the couch next to me and said, "We have to watch my favorite program. I never miss it if I can help it. The guy in it is adorable, wait'll you see him." David Duchovny in *The X-Files*. "See what I mean?"

And I, having promised myself and the world to grow up, said, "Want to see what Graham looks like?" I pointed to David Duchovny on the screen.

Caroline raised her eyes to the heavens. Would this visit never end?

Late that night, I lay on my air mattress in Caroline's living room and listened to New York clattering, banging, humming its way toward morning. I wondered: Was a night with Graham worth the loss of my niece and probably my sister and maybe even my son? From my memory came Edna St. Vincent Millay, who, not so long ago, lived a riotous and beautiful life in Greenwich Village, not so far from here:

It well may be that in a difficult hour . . .

. . .

I might be driven to sell your love for peace,
Or trade the memory of this night for food.
It well may be. I do not think I would.

From the corner of the room, just behind my left ear, came another voice. My, it was getting crowded in here. The voice, deep and sonorous, melded with mine; in the past it was so querulous and tentative, but now it was so steady and sure, it was impossible to tell one from the other: "Do you like Graham?" Yes. "Does Graham like you?" Yes. "Then I fail to see the problem."

Graham has an old soul in a young body, I the reverse. We are a perfect fit.

NINETEEN

A Wink and a Smile

Time gnaws on our necks like a dog gnaws on a stew bone.
It whittles us down with its white teeth,
It sends us packing, leaving no footprints on the dust-dour road.
That's one way of putting it.
Time, like a golden coin, lies on our tongue's another.
We slide it between our teeth on the black water ready
for what's next.

—CHARLES WRIGHT, from "Nine-Panel Yaak River Screen"

And so I left Bach at Carnegie Hall and Sidney in his office on the twenty-fifth floor and Graham on the greensward of Battery Park and everybody else and everybody else. You don't even need to ask if I cried on United Airlines Flight 91, departing 9:00 A.M. JFK, arriving 2:00 P.M. SFO.

THE PROBLEM WITH coming home is that there's no one in the next room. Oh, yes, it's nice that all the dresser drawers are for your underwear only, nice to sleep on sheets as clean as you want to keep them, nice to shit in a bathroom where the pubic hairs are yours alone. But then seven P.M. comes. Until then, I am busy. But at seven I am alone and terribly lonely. What do I do until I fall asleep? A friend, a young husband and father, once asked me, "What's it like to live alone? It must be hard." I answered, "It's like living with another person; it's just that the other person is me. Most of the time we get along fine; other times, we argue and get angry, but eventually we make up." My friend liked that answer, and so did I except now me, myself, and I are all of us separately and together lonely. How does one grow old alone? In sickness and in health, for richer or for poorer, until death do us part.

I GOT USED to being around another person. I got to like sliding behind Robert to get to the kitchen. I liked hurrying to Wall Street to meet Graham for lunch. I liked Caroline's coming through the door of her apartment. I liked Sidney's nightly phone call, his gravelly voice asking, "Tell me about your day." I am obviously feeling sorry for myself when, in fact, not one of them has abandoned me. Sidney will call every week and talk about politics and theater and my "magnificent breasts." Robert and I will write, as friends, often two and three times a day. Graham will write from wherever in the world he is. But gee, while it's sort of touching, it's not the real thing. Maybe I should have tried to get married. I would have gone about this whole thing differently: no Graham for sure, and what a loss that would be; and, of course, the ad in the *New York Review* would have read differently—something about a lasting relationship. But I didn't want marriage; I wanted exactly what I said I wanted and I got it: a lot of sex with a man I liked—who would have thought it would be so plural? Maybe I should have specified the region, "San Francisco Bay Area," adding eighteen dollars to the cost of the ad, but perhaps giving me a man in the next room. But then I wouldn't have entered into what will be the longest-lasting love affair of my life—with New York. "Why don't you move to New York?" Sidney asked. Because my son is here in California, my work is here, my money is not up to New York comfort, and, with few exceptions, I like my life here. It's just that I love New York.

So I BUMP around my cottage, read, write, see friends, and wonder what use I am to anybody, for it is summertime and school's out, the chorale is out, and I am out of work and play. Seeing friends is interesting. Some know about my doings, others not. Sometimes, when I am in the midst of an uninteresting conversation with people who have become uninteresting—why is it that aging is so often accompanied by a loss of curiosity?—I listen for the question "So, tell us, Jane, what have you been up to?" My answer raises eyebrows, opens mouths, and, always from women, elicits something like "Have you found Mr. Right?" And I answer, "Yes, I have; he comes in four different bodies." The husbands, for the most part, are quiet, though they look at me differently; they are curious, what would it be like to . . . and at the end of the evening the good-to-see-you embrace, once a brushing of cheeks or a pat on the back, is now warmer, with sometimes a murmured "I admire what you've done." Only a very few of my friends, all of them women, have known about this from the very start. They have encouraged me, been interested in this life I have led, and are curious now. I tell them stories that are true but that leave out the sad parts. Only to one or two do I confess the whole truth. I do not cry, though my voice shakes a lot. I save up for United Airlines. And I masturbate a lot. Not to Philip Roth's music, Schubert, Mozart, and the like—Mr. Roth is a high-class onanist, though spilling his seed all over his piano keys must make a mess—but to the cast recording of *Wonderful Town,* to the museum buttons from the Metropolitan and the Morgan I have affixed to the hood of my stove, to Bob Herbert's column in the *Times,* and sometimes, more often than all the rest, to the memory of Robert's touching me to the music of *Tosca.* It is said that the strongest orgasms are the ones we give ourselves. I deserve a medal.

Willa Cather says it right, as she so often does: "Human relationships are the tragic necessity of human life; they can never be wholly satisfactory, every ego is half the time greedily seeking them, and half the time pulling away from them."

In the beginning of all this, I had thought to make my life fuller, not just happier. I had thought that my passion, which had served so many people so well when I was a teacher, might find a place to put itself before it subsided into the contentment of old age. I thought right; I got what I hoped for. What is just as far away as ever is the contentment of old age. I doubt that it comes, ever. There is the inevitable falling off of energy, I suppose, certainly the falling away of flesh from the bone, and in some of us a flagging of the spirit. It's called dying. But contentment? Peace? I think we just get tired, and people who write junk about us, because contentment makes better greeting cards, mistake fatigue for serenity.

I'M NOT TIRED hardly at all, so I take pleasure in the memory of lying next to a man who knew what to do with me. I recall with equal pleasure the conversations with intelligent men who were lively and curious and thoughtful and who liked to talk with me. That was a surprise. I never thought we would actually, as my ad offered, "talk first." But we did, first and last and, sometimes, in the middle. All my parts have been fed by these men. They have made me a rich woman. But rich doesn't mean full, and rich as I am, I am not full.

The thing is, once you have had a lot of sex with a man you like, how do you stop wanting him?

ONE RESTLESS NIGHT, I woke, my nightshirt damp from twisting and turning, my arms caught in the sheet that had pulled out of the end of the bed. The clock read 4:35. I rose, walked the three steps to my computer, sat down, and began to write. "Dear Graham, I have rented a cabin, a cottage, a house on a lake in the Sierras. The first week in August it will be filled with my family, the second only with me. I can offer you mountains and lakes and as much of me as will make you happy." Then I wrote the dates and returned to my bed, where I fell sound asleep.

LIFE JUST KEEPS COMING at you. Make no mistake, it's out to get you, and in the end it will. But every so often, you can catch a piece of it and make it do what you want it to, at least for a little while. You've got to stay alert, though. Heads up so you don't get caught off base, though if you do, what the hell, it's not the ninth inning, until it is.

NEXT DAY BRINGS Graham's answer: "Paint your wagon, I'm coming."

Born in Ann Arbor, Michigan, in 1933, JANE JUSKA grew up in Archbold, Ohio. In 1955 she moved to California, where she has lived, with brief intermissions, ever since. She has taught English for more than forty years in high school, in college, and in prison. Many of the articles she has written about teaching and students have appeared in professional journals. *A Round-Heeled Woman* is Juska's first book. She lives in Berkeley, California.